JEFF ̄ ̄ ̄ ̄ ̄ 3

Is the prof ... as much ... as this?

With Chris Rogers

Visit us online at www.lulu.com

A Lulu.com book

ISBN 978-1-4477-4607-2

Lulu Enterprises, Inc
3131 RDU Center Drive
Suite 210
Morrisville, NC 27560
United States

This book is also available in e-book format, details of which are available at www.lulu.com

ACKNOWLEDGEMENTS

I've spoken to lots of people while researching and writing this book … far too many to mention by name. However, I would like to say a special thanks to my former players Derek Jones, Jeff Meacham, Richard Fey and Barry Yeo for taking a lot of time out to help me retrace my steps throughout the various stages of my career. I'd also like to thank my old assistant Mike Ford, whose help was invaluable as well. I must thank Chris Rogers for helping get all the stories and thoughts from inside my head into print, and the various newspapers who have offered assistance through supplying information, photographs and archive stories… Andrew Jones and Mark Jenkin at the North Devon Journal, Dean Stacey at the Dawlish Gazette and Owen Houlihan at the Wiltshire Gazette & Herald. Finally, I must thank my family for all their support during my 50 years in football, and the players and managers I have met during that time… without you, there would be no book!

Researching the book over a few beers are (from left) me, Richard Fey, Chris Rogers, Jeff Meacham and Derek Jones.

CHAPTERS

1... Premier League managers can keep their money

THE start of any football season is always met by excitement and optimism, but for me the opening day of the 2010/11 campaign brought with it a scenario I hadn't seen in more than half a century. I wasn't at a football ground. I wasn't lacing my boots up, I wasn't stood in a dugout, and I was nowhere near a changing room or a team sheet. For the first time in 50 years, I had no involvement whatsoever come 3pm on that eagerly-awaited Saturday in August, when thousands of players and managers up and down the country – professional, semi-professional or amateur – start out on that annual journey that dominates the next nine months of their lives.

Instead, I was sat with a beer in my hand at Gatwick Airport, staring at a departure screen that was showing a long list of delayed and cancelled flights. Okay, so I was still among a crowd of frustrated and angry people, but that was where the similarities with football ended … I couldn't have been further away from the big kick-off. I had made my mind up that it was now time I officially retired from football. Sure enough, I'd 'retired' before only to be lured back into the game for 'one more' challenge. But this time I knew it was time to go. I was 65 years old, and just a couple of weeks earlier my season-long spell as manager of Western League side Dawlish Town had come to an abrupt end when I was relieved of my duties due to budget cuts. Suddenly, I had the strange sensation of being a free man for the opening day of the season, which explains why I was at the airport – I decided to make the most of this unexpected spare time, and take a short holiday to Italy with some of the family.

I had started playing competitive junior football in my early teens back in the 1950s. As a youngster I had three years with Bristol Rovers, the club I had supported since I was big enough to kick a ball, and then spent the next 15 years developing a semi-professional playing career in and around Bristol. One of those clubs, Abbotonians, gave me an early opportunity to go into management at the age of 35, and that decision ended up extending my football career by three decades! When I first started thinking about writing this book, I looked back over my career and tried to work out exactly how many games I'd been involved in. I'm fairly sure it's between 1,450 and 1,750 senior games as a player, with another 1,350 to 1,500 as a manager.

So, with more than 3,000 senior games under my belt, I think it's safe to say I'd experienced all I could in the non-league game. But more importantly, I loved every minute of it. You don't stay involved in any senior sport for 50 full years unless you truly love it, and that's what has kept me hooked for so long. Sure, at some places I earned a few quid, but at other places I got peanuts – it was never about the money, and sadly that seems to be the difference between football in my day and the professional game today. You have to wonder how many professional players in the Premier League would still be playing football if there weren't millions of pounds to be made. At some semi-professional clubs I have been at during my career, the expenses paid out wouldn't even cover your petrol costs. But it didn't matter. You were there for the enjoyment of being involved in the game of football.

Whether I was playing or managing, there was always the same banter and the same buzz in the changing room before the game. At half-time, it would go one way or the other – you'd either done what was needed and everybody was in high spirits, or the tea cups would go flying – but it was all part of the game, and I loved it. As a player, for me the lure of the game was all about the challenge of trying, as a team, to beat the opposition.

Later, as a manager, it was about keeping sides together and building a team spirit. Once I'd built that team spirit, I then had to educate my players on how to beat the opponents, and test my wits against the opposing manager. I've always been a person who wanted to win, no matter what I was doing, but the Premier League managers of today can keep all their money. With the worries Sir Alex Ferguson has got in charge at Manchester United, that's not a football job any more. It's a business. What I've been involved in for 50 years, both playing and managing, is a sport – played at a very good non-league level – you could enjoy, while still wanting to be a winner at the same time.

As well as numerous promotions throughout my career, I've also been involved in 16 cup finals as a manager – my record is six wins and ten losses. I had a further 25 finals as a player, so I can look back and know I haven't done badly in the game of football. As a senior player, I was 24 years old when I made my first cup final appearance, which was a 4-0 win for Iron Acton in the 1969 Berkeley Hospital Cup. I had another cup win during my brief spell in New Zealand with East Coast Bays a few years later, and a load of successes during my Wednesday League days in Bristol.

While I was doing my research for this book, I really enjoyed looking back over my playing career. There were some memorable moments and more than a few laughs in there. However the fun really began when I turned to management with Abbotonians in the late 1970s. They were an absolute crazy gang, long before Wimbledon coined that phrase. I had a similar team of nutters at Trowbridge Town, and again at Torrington in the Western League some 20 years later. Along the way, I had spells in charge of two clubs who are now playing in the Football League Conference – Bath City and Forest Green Rovers, during the short spell they were known as Stroud. In total my managerial career took me to 11 different clubs in one position or another, capped off by five years as joint manager of the Devon county side with Peter Buckingham.

Of course, the highlight of managing Devon came with our South West Counties Championship triumph over Cornwall in 2003. The win was made even sweeter because it was played at Barnstaple Town, the club side I was in charge of at the time. A year later we just missed out on retaining the title when we lost to Cornwall in the final.

The contrasting emotions experienced in those two games – the celebration of success followed by the heartbreak of defeat – were both common themes throughout my managerial career. It started at Abbotonians with losses in the finals of the Gloucester Senior Cup and Sutton Transformer Cup, and a win in the Somerset League Cup. Later, at Trowbridge Town, we reached two South Wilts Senior Cup finals – winning one and losing one – alongside a South West Floodlit Cup win and a Southern League Cup defeat over two legs against Bromsgrove Rovers. As manager of Mangotsfield Town I won a Gloucester Trophy but lost a Western League Les Phillips Cup final, and at Bath City we won the Somerset Professional Cup. The last four cup finals with me in the dugout all ended in defeats – two Wiltshire Premier Cups with Chippenham Town, the Devon St Luke's Bowl with Barnstaple Town and the Les Phillips Cup again with Welton Rovers, where I had a brief spell as director of football.

You realise you are doing something right when, after 30 or so years in management, somebody still wants to pick up the telephone and offer you a job, which is what happened when I took charge of my final club, Dawlish Town, in 2009. Having said that, you know it's the right time to retire when there are players out there you would be trying to sign, who are about 50 years younger than you!

Of course, I'll go into all the above cup finals in more detail later on. However I want this book to be as much about the characters I've encountered along the way, and the laughs we have had, as it is about results on the field. It's the banter and team spirits that have made my 50-year journey so memorable. I really think my time in the game was the golden age for local football characters, and you'll hear about a lot of them in the coming chapters. One of them is Richard Fey, who was my goalkeeper at Torrington, and was a tremendous character to have in the changing room or on a team bus – he was always after a laugh. Richard is now starting out on his own managerial career with Bitton in the Western League, and he rang me up recently to ask for advice on how to build a team spirit like the one we had back in the Torrington days.

It's so much harder to do these days. For a starter, I don't think there are nearly as many characters in the modern game. I was always a firm believer that bus or minibus trips to away games played a crucial part in building any team spirit. But it's so difficult for Bristol sides today, especially in the Western League where you only really travel a long way out of the city two or three times a season – and perhaps a couple of extra times if you draw away games in the FA Vase. When coach trips are so few and far between, it really limits you in terms of creating camaraderie. It doesn't help, either, that most players these days tend to stick their headphones on within seconds of getting on the bus. It may be an old-school approach, but I would suggest that the best way around it is to chuck all the iPods and personal stereos out of the bus window!

Richard was the first person to call me up about football when I returned from my holiday to Italy at the start of the 2010/11 season. He asked me if I fancied going to watch Downton, who Bitton had drawn in the FA Cup. I went to watch them play Shaftesbury and compiled a report as professionally as I could for Richard, who then took Bitton there a week later to win 2-0. I've watched a few games for them since then and, although I know I'm never going to be stood in a dugout again, it helps me keep involved in a smaller capacity. Knowing I won't be a part of that banter in the changing room was the hardest thing to accept when it came to retiring, although to be fair the drinking and socialising aspect of football was starting to drop off for me in recent years as I got older. A bloke of 66 can't really go along to a teeny-boppers place, which is where all the players seem to want to go these days!

It's a shame to see such a shortage of real characters in today's game. In the latter days of my career, I've been sat in a clubhouse after a game, and looked around wondering where the away team are. Sometimes they wouldn't even come in after a match, and other times they may pop in for the quickest of drinks while they have some food, and then shoot off. It couldn't have been more different 20 or 30 years ago. At Abbotonians, for example, the whole team would still be in a clubhouse at 11pm and we would all be having a fantastic time. I'm not a gambling man, but I'd wager a substantial bet that it was the beer consumed in these clubhouses over the years that account for a huge majority of the stories I will tell over the next 200 or so pages!

Anyway, I hope you enjoy the book and a glimpse into my 50 years in football. It may not be the story of a professional career, like all the other football books on the shelves these days, but I want to show the side of the game that has been all but eclipsed by television deals, multi-millionaire players, and billionaire takeovers – real people, real football, real enjoyment and, above all, the love of the game.

2... A chance meeting with a Rovers legend

I COULDN'T have been more than about nine or ten years old at the time, but I can still vividly remember the first moment I was captivated by the magic of football – the game that was to become such a major part of my life for the next 55 years. I was with a group of lads kicking a ball around in a street called Ida Road, just around the corner from where I grew up and about a mile away from the centre of Bristol, and a mile from the old Bristol Rovers ground at Eastville. Whitehall Road was the main road at the bottom, and there were three residential streets that joined together in a loop off Whitehall Road – Herbert Street, Ida Road and Ivor Road, which was where I lived. There were no cars parked on Ida Road at the top, though, so that became our football pitch.

Like all the kids in those days, we didn't have computers to distract us, and we didn't have iPods ... but we did have a football. First thing every morning, as soon as we'd all climbed out of bed, I would meet up with my mates and we'd immediately be kicking a ball around at the bottom of the road. One morning, during our school holidays, there was a smart-looking ginger-haired lad who was walking past, and he got the ball for us as it started rolling down the road. He flicked the ball up on to his knee, then up on to his shoulder, back down again and passed it back to us. We all just stood in amazement – it was fantastic and we'd never seen skill, or ball control, like it. We started passing the ball back to him and we ended up having a good kickabout ... by the time he left, there were about four or five of us getting in on it. When he left, I remember turning around to one of the other kids in awe. "Who is that?" I asked.

The boys excitedly told me that he was Peter Hooper, who was then a young Bristol Rovers left-winger already well on the way to becoming a club legend. He had a left foot like a cannon – in fact, when he was invited on to the pitch as a special guest at half-time in a League One home match against Yeovil Town last season, he was introduced as the player with the hardest shot in the club's history. Hooper made 297 appearances for Rovers between 1953 and 1962, and became one of only seven players in the club's history to score more than 100 goals. Anyway, as a young lad I was awestruck after exchanging passes with a professional footballer so, from then on, every day at the same time, around 9.30am, we made sure we were there with a ball at the bottom of the road in case he went by. He was an absolute gentleman, a great player, and I will never forget that meeting.

At the time, I'd never been to see Rovers play at Eastville but I knew I had to go after seeing Peter Hooper. I can remember going to watch Portsmouth play there in the FA Cup on January 8, 1955, which was probably only the second game I'd ever been to. There was a crowd of more than 30,000 there and, at the Muller Road end, there was a special part of the stand designated for children. The Pompey star at the time was the England left-half Jimmy Dickinson, who went on to earn the nickname Gentleman Jim after racking up a phenomenal 845 club appearances and 48 international caps without ever being booked or sent off.

At the age I was, you probably can't watch a match and really know that it was a good game of football, but I loved it. The match, the occasion, I loved everything about it ... not to mention the fact that Rovers won 2-1. The atmosphere outside the ground was the other thing that sticks in my memory about that FA Cup game. Before they built the new stand at Eastville on the River Frome side, all the kids had to walk along the back of the stand. As I battled through the thousands of people, I can remember one bloke shouting out at me. "Are you on your own, son?" I told him I was and, whenever the crowds of people got too close to me, this guy would bellow out and warn everyone. "Watch it, there's a child here," he yelled, and the mass of bodies would just split apart to let me go through.

I can also remember being sat on the terrace at Eastville for a reserve-team game among a crowd of about 11,000 – that's about 5,000 more than the club get for a first-team game these days – at the end of the 1955/56 season. We were all listening to the radio, because the first team were away at Leeds United knowing a win would put them in the driving seat for promotion to the old First Division. It was the penultimate game of the season, but Rovers lost 2-1 and Leeds ended up getting promoted instead. But that's how good that Rovers side were back in those days, to get that close to top flight football. Alfie Biggs, Geoff Bradford, Jackie Pitt, Peter Hooper, the goalkeeper Howard Radford … there were some very talented players there.

My trips to Bristol Rovers games at Eastville were few and far between, mainly because it was a time not long after World War Two when there wasn't that much money about. I had to save up my pocket money to go, or ask to borrow money from my dad who also had a mortgage to pay and a family to look after.

I was the first of four children, born on September 8, 1944, to my mother Noreen and father Stanley. My mother was born and bred in Bristol, in the same area where we all grew up as a family. My father was from Wales and, as I always tell him, he had to come through the Severn Tunnel – there was no bridge back in those days – to meet a good woman! They've been married now for 68 years as I write, and I came along about 10 months after their wedding. My brother Keith arrived soon after, followed by my sister Diane and youngest sister Sheila, who was born when I was seven years old.

Dad worked with the Post Office, working his way up to become an inspector and then went off to be in charge of the mail train going to Plymouth. When that run was closed down, just before he retired at 60 years old, he took charge of the mail train that went up to Birmingham, into Derby before swapping over with the Newcastle-upon-Tyne train and heading back down. He'd actually left Wales during the war, and was at an airbase in Gloucestershire when he was invited down to Bristol and introduced to my mother.

By the time I was old enough to start my school life, we were living in Ivor Road and I can recall telling my mum that I would make my own way when it was time for my first day at Whitehall Junior School. I remember distinctly her following behind to make sure I went in the school. When I came home for dinner, I know she was watching me coming home too! But I insisted that I wanted to do it on my own, and that was the first part of my life growing up. As for football, I may have been some way off playing for a proper team, but we were up at Ida Road whenever possible and it was always one street playing another. We were lucky, though, as there was never a car that went up there. It's totally different today – I went up there the other week and had a job to even get through with the number of cars that were there.

There was a nice park nearby called St George's and, by the time I was eight or nine years old, we always used to get up there after school too. Down went the jumpers and coats for the goalposts and, as soon as there were enough kids for two teams of 11, away we went. If you couldn't get up there for the first game, then you had to make sure you were up there for the next two lots of 11, and that's the way it went. As I got a bit older, maybe 10 or 11 years old and approaching my final year at Whitehall School, we moved down to the Netham playing fields where a few of the older kids played. In my class at school was Tony Ford, who ended up as a professional footballer with Bristol City and Bristol Rovers. Actually, there were three or four of us who were good friends and, as a group, we stuck together and we would even end up in the Bristol Boys side together a few years down the line.

We had a great time playing football at the Netham, as all the kids were there – and sadly that's a sight you don't see today. Maybe if you took a computer or an iPod away from every child, and gave it five years, then we would start producing decent footballers again. Also, take a look at the photograph of the Whitehall School team when I won my first medal in football at 11 years old. The football boots we wore were all leather and came up above your ankle, with leather studs on them. The football was all leather, with a lace, and boy did that lace hurt if it hit you at the wrong time! And we had to learn to play football with that equipment. It wasn't like playing with the balls of today that you can bend here and swerve there. But how do you change it? How many children do you see playing football in the park these days? The answer, basically, is none, and that's this country's biggest problem with regards to football.

The first medal you win, though, is always a memorable one and I had a great time playing in defence – my preferred position was always at right-back – in that Whitehall School team that won the Junior Coronation Cup. Tony Ford was in the side, as well as Jackie Pitt's son John. Jackie was another Bristol Rovers legend who spent more than 50 years at the club as a player, coach and groundsman. You could tell both Tony and John had a little bit of skill about them on the pitch. John never went on any further with his football, but with Tony you could see he was a cut above the rest of us. We all liked to think we were as good as him but, if I'm honest, we weren't.

I can remember one match in particular during that cup run, on the Downs in Bristol. I'm not sure which team we were playing, but we were 1-0 up and I remember heading the ball off the line to keep us ahead. The next day in assembly, I got a message of thanks from our headmaster Mr Dixon for clearing the ball off the line and helping to get us to the final. But if I'm telling the honest truth, I didn't even see the ball coming – it walloped me in the face and went out of play. Job done!

The Coronation Cup was actually a very prestigious competition for school teams, with junior and senior competitions involving schools all across the city. For a Bristol schoolboy at that age, lifting a Coronation Cup was like lifting the FA Cup. Other finals had been played at both Bristol Rovers and Bristol City, but our final that day was played in front of a very large crowd at the Electricity Sports Ground against Connaught Road School. Connaught Road is in Knowle West, which is a very hard area, but we went there and won 1-0. We went back to school the next day as returning heroes, and the school were all over us. We were on top of the world – it really was an unforgettable and wonderful feeling, and it was my first taste of success, achieved working as a team. The headmaster promised us all a meal out in Bristol, which turned out to be a cup of tea and cakes in the afternoon, while our sports teacher Mr Garland laid on a load of food to celebrate at his house in Hanham. We had a great time, although sadly it would prove to be our last experience together as a squad.

Soon after, it was time to go to senior school and everybody got split up. I went to Speedwell School while others went elsewhere but, because we all lived in the same area, we were still able to keep in touch and would regularly meet up for kickabouts on the Netham. To be honest, I had a bit of a rough time at Speedwell ... mainly because I couldn't play football all year round. The first three months were football, but the second three months were rugby and then it went on to cricket. I either had to go with it or fight against it, and in the beginning I tried to fight against it, showing that I didn't want to play rugby by going off and playing for other teams.

We had a sports teacher at Speedwell called Mr Harris, and he pulled me to one side to remind me that I was there for four years and it really wasn't worth fighting it. He said he'd ease me through the other sports and promised me he'd help me into the Bristol Boys side, which had U13 and U15 squads. Actually, by the time I got to my final year I really felt I was doing too much, because I was sports-mad. If you look at my leaving report, I did get an 'A' for maths but a 'D' for English … ask me to spell a word, it's a waste of time! But for sport I had an 'A' after representing the school at cricket, basketball, rugby, athletics, football and boxing.

Yes, that's right … boxing. I was a little bit of a temperamental lad at times, and I had a fiery belly inside me. I remember we had a sports afternoon and we'd gone down to the gym, and I'd had a bit of a punch-up with a kid in the dinner hour. Mr Harris found out about it. "I think it's time for a bit of discipline," he said, and threw me a pair of boxing gloves. I at least had the manners to ask him first if I could hit him, and he replied: "If you're quick enough, yes!"

As it happens, my best mate at Speedwell was Steve Webb, who was a schoolboy boxer. I always used to spend time at his house where we'd mess about boxing, so I thought I'd get my guard up and give it a go – and I gave Mr Harris a good scrap. Straight away he told me that I'd be going to Cotham Park School the next Thursday and representing the school at boxing with Steve. By this time I was playing football for Bristol Boys and, looking back, it was all too much. I won the Bristol Championship, and then had a West of England Championship fight at Colston Hall. Steve was a member of Patchway Amateur Boxing Club, so I asked him if I could go along and speak to the coaches down there.

As it turned out I could handle myself quite well there and went on to win the West of England Championship, earning the right to represent the region against the South. I would have had to go down to Plymouth to fight a kid there, but I ended up getting ill the week before. I was gutted I couldn't go down there, and that was really the end of the gloves. I went away with Patchway ABC a couple of times after that, once down to Cornwall and once in Avonmouth, and I held my own. I think I only lost two bouts and won all the others but, at the end of the day, it was another sport that needed to be chucked in so I could fully concentrate on football and keeping my place in the Bristol Boys side.

I remember my first ever game with Bristol Boys. It was at Cheddar, and it was freezing cold with snow on the pitch, but we had to get it out the way because it was the first round of the English Shield. I can't recall who we played in the following rounds, until we went away to play East Ham Schoolboys in West Ham. It was the first time that I had to stay away from home for football, and we left Bristol Temple Meads on the Friday night to head up to our hotel in London. There we all were, 15-year-old 'Jack the Lads' in London desperate to sneak out and see what life was all about in the city, but we had no chance – there were teachers watching every door!

We played the next day. Well I say 'we'. I didn't play. I was dropped, and I was absolutely gutted. I asked our manager Ted King why, and he told me he thought I was doing too much and needed a rest. He assured me I'd be brought back in as we progressed further in the competition, but in the meantime he advised me to tell my sports teacher that I didn't need to play any other sport. Ted wanted me to concentrate on Bristol Boys, which was what I needed to hear – I was burning myself out. Anyway, we drew the game 1-1 against an East Ham side that included John Sissons. John was a young winger who would later play for West Ham United, and at one time he became the youngest ever player to score in an FA Cup Final when he scored for the Hammers in their 3-2 defeat of Preston North End at Wembley Stadium in 1964.

With the game drawn, we brought East Ham back to Eastville for a replay. I was still on the bench, even though there wasn't a substitutes' bench in those days – I think 'travelling reserve' was the correct phrase – but Ted King told me to get changed and help to warm the goalkeeper up. Our keeper was Dick Sheppard, who went on to have a good pro career at West Bromwich Albion.

In fact, Dick played in the 1967 League Cup Final against Queen's Park Rangers, when West Brom went 2-0 up at half-time against a Rangers side who were two divisions below. However Dick was beaten three times in about 15 minutes near the end, including a great solo goal from Rodney Marsh, as QPR won 3-2 in what was a pretty major upset at the time. After 39 appearances for West Brom, Dick returned to Bristol when he signed for Rovers in 1969. He went on to make 150 league appearances before suffering a fractured skull in a game against Tranmere Rovers at Eastville. It kept him out for more than a year, and he only made a few more appearances after recovering, including a couple while out on loan at Torquay United. Sadly Dick died at just 53 years old in 1998, following a battle with cancer.

Going back to the replay with East Ham, I can remember us being well on top at Eastville, but Dick let a back pass in and Bristol Boys lost 1-0 in a game we were expecting to win. I went home, went to bed and the next day strolled off to Speedwell for what I assumed was going to be just another day at school. We had the assembly, with the usual thanks expressed to Jeff Evans for representing the school at Bristol Boys, and then I was asked to go into the office. I thought I was going in there to pick up a little cup or certificate for my achievements, but when I got in there I was handed my leaving report – by now I was old enough to leave school – and given the school's best wishes for success in my working life. Just like that, in one split-second, my school days had come to an end.

By this time I'd already got some experience of senior football through playing for a side called St Matthew's Church in the Church of England League. There were probably four or five lads from the Bristol Boys side playing for that team, while the rest were all regulars at the church. Basically, I still had my football up to the end of the season, when all the names of the lads who were 'released' from school football because of their ages would be circulated around the big clubs like Rovers and City. Soon after, I had a letter from Bristol Rovers manager Bert Tann asking me to go along and see him, which I did, and I ended up signing for him.

Little did he know, but Bert Tann had actually invited me to that very meeting a decade or so earlier. My father and my uncle Jim – he's one year younger than dad and, at 88 years old, is still a Rovers season ticket holder – decided to stop and watch Bristol Rovers train one morning when they were taking me for a walk around Eastville Park. I was too young to remember it, but I've often had the story told to me. Bert Tann came over for a chat and, spotting me, told my dad to bring me back when I was 15 to see if I was good enough. Well, I must have been good enough, because all those years later I kept him to that promise, and he signed me!

Uncle Jim had also helped to fuel my interest in all things Rovers at a young age, mainly because he played in the same skittles team as the club's big, tough, centre-half Paddy Hale. Whenever I went to visit him, I always used to ask if we could go around and visit Paddy's house, so as soon as we got there the ball would come out and Paddy would be having a kickabout with me.

For me, memories like this highlight another thing that's wrong about today's game – I feel that pros these days don't have enough time for the kids on the street. In my day they would talk to anybody, there was no problem at all. Take my Peter Hooper meeting that I mentioned earlier … can you imagine a Premier League player, or even a player in League One or League Two these days, doing the same thing? I'm sure there are players out there who would, but I bet they are in the minority. The rest wouldn't be walking out of the ground and offering to kick a ball with the kids; they'd be walking past with their heads down listening to music on these giant over-sized headphones, or driving past in a Bentley or Rolls Royce.

Several years on, and although I was only signing amateur forms for Bristol Rovers, I still felt like a man mountain when I put pen to paper. Looking back on it, maybe that was one of the problems why I didn't ultimately make it as a pro. I always enjoyed training, and I had no problem keeping to the weights they set because you couldn't keep me still. In pre-season the amateurs used to train with the pros, and I felt I was just as fit as any of them. But, through a combination of factors including bad luck and bad timing, it never quite happened.

When I started my first season, I played for the Rovers side in the Bristol Premier Combination. Now that may not sound like the best standard in today's terms, but back then non-league football was structured in an entirely different way. You had the Bristol Premier Combination, you then had one Western League division and one Southern League division, and then you were at the Football League. Basically, you were four steps away from league football. These days, four steps down from League Two in the South West takes you as far as the Southern League's first division, so I was effectively playing what we'd see now as Southern League football. There were some good, good teams in there … Weston-super-Mare, Clevedon Town, Keynsham Town and Bristol St George to name a few. At 15 or 16 years old, it was a hard league to go into straight from school and perform. But I must have done something right in my first season, because at the end of that year I played two games for the full Bristol Rovers youth team.

The next season, I really thought I had a very good year. I played a lot of youth team football, and also played a lot of games for Bristol Rovers Colts – they were the club's third team and they played in the Western League, alongside sides such as Torquay United Reserves,

Bristol City Colts, Yeovil Town Reserves and a load of top local sides like Chippenham Town, Salisbury and Dorchester Town. The best thing about it was, at the end of this second season, I was retained for a third year, so I was going to turn 18 years old with a real chance of picking up a contract with Bristol Rovers.

With the youth team, we'd go away to play Plymouth, Oxford, Swindon, Southampton, and over to Newport. It doesn't sound that far these days, but you've got to remember that back then there were no motorways, and no Severn Bridge. Even the trip to Plymouth was at least four or five hours. We didn't have any luxury air-conditioned coaches either – all we had to get us there was a charabanc. There was nobody there to take your bags for you and load them up, and there were certainly no tables for card games. All we had to sit on were rock-solid benches, and then we had to go and play top-level football to try and earn ourselves a living. I often wonder how the young professionals in today's game would cope with such preparation.

Anyway, one such gruelling charabanc trip that took us up to London and back will always stand out in my memory – and it had nothing to do with the football. During my second season I was told I had to travel with the Rovers reserve team up to the capital, and I'm sure it was a game against Tottenham Hotspur. I was travelling reserve, and was told to bring my boots because there were players missing from the first team, and several reserve players were carrying injuries. As it happened, I never got on but I had the experience of travelling with the reserves, which I was delighted with.

It was 10pm by the time we got back to Bristol. Unlike today, when nightlife in the city starts at about 10pm and goes on until the sun comes up, all we had time for was a quick half at the local and that was it, home we went. I'd arranged with Vic Gardner, who was a first-year pro at Bristol Rovers, to go out for a drink the following evening. Ivor Road was only a mile or so from the centre of Bristol, so Vic and I wandered into the city and it was a typical Sunday night – the place was empty. We ended up in the Plimsoll Bar in the Grand Hotel for a beer and a chat and, out of the corner of my eye, I noticed a couple of girls coming in. We started chatting, and I've been chatting to her ever since. That's the night I met my wife Josephine – she'll crucify me for saying her full name, but it is her real name, even though I've always called her Jo. She was 16, I was 17, and we've been together ever since.

Of course, the downside of signing amateur forms was that I still needed to work during the day to keep the money coming in. Most of the time I worked in fruit and veg, although I did have one year at GB Britton & Sons – a shoe manufacturer in Bristol – and did get paid rather well there. The average wage of the time was probably about £3 or £4 per week, but with bonuses at GB Britton I was probably taking home about £11 per week, so I was a very wealthy lad ... although still moaned when I had to come home and give my mother £2!

I worked all the way through my time at Rovers, but I knew as I started my third year that I had to give it a really good go to get this contract nailed down. So I did just that. Once again I played a lot of Colts football and the standard really was very good. One striker I remember having to mark was Robin Stubbs for Torquay United Reserves. Stubbs had just signed for the Gulls ahead of the 1963/64 season for a then-record club fee of £6,000, and he went on to score 120 goals for them over the next six seasons with a strike-rate of more than one goal every other game. Later in his career he signed for Rovers for £10,000 and had a pretty decent time at Eastville too. That was the standard of the Western League in those days, regularly coming up against £10,000-rated players.

Things were going well, but it all blew up after Christmas. We had two games against Swindon Town in fairly quick succession, against a very strong Robins youth side that featured several players already brimming with first-team experience. Their inside-forward Ernie Hunt had made his league debut as a 16-year-old, as had Mike Summerbee. They both played that day, and went on to have very good careers. Hunt scored lots of goals for Wolverhampton Wanderers, Everton and Coventry City, while Summerbee won eight England caps and also lifted the European Cup Winners Cup with Manchester City in the 1969/70 season. As if they weren't enough, there were also two future Swindon legends in the Robins' slick youth side that day. Left-winger Don Rogers went on to make more than 400 appearances and score 147 goals for the Robins – and have a stand named after him at the County Ground – while John Trollope played a staggering 770 games for the club, mainly at left-back. John's son is none other than Paul Trollope, who had a successful spell as manager of Bristol Rovers until his sacking midway through the 2010/11 season.

We played a great game against them in front of a big crowd at Eastville, and then went up to their place maybe a month or so later. Much like in the first game, my main job at right-back was to take care of Don Rogers and I'd had a rollicking from Jackie Pitt, the Rovers youth team manager, at half-time for not marking Rogers tightly enough. He told me that if didn't get tighter to him he'd bring me off, so I went out and tried to stick to Rogers like glue. I thought I was doing the job pretty well, but with about 25 minutes to go our goalkeeper went down injured. Back in those days we didn't have substitute goalies hanging around, so all the players were looking around wondering what we were going to do. All of a sudden I heard Jackie Pitt shout over: "Go on Jeff, you get in goal." In the past Jackie had seen me mess about in training, when quite often I'd put the gloves on for a bit, so I guess I was the first name that popped into his head when looking for an immediate solution. Sadly, it wasn't just a quick fix either. I finished the last three months of my third season with Bristol Rovers as the new youth team goalkeeper, deputising between the posts at Eastville, at Torquay, at Plymouth. I also ended up having to play in goal for the Colts team too, because our injured keeper played for them as well.

Looking back now, it was like receiving my own Dear John letter. The final three months of the season were absolutely critical in the race to secure a professional contract with the club I had supported, and played for, ever since that fateful meeting with Peter Hooper. But rather than putting my heart and soul into my performances in a preferred full-back position, I found myself playing in goal. With hindsight, I wish I had stood firm after that one game against Swindon and said: "I'm not playing in goal, I'm a right-back so you need to grade me on playing at right-back." I didn't, and sure enough, that letter came through the post telling me that I'd been released from Bristol Rovers Football Club. After standing in as goalkeeper, I'm sure they just viewed me as a 'Jack of all trades, master of none'.

I can sympathise with any young player who gets that dreaded letter from a club. It's a horrible feeling that I can't really describe when you first learn that your professional dreams are over. You pick up the letter when it pops through the door at home, and you can just feel the colour drain out of your face as you read each line. It couldn't be more opposite to the feeling three years or so earlier when I went down to Eastville to see Bert Tann. From feeling like I was on top of Mount Everest, suddenly I wasn't even standing on the top of a pebble at the beach and for the best part of the summer that followed, I would have been quite happy if I had never even seen a football again, let alone play it.

Check out the boots! That's me (second from right in the front row) in the Whitehall Junior School side, just after we won the 1955/56 Coronation Cup.

Me (second from left in the front row) pictured in the Speedwell Senior School side of 1956/57.

Chilly work indeed! I'm in the back row (second from left) of this Bristol Boys team picture, taken on a snow-covered pitch at Cheddar.

This photo has seen better days! But through the creases and tears, you may just be able to recognise me in the back row (third from right). This is the St Matthew's Church of England side I played for.

3... Farewell Bristol Rovers, hello Bristol Prem

IT TOOK me a very long time to get over receiving that letter from Bristol Rovers at the end of the season. I didn't attempt to find another club, I didn't tell any of my friends – I was just very quiet all summer, until around September time when I happened to be in a pub in Sea Mills, near where Jo lived. A bloke in there recognised me from my time at Bristol Rovers, and asked me which club I was at. When I told him I wasn't playing, he immediately invited me to go along to training with Sea Mills in the Bristol Premier Combination.

As I mentioned in the previous chapter, in those days the Bristol Prem was a really strong league. When I started with Sea Mills, there were teams like Weston-super-Mare, Clevedon Town, Keynsham Town and Mangotsfield Town in it. It was a quality league, because there were no major forms of transport for the better local players to go further afield – cars were still few and far between in the early 1960s. Nowadays, you have the Conference, Conference North and South, three divisions in the Southern League, two in the Western League and then county league football, all before the Bristol Prem. How times have changed... when I made my Sea Mills debut, we were just four steps away from the Football League and Division Three (South). There was quality football there, and you often played local derbies in front of crowds of 400.

I went to training and signed on, and the manager at Sea Mills was delighted. I must tell the honest truth, though. I probably played five or six games, and he said to me: "I think you need to go and play in the reserves, and get your head together." He was right – I couldn't get my head around the idea that I wasn't a Bristol Rovers footballer. I was brought up as a young lad determined to make it professionally, and I was sure that was where I was going to end up. All of a sudden, I had to get used to the fact that I hadn't made it, and that the dream had been taken away from me.

I remember one cup game early in that first Sea Mills season that we had to play against a side from the Bristol Downs League. With the greatest respect to the Downs League, the standard wasn't that great. At 66 years old, I could probably still get a game there. However, in this one cup game we were playing, we were overlooking the Clifton Suspension Bridge and playing right over by the sea wall. I found more enjoyment trying to kick the ball over this wall than I did playing in the game – I just didn't want to be there. At the end of the game, I was walking off the pitch and a guy walked up behind me and clipped me round the back of the head. "What the hell are you doing here?" he asked as he put his arm around me.

It was Mick Gerrish, who had been a pro with Bristol City for many years and who had just taken over as landlord of the local pub where the Sea Mills lads would drink. "The last time I saw you, you were playing for the Rovers youth team at Ashton Gate against the City," he added, telling me to get over to the pub for a chat in the evening. I did, and he gave me the biggest grilling I'd had in years, which helped straighten me out a little bit. I got my head around the idea of playing football again, and I even went to see the Sea Mills manager to apologise for my performances during those opening few games. Mick basically told me to get on with my football and that, if I enjoyed the game – which I obviously did – then it didn't matter where I was playing. He named several players who had been blown out by Rovers or City as youngsters who had never laced up a pair of football boots again, and I quickly realised that I didn't want to be added to that list.

I went on to play two years of football with Sea Mills and, in that time, I got married to Jo on March 6, 1965. I may never have made it as a pro and, although I received my Dear John letter from the Rovers, I also gained a Dear Jo. We met because of my time at Rovers, and she's been with me ever since. We went on to have three wonderful children – Paul, Amanda and Clive – but I'm getting ahead of myself a bit! After getting married, firstly we moved over to a flat in Kingswood which Jo absolutely hated, but it took me to the other side of the city. While over there, I bumped into a couple of old school mates and they told me they were playing for Hillfields, who had just got promoted into the Bristol Prem. It made a lot of sense to play at Hillfields – not only was I saving the journey back across the city, but I was also able to play with a few of my old mates again. Perhaps I needed to prove to them that Jeff Evans was just as good as when I played for the school and Bristol Boys. I think I managed to do that, and I had a good first season playing with friends like Andy Perrett and Tony Sweet, to name a couple.

About two thirds of the way through my second season with Hillfields during the 1966/67 campaign, I remember playing a side called Iron Acton and, to be honest, we couldn't handle the football they were playing. I was at right-back, and was up against a quick left-winger by the name of Brian Birchall. I didn't know him from Adam, but I knew there was only one place for him – off the pitch! It's hard to believe we would go on to become best mates. In those days, you could always get away with the first few rough tackles before the referee would give you a warning, so I thought I'd nail him. There was only one problem with this master plan, though – I couldn't catch him! He was either laying the ball off, or was taking the ball past me and doing me with his pace. I couldn't get near him, and they beat us 2-1.

As I was walking off, I felt this arm come around me and it was Brian. I immediately thought he was looking to have a pop, but how wrong I was. "It's a bit late this year now, but next year you're coming to Iron Acton," he told me. "Why?" I asked. After all, I couldn't catch him over the previous 90 minutes. But he told me he'd teach me how to play properly at right-back, and took my telephone number. I really didn't think any more of it, until I got a summer call from Brian who was following up his pitchside invitation that he'd made a few months earlier. So began three years of very enjoyable football with Iron Acton.

Iron Acton is a little village just outside Yate, which in those days was a fairly small village itself. We played behind the Rose & Crown pub there, which was perfect – we'd play our game, get showered and head straight into the Rose and Crown for our beer. Coincidentally, Iron Acton was the club where I made my one and only appearance for the Bristol Rovers first team a few years earlier. The Rovers took a side there to officially switch on Iron Acton's new floodlights. Amazingly, these floodlights weren't on stanchions as you might expect – instead they were up in the oak trees! But they worked well, so fair play to them for their resourcefulness. I remember the game as plain as day, especially the faces on the Rovers first-team players when we all went to change after the game to find a tin bath full of hot water – and that was it!

When I returned to Iron Acton to play for them a few years later, you could tell the club had worked extremely hard. The pitch was still the same and the floodlights were still in the trees – although they were rarely used for health and safety reasons – but there were now changing rooms and showers. On the pitch, we put a side together that was competing with the top sides in the Bristol Prem. I can remember going to places like Bristol St George on a Boxing Day, and being watched by the best part of 1,000 people. They had a great side there, and won the Bristol Prem five seasons running from the 1963/64 campaign, right through to 67/68. They also had a very good run in the FA Amateur Cup, which went on to become known as the FA Vase. The crowds were amazing compared with the gates you see at a similar level today. We would go to Hanham and play in front of 450, and even little Iron Acton used to get at least 150 turning up every home game.

I played at right-back, and Brian Birchall played in the side too. There was a lad by the name of Bunker Hill, who was a solid centre-half. Brian Shepherd was our other centre-half, and he could also play some good football on the floor. The goalkeeper Jeff Gale was the chairman's son, and he was more than adequate. We had two good wingers in Bernie Slade and Carlos Hall. Bernie was so fast he made a cheetah look sluggish, while all Carlos wanted to do was beat his full-back five times, tie him up in knots and then beat him again! Carlos was the brother of Bernard Hall, the goalkeeper who got a chance to become Bristol Rovers' No.1 after Esmond Million was hit with a lifetime ban from football in 1963 for accepting a bribe to throw a game against Bradford Park Avenue. Bernard went on to play 134 consecutive games for the Rovers before having his career ended by a horrific injury at the very early age of 24. Bernard collided so heavily with Middlesbrough forward John O'Rourke, that he was knocked out and spent the next 16 days in a coma at Frenchay Hospital. Fortunately he made a good recovery, but his football career was over.

At Iron Acton, we did okay in the first year and were a comfy mid-table side. The second year I was there – the 1968/69 season – we pushed ourselves very close to the top of the Bristol Prem, and also reached the final of the Berkeley Hospital Cup against Glenside Hospital. It was a good competition to do well in, because it featured a lot of good sides from Gloucestershire like Shortwood United, Stonehouse Town, Tuffley Rovers and Slimbridge.

Anyway, we had a pretty major problem ahead of this final. Our midfielder Brian Harper was at Wembley for the day, and there were two other lads who had taken their holidays early. By now, Brian Birchall was concentrating more on managing than playing, so on the Wednesday before the game he met with me – I was his captain – and vice-captain Brian Shepherd to discuss what we were going to do. We knew we were up against it, but things got worse on the morning of the game when we lost two more through illness. The photo of the team before the final tells its own story – we had our goalkeeper Jeff Gale playing at right-back so the reserve team goalkeeper had to come in between the sticks. The third team goalkeeper was also drafted in, so we had three goalies in our squad of 12! Age had finally caught up with Birchall too, he'd picked up an injury and couldn't play, so we really did have our backs against the wall. Despite all this, though, we somehow found ourselves 4-0 up after 20 minutes, and took that lead into the half-time break! We came off at half-time and there were players who were already on their knees, so it called for desperate measures in the second half – whenever the chance arose, we had to go down like we'd been shot, as if we were dying!

Glenside were moaning and groaning because they knew exactly what we were doing. But it got the job done, we won 4-0. They had the champagne ready in their changing room, but fair play to them – they brought it in for us so we went back to Iron Acton in very good spirits. There were only two pubs in Iron Acton, but I'd told the missus not to expect me home early … in the end, I think she picked me up around 7.30am the next morning. A good night was had by all, I can assure you. The two pubs opened all night for us, and it was a great end to a fantastic season.

We were never really able to carry on building after that. Brian Birchall was really struggling by now with wear and tear. Bri Shepherd was a couple of years older, as was Bunker Hill. In my working life, I was a fruit and veg salesman working out of the back of a lorry, and one of my customers, Miss Jarrett, offered me a shop during one visit. I asked where I was likely to get a mortgage from at my age – it was 1969 so I was around 25 – and couldn't believe my ears when she offered me a 100 per cent mortgage, with me paying her directly. It was an incredible gesture, and that was my real start in business. I moved to this shop which Jo used to run with the help of my sisters Diane and Sheila on Saturdays so I could play football.

At the same time I used to drink in a pub called the King Billy, which was right opposite the DIY shop that Brian Birchall ran. Lots of football teams used to drink at the King Billy on a Saturday evening after games, and it was in there that I met Soundwell chairman Rex Penrice. Soundwell were in the Bristol Prem, but had been a Western League club in the 1940s and 1950s, and in that time they produced more than their fair share of Bristol Rovers professionals. Anyway, Rex explained to me that Soundwell were keen to go further again, so off I went to join them.

I enjoyed it at Soundwell, but I have to be honest, the manager Brian Usher wasn't really my cup of tea and I knew I wasn't going to have a long stay there. However, it was the start of a long friendship with Rex Penrice. Bristolians will need no introduction to the surname – Rex's son Gary went on to be a top professional footballer with Rovers, Watford, Aston Villa and Queen's Park Rangers. Gary was probably only about six or seven years old when I was playing at Soundwell, but he could already hit a ball like a bullet!

Back at the shop, I would quite often hear Jo inform me that "that bloke's at the door again" and she would regularly be told to tell him that I was out or unavailable. Now, 'that bloke' turned out to be Ralph Miller, and if you ask anyone in Bristol football about Ralph Miller they will all tell you what a proper character he was. There was certainly no nonsense with Ralph … if a player didn't do what he wanted them to do, boy would they know about it! Ralph was in charge at Cadbury Heath, who were playing in the newly-formed Gloucestershire County League, so I thought I'd give them a go.

By now the Bristol Prem had a completely different look about it. It was still there, but the formation of the Gloucestershire County League for the 1968/69 season had hit it really badly. Having just won five Bristol Premier Combination titles on the trot, Bristol St George were among the top quality sides who made the jump to become founder members of the Gloucestershire League. The reason? Teams had to move to hold their level in the non-league pyramid – staying in the Bristol Prem would have meant dropping a grade.

Anyway, if there's one thing I'll pull Ralph Miller up on, it was his organisation. I remember one away game at Matson Athletic, and we only had nine players available. I spoke to Ralph in advance and asked what he was going to do about it, and his reply? "You know where the pitch is … you get there, and I'll worry about the three new players." So we arrived for the game and, sure enough, there's Ralph walking across the car park with three new players. None of them were signed on, but that didn't matter to Ralph as nobody knew them at Matson! We got into the changing rooms and Ralph was barking out the orders as to where we were all playing. Then it suddenly hit me: "Oh no, he's forgotten the goalkeeper!" No sooner had the thought entered my head, I saw Ralph's finger pointing straight at me. "By the way Jeff, you're in goal!" It could have been worse … I did manage to keep a clean sheet!

By now I had three shops on the go, and I found it an increasing struggle to give up the time Cadbury Heath needed – especially with the constant travelling all around Gloucestershire. So when my old mate Brian Birchall told me he was taking over as manager of Ridgeway Rovers, it didn't take me long to link up with him again. Credit to Ralph Miller, though, he built an excellent side that went on to win four Gloucestershire County League titles back to back between 1970 and 1974, before taking them into the Midland Combination.

On the surface, my decision to join Ridgeway Rovers for the 1970/71 season made perfect sense. All the travelling was in and around Bristol, and they played their home fixtures on a local playing field that was just down the road from one of my shops. Looking back, it was one of my worst decisions because I don't believe you should ever choose to go downhill, in terms of standard, in anything you do. That's a belief I've continued to tell players who play for me through all my later years in management, although I'm sure I've contradicted myself a couple of times since! Ridgeway, though, were playing in the Bristol Suburban League and there were really only two teams in it – us and St Aldhelms. We drew at our ground, they beat us at their place and that decided the title, so we were runners-up.

I didn't enjoy it one bit, and said to Brian at the end of the season that I'd rather not play at all than play at that level. He quickly reassured me that I wouldn't have to, because he was taking over as manager of Hanham Athletic. Much like Bristol St George, Hanham had switched to become founder members of the Gloucestershire County League in 1968, and had finished third in their first season. It was at Hanham where I met Bill Holloway for the first time. Bill and I were to become very close in my early managerial career, but I'll get to that later. I also got to know Bill Pomeroy well during my spell at

Hanham, and he will always stay in my mind for his simple footballing phrase that sticks with me to this day … if in doubt, three miles out!

Brian put a great side together at Hanham with Alan Burborough up front. There was a younger lad called Johnny House, who was in and out of the side with us. On weekends when we didn't have a game, we would sometimes get a call from Bradford-on-Avon's manager Bob Mursell, if he was short of a few players. Johnny had a terrible habit of swinging his elbows when going up to win a header, and Bradford's fans were treated to a House special in the first half of one particular game when he went up to play for them. He was shown a straight red card for the challenge, and the referee came over for his name. "Alan Burborough," was the answer from House. "How do you spell that, son?" quizzed the referee. "A-L-A…" came the smart alec reply, which was cut off by the referee before he could finish it. "Don't take the mick. How do you spell Burborough?" Johnny was struggling. "B-I, erm, B-U, erm, B… oh fuck it, it's House!"

Johnny got suspended for that, and I think Bradford got in a lot of trouble for it too. It was during the first of only two seasons in the Western League for them, as they dropped out at the end of the 1973/74 season after finishing second from bottom. Bob Mursell certainly went on to greater things though, winning the FA Vase as manager of Forest Green Rovers. Bradford are back in the Western League now – they changed their name to Bradford Town in the 1990s.

It was playing with players like House and Burborough, and at a decent standard again, that got me back enjoying my football. We'd finished fourth in the table in the 1972/73 campaign, my second season with them, but after the final game I told Brian Birchall that I wouldn't be with them for a third season. "I'm going to New Zealand," I explained to a baffled Brian. Now this was no spur-of-the-moment excuse – it was something Jo and I had been discussing for a while. I'd had some colossal electricity bills at my three shops, so we'd decided to go out there and see if we could find a better life for ourselves. Jo had two sisters out there, so we decided to sell one of the shops and keep two others that my sister Diane agreed to run in my absence.

Brian and I had always talked about going to the FIFA World Cup in 1974 in West Germany, so I assured him that, even if I made a go of it in New Zealand, I would come back the following summer to sell my other two shops and combine it with our long-planned footballing holiday. But it was something I had to do. I wanted to see if there was a better life for Jo and I outside of England.

It must have been early May, 1973, when Jo and I waved goodbye to Britain. Jo's sister Ruth and her husband Paul also went to New Zealand with their first child Nigel, so all four sisters were going to be reunited there. I felt a bit sorry for Paul, as I wasn't sure if he was entirely happy about going to New Zealand. As a footballer, he wasn't the best but he certainly wasn't the worst. After hanging up his playing boots, however, he took up refereeing and took it very seriously. He got to Class 1 level and was being pushed up the ladder, at a relatively young age for a referee in those days. I've never told him this, but I really do believe that he had a great chance at becoming a Football League referee had he carried on. He was probably only around 26 years old when we all flew out to New Zealand.

We arrived at Jo's sister Christine's house in North Shore City to stay, and we had only been there for 24 hours when there was a knock at the door from a bloke asking for a word with Jeff Evans. He didn't know me personally, he hadn't seen me play, yet there he was offering me money to sign for his club! Word had got around that I had played football in England, so they had done their research and realised it was at a fairly decent level. The team was called East Coast Bays, and they played in the Rothmans National League. I went along for training and signed on, and when I asked what the arrangements were for the Saturday, the manager told me to meet them at the airport because we were playing at Wellington. I was awestruck – flying to a game was something I would never have even dreamed about back in England. But playing in that league took me all over the island. Some of the flights took 90 minutes, so you can only imagine how long it would have taken to drive to away games on those old roads.

Playing for East Coast Bays was absolutely superb as I was able to see the whole of the North Island. When I describe it as superb, I do so in a rather selfish manner because the wife didn't see any of it! To be fair, she didn't take to New Zealand at all. We had an agreement when we first went out that the move out there was purely temporary for the first few months, so that we could both find out whether we were going to like it. We promised that, if either one of us didn't settle, then we would both move back to Bristol. If it had been down to Jo, I think we would have come back after the first week or two! We actually went back for a visit a couple of years ago, and she still couldn't get a feeling for the place, which was a good thing really – it reaffirmed that we made the right decision in not staying out there longer than we did.

The football with East Coast Bays was good, though. It was effectively the second division of the Rothmans National League, but it did put money in my pocket each week so that I didn't have to touch my money from home. Anyway, Jo agreed to let me see the football season out before we came home. I had bought an old Austin Cambridge car to get about in, and I managed to sell it for the same price that I had paid for it. It meant that when we returned home in October 1973, we were in a pretty comfortable position in terms of savings and having the two shops still going. Brian Birchall picked me up from the airport on a Friday night, and the next day I turned out for Hanham!

It was pretty much business as usual. Although I'd missed the opening few games, I slotted back into the side and saw the season out. It didn't end in a happy way though, because Brian was sacked as manager of Hanham Athletic at the end of the season. I think every player, bar one or two, walked out after that decision was made.

The next stop for me ended up being Mangotsfield United. One of my shops was in Mangotsfield, and a player for the club, Chopper Hill, stopped by one day and suggested I should pay them a visit in pre-season to see if I could get in the side. I was happy to, and it was a lovely place with some quality players. Keith Gleason had to be the best centre-half I have ever played alongside. His footballing brain was second to none, and his talking was irreplaceable. I had to play at centre-half for one game when we were short in defence, and I wasn't all that comfy with it. During my career I'd played at right-back and in midfield, but I'm only 5ft 8in and the idea of playing as a centre-half had never entered my head. Keith was incredible, though – I've never met anyone who could talk you through a game so well. Pat McKeown would have kicked anything that moved, but he could play football, and Chopper Hill was up front and always scoring goals.

Mangotsfield was certainly one of the better clubs I'd played for, both on the pitch and off it. The pitch there was always fantastic and just seemed to get better and better with each game we played on it. The side was competitive and well organised too, although when there was a problem, it was definitely sorted out in the old-fashioned way! In one game, I remember going in for half-time 3-0 up, but Chopper Hill was having a right go at little Jeff Long, who had messed up a pass. By the time we got to the changing rooms, it was all-out war in there. Pat McKeown pushed a group of them to one side, and I did the same at the other. You've got to remember, we didn't have a manager at that time. Bert Hill was the chairman and, once the side was picked, it was down to the players to get out there and do it. This group of players would drink together in the bar and they would go out together on a Saturday night, but when things had to be sorted out – believe me, they were sorted out!

By this time I knew I wasn't getting any younger. I was in my early 30s, and I just felt I wasn't the right player to help Mangotsfield chase their ambitions. They hadn't switched to the Gloucestershire County League like many sides had done a few years earlier, but now they were looking to make their way in the Western League. With my businesses at the forefront of my thinking, I decided to go back into local football and linked up with a chap called Mick Millard at Abbotonians.

Abbotonians had been formed back in 1947 as a junior side, launched by pupils at Hanham Abbots School. Mick then took the club into adult football in the early 1960s before later handing over the reins to his son, Steve. Abbotonians were based at the Longwell Green Community Centre in Shellards Road when I arrived and, in my second season there, I agreed to become assistant manager to Steve Millard. Steve had played Southern League football, and brought with him several experienced players to bolster that Abbotonians side. He was an enthusiastic lad, but could be a bit of a loose cannon at times. You couldn't keep him down – if he wanted to do something, he went ahead and did it. He and his dad were always arguing about something, and one Saturday morning when I picked him up he suddenly blurted out that he was finishing with immediate effect. He told me he had signed for Forest Green and that he was off. It was a big shock.

A few days later I went around to Mick's house to chat about what we were going to do. Mick said he didn't have the contacts to go back into management, and said he'd had several sleepless nights worrying about finding someone to replace Steve. I looked at him and asked: "Would I do?" Now Mick was about 6ft 2in tall and almost as wide, and he stomped across the room to me and picked me up with an almighty bear-hug. He threw me back down into the chair and said: "Why the hell didn't you tell me that a few days ago? I may have got some bloody sleep if I'd have known!" With that, I had my first managerial job at 35 years old. No lucrative contract signing, no scarf-waving in front of the main stand ... just a colossal bear-hug from Mick Millard!

Iron Acton before the Berkeley Hospital Cup Final triumph in 1969. I'm in the front row, second from right, with the ball. My great friend Brian Birchall was the manager of the side – he's the smart-dressed one on the left!

4... Every day's a football day

IT WOULD prove to be the bane of my life throughout my playing career but, as you've probably guessed by now, my love of the game and my enthusiasm to kick a ball whenever I got the chance made me easily susceptible to the lure of Sunday morning football. Before I get stuck into the managerial side of my football journey, I wanted to take some time to look back on a few of my other experiences in the game, away from the semi-pro side of things, and Sunday football certainly played a big part.

For me it all started when a lad by the name of John Reeves decided to start a Sunday morning team based at the King Billy. Back in my early playing days, there weren't many local sides around who had their own clubhouse, so you had to find a pub to do your post-match drinking. The King Billy was a popular choice in Staple Hill, and probably had about ten or eleven sides who would meet there on Saturday evenings after games – the landlord Ralph Jefferies had spotted a gap in the market, and really promoted the football side of his pub. Ralph and John came up with the idea of starting a pub side and, being one of the more senior players who drank there, I was obviously asked to get involved.

It started off as a great venture and a big laugh, but I can assure you that getting up on a Sunday morning to play a game after a night out with the wife, or a night on the beer with your Saturday side, was not the best decision I ever made. But I got on with it because I enjoyed playing football, although I soon realised the side wasn't going to go anywhere without forming a committee and getting a bit of money in for proper kit, balls and other equipment.

Our first year was a venture into nothing. We started in whatever the lowest division of the Bristol Sunday scene was at the time, and it was a real education. John had never played a decent standard of football in his life and was really trying his best, but after forming the committee we decided to dispense with his services and brought in a manager by the name of Les Britton. It was the best thing to do, but letting John go was a painful decision for us to make – sometimes though, to move forward in football you have to make decisions that aren't always liked. Under Les, we won promotion in our second season and we also gained a team sponsor when a friend of mine called Bob Marshall, who had a tyre business, got involved. From then on, it just snowballed.

We got ourselves into the Sunday League's top division, and we were playing some big games – I remember playing in one match at the Netham against the Pack Horse, one of the city's top Sunday sides, and there were about 400 people stood around the outside watching. It was incredible … you certainly wouldn't get crowds like that for Sunday League games today, I can assure you.

The laughs along the way were fantastic, and one that always stands out for me involved a young lad called Martin Evans, who was celebrating his birthday one Sunday when we were playing at Page Park. In the changing room after the game, the lads got all Martin's clothes together while he was in the shower and we all hightailed it back to the King Billy, which was about half-a-mile away. The only thing we left him was a hand towel – and a message that his clothes were at the King Billy, and we'd see him there shortly! By the time Martin came scuttling up the road, with nothing but a dainty little hand towel sparing his blushes, we'd all got back to the pub and the entire place had emptied onto the street to cheer him on. Into the pub he came, where he gratefully received his clothes, and from that day on Martin has always been known as Pinky Evans!

Off the pitch, Ralph informed us that he was retiring at the end of the year and the incoming landlord was not keen on the idea of football in the pub, so advised us to start searching for an alternate venue. We looked at the Labour Club next door, but a couple of our sponsors weren't happy with that, so ultimately it ended with the club splitting in two. By now we also had a reserve team full of local lads, so they went to the Labour Club while the first team went over to a pub called The Folly on Westerleigh Road. The Folly's owner Dave Nunn was into football and was going to back us, and our two main sponsors came with us too. We had to get a pitch and a changing room, and the latter was found by my old mate Brian Birchall … a mobile home! As for a ground, I got on to one of my customers, Mervyn Dann at Danco, who had more than enough space for a pitch. I said we would happily look after the upkeep of the grounds and return it as we found it, as long as they wouldn't mind a groundsman coming along and marking up a pitch. Danco were fantastic, and even offered to get some running water so we could bring down our 'mobile changing room' and place it pitch-side – the original plan had been to keep it at The Folly, and walk the half-a-mile or so down to the pitch.

So that's what we did, and we even managed to get some electricity there so we could have a hot shower after matches. We got a couple of guys involved as groundsmen who would look after the pitch for us and advise us whether or not we could play – the venue was prone to waterlogging after a lot of rain – and the first year there was superb. We all had a fantastic time and everybody enjoyed it. Unfortunately, in the second year there were one or two teams coming to play us who couldn't control their mouths. We asked every away team to control their effing and blinding out of respect for the people who were living next to the pitch, seeing as they were letting us use their ground for nothing. In the end, Mervyn's wife put a stop to it. She said she was happy for us to play football there, but wasn't so happy about the language and having a load of blokes wearing next to nothing going in and out of the changing rooms every Sunday.

We reverted to our original plan of basing the mobile changing rooms at The Folly. Although it was a pain having to walk to the ground and back, more often than not I was able to load all the lads into the back of my fruit and veg van and ferry them there and back. This went on for around four years and produced some good times, especially one involving a game against Hengrove. The pitch was waterlogged down one side, so much so that you could have been forgiven for thinking it was a swimming pool. To get the game played, we convinced the referee to class the ball as being out whenever it hit the water! To be fair, he agreed and I remember a couple of Hengrove lads going in for sliding tackles and aquaplaning the best part of 15 or 20 metres! There were no complaints though. They would just get out, shake themselves down and get on with it – that was the spirit of the game back then, and there were nowhere near as many prima donnas as there are now.

Looking back, Sunday football was a very good experience for me, despite the early starts. I played with the likes of Dick Savage, Kenny Savage, Oscar Ponting and Eddie Griffiths, who were all good players in their own right and we played some really good stuff. I also played with Terry Rowles, who later went into management and took Taunton Town to Wembley Stadium for the 1994 FA Vase Final, which they lost after extra time to Diss Town.

But in the end, running around on a Sunday morning and collecting players just got a bit much. Picking up Kenny Savage was an experience in itself. He lived out near me in a village called Pucklechurch, but in a caravan! When I used to open that caravan door on a Sunday morning, you've never ever smelt anything like it – it really made you proud to be up and about early on a Sunday morning! So after four years of Sunday League football, I'd decided that was my lot and I jacked it in.

Before you start worrying about me not playing enough, don't panic ... I haven't even got to Bristol Wednesday League football yet! It was set up in the main to accommodate players who, for whatever reason, were unable to play at the weekend, and there were a lot of teams from the city and surrounding areas who got involved. The police and fire brigades had sides, there were factory sides entered who saw the league as an advertising opportunity, and then there was a side called Clifton Wednesday. Once again, Brian Birchall was a prominent figure in getting me to play for Clifton Wednesday. He played there himself, and kept on and on at me to go along and join in. As luck would have it, the latest I would finish work on a Wednesday was around 1pm. I only had one fruit and veg shop at the time, and was also working as a fruit lorry salesman for a company called Smith & Son, and in those days we would close on Wednesday afternoons.

Once again, I was very easily persuaded to go and play Wednesday League football, but I have to be honest ... those ten or so years were the most enjoyable time of my entire playing career. It was an added chance to play with quality players week in, week out, and although the opposition were sometimes poor we would always take the opportunity to make a real go of it by building up an early lead and then playing for our own enjoyment. In that Clifton Wednesday side, there was a bloke by the name of Ronnie Rampling who played right in front of me. Ronnie was basically a carbon copy of Dave Mackay, who George Best always described as the hardest man he'd ever played against. As the weeks and months wore on, I soon learned that, by the time any player had managed to get past Ronnie Rampling, he was so dizzy and beaten up that I was just able to nick the ball off him and play football. Ronnie made my life as a full-back so much easier, although this was back in the day when you could put a proper tackle in.

Another lad in the side was Barry Dudbridge, who was a couple of years older than me and had an arsenal full of tricks and flicks. I remember Mick Millard chasing him with a corner flag once because he wouldn't pass to him! Mick didn't even wait for the end of the game ... there we were, trying to play with nine men while Barry was legging it with Millard in hot pursuit, waving this corner flag at him! Barry was doing him for pace easily, and that just made Mick angrier – every time he got close, Barry just cranked up the pace and pulled away again!

Les Britton, who we'd brought in to manage the King Billy's Sunday side, was also in charge of Clifton Wednesday and he played a bit too. Despite being in his 50s, he had a lot of skill I can assure you. With young Dudbridge, Brian Harper and Brian Birchall involved too, there was a lot of quality in the side and more good players joined over the following decade. Mark Graydon, Kenny Phillips, Phil Powell, Steve Millard, Johnny Bamford, John Slocombe, Mickey Noble, Steve Summers, Steve Frith and Paul Bennett, to name but a few. Many of them were playing as high a standard of Saturday football as they could, without having to endure the travelling that the Southern League brought. What a player Mick Millard's son Steve turned out to be. He only played for Clifton Wednesday on a few occasions – he was only 15 years old at the time, and Mick used to get him out of school early when we needed to make the numbers up. He went on to be an outstanding player, and achieved what so many dream of but so few realise – playing at Wembley Stadium when Forest Green Rovers won the 1982 FA Vase with a 3-0 triumph over Rainworth Miners Welfare.

There were three medals to be won each season – the league, the league cup and another countywide cup that teams outside of the Bristol Wednesday League could enter. Over the course of ten Clifton Wednesday seasons, with 30 medals available, I have a box hidden away upstairs with at least 24 in. I remember giving one medal away too, after one cup final win at Keynsham Town's ground. I told Mickey Noble's son Bunter, who went on to play for Bristol Rovers, to keep the medal safe for me.

There were also representative games, and I was picked to represent a Bristol Wednesday side against leagues from Cardiff Wednesday, Gloucester Wednesday, Taunton Thursday and others. I can remember sitting in the charabanc going to those games which, much like my away days with the Bristol Rovers youth team, was an experience I can only liken to sitting on a wooden stool in the back of a truck! For one game away at Taunton, we all had first class train tickets to get there – that really made us feel like prima donnas!

We were a very close-knit bunch at Clifton Wednesday, held together by our gaffer Les Britton, who we all had a great amount of respect for. So tell me ... why, without fail, did we always have to pinch his hair dye and his lacquer after every game? In he'd come afterwards, shouting and balling about his missing hair lacquer! In games, sometimes we'd all deliberately keep the ball away from him when we were well on top, trying to let anybody score but poor old Les! Whenever he did find the net, boy oh boy did we hear about it in the clubhouse afterwards! Having said that, on one occasion we kept him so busy that he scored six goals – and he was 56 years old at the time. We wouldn't pass to Barry Dudbridge, or any other forward, and we just kept giving it to Les. He'd give it back, go again and the next minute he'd have an open goal or only the goalkeeper to beat. He scored six goals at the age of 56 – now that's some achievement.

In some of the cup games, Les would play me in midfield and my job was to upset the opposition, back in a time when football wasn't the non-contact sport it has seemingly now become. I first came across Kenny Phillips, a quality midfielder, while performing this role for Clifton Wednesday, against a side called Robinsons I think. I had to mark Kenny tightly which he didn't appreciate, but I was following orders! We wanted to win, we did win and it was soon forgotten when we got back to the clubhouse and had a good drink. That was the beauty of playing Wednesday League football. There were some really entertaining teams involved, with great characters. I always enjoyed playing the police teams. We had a healthy respect for those sides – after all, chances are one of us had a speeding ticket or something, so we made sure we didn't kick the police players too high!

For the last four years of my time with Clifton Wednesday, I played in goal. It was the same old story ... our goalkeeper gets injured and I stand in, so Les decided to keep me there. By that time I could handle it easily though, so much so that on more than one occasion I used to take a chair with me! I'd set it up in the net, sit down and enjoy the football that was being played in front of me. Our lads were so far superior to any of the other teams involved. However, that brought about problems in itself, because any new team coming into the league had one mission – to beat Clifton Wednesday. One such side were called Harris Furniture, who had a very chirpy manager, all 5ft 6in of him, who told anyone who listened that they were going to beat us and take the league title.

When we played Harris Furniture on our ground, which unfortunately was Page Park in Staple Hill, we'd opened up an early 2-0 lead when their manager decided to bring himself on. It actually picked up their spirits a little bit, and they had us under the cosh. Their winger went down the line and whipped in an inch-perfect cross. Their manager, meanwhile, had galloped into the box like a man possessed and rose to meet the header. What happened next was probably one of the funniest things I've seen in football. Our goalkeeper that day, Joe Goldburn, instinctively flung himself at what he thought was the ball, but we could all see that the ball had sailed wide of his other post. For a split second everyone was confused, until Joe looked down at his hands and realised he had smothered this guy's wig! I've never seen 11 blokes laugh as much. Even their side were laughing. In fact, the only guy not laughing was the one who had lost his hair … he was clearly less than impressed by it all! I think it took Les Britton about 20 minutes to calm us all down, but once we regained our composure we managed to stick another couple of goals past them.

Different players came and went during my ten years with Clifton Wednesday, but the team spirit remained as strong as ever throughout. We used to hold presentation nights at the end of every season at whatever pub Dave Nunn was running at the time, and our nights out on the town quite often involved a visit to a snooker hall that was down behind Bristol Hippodrome, before doing the pubs in the city centre. However the most memorable knees-up of all time had to be my two-week tour of Germany for the 1974 FIFA World Cup, which also took in a bit of Belgium and Holland. As I mentioned in the previous chapter, Brian Birchall and myself had often spoke about doing this trip, and we were joined for the adventure by Micky Lee and Fred Hacker when we left Dover for Ostend.

On that four-hour ferry trip, we decided that instead of having a kitty for the whole fortnight, we would rotate and make one person responsible for spending money on all the food and beer that day. At the end of each day, we would work out the total spent, divide it by four and the person in charge of the day's spending would get three-quarters of it back. Brian was in charge for the first day at Ostend, which I'd liken to a Belgian version of Weymouth. You wouldn't believe that, in such a popular seaside resort, we managed to book up in a hotel where we appeared to be the only paying guests ... all the other rooms appeared to be for ladies of the night! Walking down the corridor was an experience in itself, and you'd see every Tom, Dick or Harry coming out of the rooms. It's a shame we didn't have video phones in those days! Downstairs, the bar was full of sleazy women too, so we quickly headed out for some beers in the bars around the town. Less than impressed with our digs, we decided to abandon our scheduled second night's stay there and I think it was Fred who suggested we take in Amsterdam instead, on our way to Frankfurt.

The next day, the four of us piled into Brian's Mercedes and set off on the jaunt to Amsterdam, where we found a nice little hotel on the outskirts of the city. The main reason for visiting new places is to see different things, and it's definitely a safe bet that you'll be able to do that in Amsterdam. I'd never seen anything like it before, and I haven't since, walking down one side of the river seeing all the women in the shop windows. We were leaning against a rail watching all the blokes who were shuffling in and out – Micky and I timed one of them, he was in and out in less than four minutes! All the windows were doing the same brisk trade, but I can assure that none of us four went shopping that night!

The next day we were off to Frankfurt for one of the most memorable moments of my life – being present for the opening ceremony of the 1974 FIFA World Cup on June 13. We got the tickets through an agency in Bristol and we were worried about how good they would be, but we were sat just a few rows back from the Royal Box. It was an unforgettable moment, being part of a 62,000 crowd to see the launch of the biggest sporting event on the planet at the Waldstadion. After the ceremony, we saw a Brazil side featuring Jairzinho and Rivelino draw 0-0 with Yugoslavia although, in all honesty, the football action on the pitch was almost a by-product of the whole experience of being at a World Cup. Out on the streets of Frankfurt afterwards, I've never known an atmosphere like it. Even the police were having a laugh and a joke with you. In fact, I can remember being sat in a police car while Micky took my photo, and the police didn't mind at all. I think you'd probably get clubbed over the head for that these days.

About a year earlier, the four of us had to come to terms with the idea that England wouldn't be at the World Cup. 'Bite your legs' Norman Hunter decided not to tackle on the halfway line, Peter Shilton performed a belly-flop instead of saving a shot, and Poland had nicked an unexpected 1-1 draw at Wembley Stadium – a result that sent them to West Germany at England's expense. Although our home nation weren't able to make the trip, we knew it was a once-in-a-lifetime tour and that we'd have to make the most of it. The party atmosphere on the streets of Frankfurt was infectious, and it set the scene for the rest of the holiday.

While England weren't there, Scotland were so our next port of call was their opening game against Zaire the next day in Dortmund. As it turned out, this was the game that cost them qualification to the second round – even though they won 2-0 and were the only team in the entire tournament who didn't lose. Like Yugoslavia and Brazil, Scotland ended the group on four points so it went down to goal difference and, effectively, who put the most goals past Zaire. Yugoslavia walloped them 9-0 and Brazil beat them 3-0, and that latter result emphasised the fine line between success and failure in football … one goal.

I can remember Scotland being completely on top for the entire game, and big Joe Jordan probably missed a hat-trick of headers. If it had been a boxing bout, the referee would have stopped it and Zaire couldn't have complained had they conceded double figures. Football can be a cruel game and, as we were to find out, so could the Scottish fans! Brian and Fred got us some fantastic tickets right on the halfway line, but the Scots were all around us. They weren't causing us any problems because we were dressed normally, but there were a few England fans visible and they were getting some real stick. At one stage, Sir Alf Ramsey walked past and the abuse he got was frightening. I felt sorry for the man really. After all, he'd done nothing wrong other than winning the World Cup in 1966, and I found the Scottish fans' behaviour extremely disrespectful.

Before the game, we were in a bar sat alongside about eight Scottish fans who were all from the same family. Needless to say, the beers were being supped at an alarming rate and all seemed fine until the young waitress came up just after they'd left. "Where are your friends? They haven't paid their bill!" I quickly assured her they were no friends of mine, but she wanted us to settle up their bill! If that wasn't bad enough, it was my day to take care of buying all the food and drink in our little kitty arrangement. Over there the bars would give you a peg and just spike it with tickets every time you ordered drinks or food. Their peg was full and I worked their bill out to be around £180. Ours was half-full so I feared that would mean an extra £90, which was a ridiculous sum of money back in 1974. There was only one thing for it… what's good for the Scots is good enough for us! I told Fred and Brian to head on down to the stadium while Micky and I paid the bill, but little did they know that the two of us just scarpered! Straight past the till, straight out the door and straight down to the ground!

After the game we went to a steakhouse to eat and, of course, by now we were full of drink and having a right laugh. When it came to leaving and settling up, there was another massive queue for the till so I gave Micky a wad of cash and told him to settle up while I waited outside. A few minutes later, out came Micky with the same wad of notes still in his hand. The cash was quickly returned to my pocket and off we went to a few more bars, where we actually ended up paying for drinks over the counter in the normal way. When we got back to the hotel and it came to working out how much was spent, I chucked all the money on the table. After a long day's session on the beer and with a fine steak involved, the only money I'd spent was for those last two beers on the way back to our room. Brian was shitting himself, he was sure that the German police would be hot on our heels and broke out into a cold sweat at the mere thought of a knock at the door! He really wasn't happy about it because he wasn't that sort of bloke, but it was a fantastic day out.

We managed to squeeze in two other World Cup games before it was time to head home. The day after that Scotland game, we went to Düsseldorf to watch Sweden draw 0-0 with Bulgaria, and also Italy's 1-1 draw against Argentina in Stuttgart. The homeward part of the trip involved heading back to Ostend and an overnight stay at that hotel we were so eager to get out of a fortnight earlier. Travelling back, we were all in agreement that we'd prefer to find somewhere else to stay, so we had a quick stopover in Bruges. It was a completely different experience to the nights in West Germany, but once again it was great fun in the bars.

When we got back to Dover the next day, we only had about four hours to get back to Bristol and watch the next World Cup game on television. After the two weeks we'd just had, you'd be forgiven for thinking we'd had enough football. Not a chance! We were held up at customs, because they wanted to look in my suitcase, and I told the guy he was welcome … if he was brave enough! After two weeks of drinking, eating and touring, everything in there was filthy. The only clean clothes I had were the ones I was wearing.

After that delay, we got onto the motorway and Brian put his foot down, although we almost didn't make it back at all. One of Brian's rear tyres blew near Reading, and to be fair to him he did well to keep the motor under control because the car was shaking and weaving quite violently. Brian managed to get the car pulled over and, with the televised match still at the forefront of our minds, that tyre change was done like a Formula One pit-stop! The blow-out had left Brian a bit shaken, so I drove the final leg home and we went straight back to my place. We got in the door, said a quick hello to the missus and put the telly on just as the game was kicking off … happy days! It was a great World Cup and, for me personally, a fantastic experience that I'll never forget. Okay, so we did a few things wrong but we were young lads all away in Germany, and I think it's fair to say they owed us a few quid anyway!

Although I never got the chance to watch England play in an actual World Cup match, I went on to become a regular at Wembley Stadium for qualification games and friendly matches. It was mainly down to a change in career. I'd sold one fruit and veg shop when I went to New Zealand, but as the 1970s wore on the other shops were finding it increasingly hard to compete against supermarkets and bigger shops. By Christmas in 1978, I had shut the doors for the last time and a couple of months later I got a job with a chemical company. I didn't know how to spell chemicals, let alone work with them, but it was a selling job and I took a chance on it (it was commission only) because it let me have Saturdays off for football and ended up giving me a good income.

Through this new job, I landed up with a privilege card for Posthouse Hotels, and at the time they had a hotel on the edge of the car park at Wembley. When I stayed there once, I got chatting to the manager and he told me he'd be able to get me England tickets if I fancied watching a game. That conversation started a five or six-year stint where myself and a motley crew of Steve Tregale, Brian Burden, Jeff Meacham and Steve Fey, who also had a few good Wembley contacts, would regularly travel to London for the games. What started as a 4pm departure from Bristol for evening games later became 2pm as we would always get invited to the hotel first for a drink, so the five of us would take turns in driving to allow everyone the chance to have a beer.

As good as it was watching England play, some of my most memorable moments of this era occurred in the Posthouse Hotel. I'd also managed to get my hands on a privilege card for a club called the String of Pearls, which was inside the hotel, and it allowed us to go in there after the game and mingle with the England players when they appeared about an hour after the game. It was a lovely experience, being able to get all the players' autographs for the kids, although I can remember at least one occasion when full-back Phil Neal probably wouldn't have described our presence as lovely. You'll hear a lot more about Jeff Meacham in the coming chapters because he played for me at several clubs, but for now let's just describe him as a proud person who always says what he thinks. Never mind the fact that Neal was a four-time European Cup winner with Liverpool … he'd had a stinker in this particular game, and Jeff may have said something along those lines a bit too loudly! Neal was within earshot and in the end, for the sake of our membership in the String of Pearls, I had to step in and separate the two of them because I thought Meach was going to stick one on him! If I remember rightly, goalkeeper Ray Clemence also came over to try and diffuse the situation, but fortunately it was all cleared up without any blows being traded!

I was the designated driver for another Wembley Stadium trip that sticks in my mind, mainly because it showed what a bunch of jokers the lads were sometimes. I can remember having Steve Tregale in the front passenger seat with Jeff Meacham, Brian Burden and Steve Fey in the back as we were driving up. Looking in the rear view mirror, I saw Brian gently sprinkle a pile of powder on Tregale's shoulder before leaning forward and coughing into it. It was itching powder, and Tregale was covered in it! So much so that he spent the rest of the trip up to London with his top off, calling Brian every name under the sun. When we got up there, we were having a meal in a Chinese restaurant and more of the itching powder was called into play on the chairs of several unsuspecting guests, who had probably the most uncomfortable chicken chow mein of their lives – no doubt the farting powder that was sneakily poured into the pepper pots didn't help!

As we got into the ground, there was one of those hardcore fans that you still see today – usually a Newcastle United nutcase at St James' Park – stood there with his top off, no matter what the weather, draped in an England flag. This particular guy was massive, shaped like a barrel, and all of a sudden I went into a panic as I saw Meacham empty the entire contents of the itching powder onto this bloke's shoulders. Tregale came along and blew it, and the pair of them made a quick exit! Although our behaviour may suggest otherwise, we always tried to dress very responsibly and wore our best suits to the matches. This helped us with another little scam, because we were usually able to blag our way in to a better part of the ground where we knew there were empty seats, and get a lovely view. We were able to again at this game in question, and we had a tremendous view of our latest itching powder victim. He was red all over from scratching, and was using his flag as if he had just got out of the shower! He must have been in a hell of a state by the time he got home. I just hope it wasn't a long journey.

One other Wembley trip where I was grateful not to be driving ended up with me meeting one of the country's great managers in the String of Pearls. Again we'd managed to talk our way in, and I'd just ordered four pints and an orange juice (Steve Fey was the driver that day) when I felt someone tap my shoulder. "It's a free bar son." It was Malcolm Allison! Who was I to argue with a man who had helped Manchester City win the European Cup Winners Cup?

The drink was definitely flowing, and we were throwing it down for what must have been the best part of an hour. It all stopped when we heard a bang on the table, and someone of great importance – even more important than Malcolm Allison – told us to take our seats for Her Royal Highness the Princess Anne. We knew we didn't have a place at any table, and we were just there making the most of an unexpected free bar. But Princess Anne was on her way in, and suddenly I felt the biggest arm I had ever seen wrap around my neck. The owner of said arm, a particularly burly bouncer, quietly suggested in my ear that I'd had a good free night, and that I should take my glass to the bar, top it up and leave quietly. When I looked at him, I knew the best option was to wholeheartedly agree. As we were quietly leaving, we saw Malcolm Allison again. "Good night, lads?" he enquired. We all nodded as we walked out, and then realised he was coming too. "I'm in the same boat boys, I wasn't invited either!"

All good things have to come to an end, though, and our England jolly-ups were gradually phased out when the hotel changed hands and the tickets started drying up. However those five or six years we spend hammering up and down the motorway were very enjoyable times. The football was good, and the laughs were even better. It's a shame that fans today probably won't get the same experience as we did 30 years ago. Today's traffic problems really do take some of the enjoyment out of it. When we first started going to Wembley, we could leave at 4pm for an evening kick-off, and be back in Bristol by midnight. There's no way it would be possible today.

I also wonder how many people in Wembley really enjoy the England friendlies and qualifiers these days as sporting spectacles. Let's face it, the vast majority come across as absolutely dire on television. But I suppose that's the problem when you've got players starting for England, but who are only substitutes for their Saturday clubs. I'm a firm believer that the only way England's international football fortunes can be reversed is if we were somehow able to introduce a rule to limit the numbers of foreign players at any one club. Of course, that's easier said than done these days, what with the red tape and European laws, but let me just ask one question. How many foreign players played in the English First Division in 1966? We must have been doing something right with our national team back then, because we won the World Cup.

Our successful King Billy FC Sunday League side. That's me, front row, second from left.

Travelling in style! Our Clifton Wednesday side get ready to board the charabanc for another luxurious journey to an away game!

The Clifton Wednesday lads celebrate another successful season. I'm in the front row, third from the right. Also in the picture are Brian Birchall (centre), manager Les Britton (front row, second left) and Barry Dudbridge (far left).

The all-stars! That's me, front row centre, as part of the Bristol Wednesday XI that went away to play Taunton Wednesday.

5... The original crazy gang!

DURING my time as a player I'd encountered more than a few moments when the nerves were jangling, be it a closely-fought cup semi-final or playing for a professional career with Bristol Rovers. But I can assure you that it was an extremely nervous Jeff Evans who took charge of his first ever game as a manager with Abbotonians. I can remember it was an away game at Watchet Town in the 1980/81 season, which was one of the longer trips the club had to make in Division One of the Somerset County League at that time.

I found it a very daunting task when we got to the changing room at Watchet and there in front of me was basically the side that Mick Millard's son Steve had put together. Steve was even there himself, and took great amusement in seeing me worry! Although he'd stepped down as manager and had said he was off to Forest Green, he actually ended up staying on at Abbotonians for at least a month before leaving. I really did feel the pressure involved and it was a weird experience, trying to give a team-talk to a group of lads who had come to the club to play under another manager, who just happened to be sitting right alongside them.

However I was under no illusions about the task in hand. I either had to do it, or not do it, so I made sure I did the best I could. Okay, so the team-talk before the game was a rather nervous one, but the half-time chat got a little bit better and when the final whistle blew we were 6-0 winners. As we were walking off the pitch, Steve came up behind me, wrapped his arms around me and hoisted me up in the air. "Jesus Jeff, is it really that easy to get these players playing? I must have been doing something wrong!" Steve was a fabulous player, and he was also a good bloke too. He didn't have to say that, but it really helped ease the nerves – along with that 6-0 win.

I've got to be honest, I had a fantastic crew behind me at the club, and that made it so much easier for me to settle in to my new role at the club. There was the man-mountain Mick Millard, and two committee members in Roger Caines and Roger Tarrant who were also extremely supportive. I really did appreciate their help because in those days I had no assistant manager working alongside me. I just carried on by myself, taking training, picking the team and managing from the dug-out. If ever I needed any help or advice, Mick was always at the end of the phone and he was always there to listen.

In the Abbotonians side there were a lot of players who already had Western League experience under their belts. Malcolm Smith, Steve Tregale, Paul Allen, Jamie Patch and Paul Hopkins are just a few players who spring to mind, who were very accomplished players within the squad during that first season. We put a few good results together, and did our best in the cups that the league had to offer. But there was one cup competition that we really seemed to excel in, and everything seemed to click at the right time. It was the Sutton Transformer Cup. This was a very popular competition back in the 1970s, and it attracted good sides from all over the South West and as far away as the Southampton area.

We put some really good results together in it, and we had a very good centre-forward in Terry Brown who I was able to persuade to stay with us when other clubs began to sniff around. Glen Bowyer and Steve Dale also agreed to stay, and I brought a young Jeff Meacham to the club. It was all part of a steep managerial learning curve for me. Not only was it arming me with experience of how to react when other clubs expressed their interest in your players, but I was quickly learning how to interact with them, and how to get the best out of them.

But one thing I knew about management was that it wouldn't always go smoothly, and that sometimes decisions would need to be made that wouldn't always please everybody. It wasn't long before I had hands-on experience in such a decision, and it concerned our goalkeeper Graham Bird. I decided to replace him with a very young Steve Fey, and it was the first of many controversial moves I would have to make over the years. Obviously I knew Steve already and he was a friend, but that was coincidental. A manager's job is to get the best players he possibly can to the club, and I honestly felt Steve would be the better asset for Abbotonians going forward. Graham was very bitter for a long time after that, and felt very hard done-by. A number of years passed before we would ever speak properly to each other again.

On the pitch, we quietly went about winning games and put ourselves in the hunt for promotion and a place in the Premier Division. As the season drew to a close, every Saturday we would be putting a call in to the local newspaper to try and pick up results involving the teams around us, and before we knew it we were sitting in second position with just a couple of games to go. I was close to winning a promotion in my first full season as a manager and, on top of that, we had a Sutton Transformer Cup final to look forward to – to be played over two legs against Holsworthy, a Devon club who at the time were a top-half side in the South Western League.

The first leg of the final was at Longwell Green and, despite having home advantage, we lost 1-0. They had some very good players in that Holsworthy side, in particular a winger who was as quick as lightning and gave us all sorts of trouble. The second leg down at Holsworthy was the following weekend, but before that we had the small matter of our final league game in midweek that could see us clinch promotion into the Premier Division of the Somerset County League. We did what we had to do, winning the game to clinch the second promotion spot in Division One. We ended up four points clear of third-placed Westland United, with 20 wins and just four defeats from our 32 league games. East Worle won the division that year, six points ahead of us. Needless to say, it was drinks all round, and in those days it was proper drinking to celebrate a promotion!

We had a few days to shake off the hangovers before the second leg of the Sutton Transformer Cup final, which was scheduled for the Sunday at Holsworthy. We were looking to overturn that 1-0 deficit so we really needed to be on our game, but I would end up making the biggest mistake of my managerial career so far. Still on the high of promotion, I decided to arrange for the team to travel down to North Devon on the Saturday, 24 hours before the game. Obviously, the team's spirits were still very high following our midweek celebration, and taking a group of jubilant footballers away for a Saturday night made it inevitable that the temptation of another night on the beer would prove irresistible. As a young man who had been used to playing with these lads for longer than I'd been managing them, I had no idea how to deal with the situation. In hindsight, I dealt with it in the worst way possible … I joined in!

We arrived in Torrington early on the Saturday afternoon, and headed straight for a pub called The Cavalier Inn. Two or three of the lads in the squad couldn't even see by the time we left The Cavalier, and it was still pretty early. We headed over to the holiday park just outside Torrington where we had booked in to stay. I think the owner was a little bit worried with how rowdy we all were, and when Paul Hopkins narrowly missed a cat by inches when we were supposed to be playing darts, he came over to us and suggested we all moved on to a pub nearby. We all staggered over to this place, I think it was called The Gribble Inn, and the guy on the door told us the entry was by ticket only. I very politely explained the situation to him, that I had an entire football squad behind me who were starving and wanted to order meals, and the pound signs quickly flashed up in his eyes. In we went, only to find all the locals in there dressed up as cowboys for a country and western night. It didn't seem to worry my lads though, they all just joined in!

To be fair we had a cracking night in there, so much so that we had all forgotten the reason why we were there in the first place – to play in a cup final. We headed back to our accommodation and a pack of cards came out, and the first time I glanced at my watch I realised it was 3am. I quickly hurried the lads off to bed, reminding them all that they had a game to play in the morning, but the damage was done. You can imagine what sort of state the players were all in the next morning and, much to my disgust, I have to say that I was feeling every bit as bad as the rest of them. I apologised to the owner of the park for our behaviour the night before, and asked if he minded providing a late breakfast for us. To the chap's great credit, he said he would so the players were at least able to get some food inside them … well, most of them!

We got to Holsworthy's ground for a 3pm kick-off and even then, when the referee blew his whistle to start proceedings, Steve Fey was still in no condition to stand up unaided, let alone keep goal! A lad called Lee Jenkins put himself forward to mark Holsworthy's flying left-winger who had caused us so much grief in the first leg, and the massacre continued. At one point I remember this player flicking the ball past Lee, running over the touchline and around the back of the dugout before rejoining the pitch and gathering the ball. Lee was just rooted to the spot, looking dazed. "Where's he gone?"

It pains me to say it, but we lost the game 7-0, and 8-0 on aggregate. The Sunday evening drive back to Longwell Green was a very quiet one, and it was definitely a reality check for me personally, and quite a few of the players. Our better players all had Western League experience, but they had become complacent and had let themselves go a bit. Okay, we had won promotion which was probably a bonus given that we didn't set out at the start of the season considering ourselves as promotion contenders. But that was no excuse for what happened the night before this cup final. For me, as a young manager, it was a huge learning experience and I made a promise to myself that I would never let it happen again. If you get to a cup final, you prepare for it properly, and if you're taking a team to stay away from home, you do it professionally.

After several weeks off, we returned for the 1981/82 season with Abbotonians ready to play in the Premier Division of the Somerset County League. It soon turned out to be a very disappointing pre-season, though, with the departure of several key players. Paul Allen's increased work commitments kept him away a lot, while Jamie Patch made the switch to management and several other lads decided to retire from playing, such as little Paul Hopkins, Malcolm Smith, Steve Tregale and Steve Dale. At one point I had serious doubts about whether we were going to be able to raise a side for the start of the season.

I was constantly on the prowl for new players, keeping my eyes open and my ears to the ground wherever I went. To this day I can still remember spotting one young player who immediately blew me away with his talent and potential. We were in the middle of a pre-season training session at Longwell Green when in the corner of my eye I saw a little lad kicking a ball around on his own in the adjacent field. He only looked about 16 years old, but I invited him over to join in with our session. He spent the next half-hour making our players look silly. His touch was superb, his all-round play was excellent and he had that little bit of a spark that meant he wasn't afraid to get stuck in. I had seen enough. I didn't care about how old he was, I just knew he was a quality act and that I had to sign him up.

I pulled the lad to one side and asked him to join us, but he told me that I needed to talk to his dad. "Where's your dad?" I asked, and he pointed over to a bloke talking to the Longwell Green club chairman, and an old friend from my Hanham Athletic days, Bill Holloway. I scuttled over, apologised for interrupting and told the chap that I wanted to sign his son. He looked at me a bit baffled and said, "What do you mean? I haven't got a son." Bill laughed, and said: "Jeff, that's my son." Even better, I thought! Bill seemed very reluctant to let his lad sign on, despite me taking the best part of 10 minutes assuring him I would look out for him and treat him as if he was my own son. In the end, a broad smile appeared on Bill's face. "Jeff, he's just signed a three-year contract as an apprentice player with Bristol Rovers!" It was then that I decided to duck out of trying to negotiate that particular deal, and as I walked away I could hear Bill having a right good laugh.

That turned out to be the first time I ever met Ian Holloway. Even though he was only 16, you could tell he was a class act. He's since gone on to become one of the English game's great characters, both as a player with Rovers and QPR, and more recently as a manager. Last season, Ian's infectious personality took the Premier League by storm after his quite outstanding achievement of getting Blackpool promoted to the top flight. Our paths have crossed on a number of occasions since then, and it was always a pleasure to be in the lad's company. He used to get involved in the Longwell Green Sixes summer tournament, and I even met him a few times in hotels and pubs in Barnstaple – while he was managing Bristol Rovers, he would quite often take his sides to North Devon for pre-season friendlies. I've also met his wife Kim and children and, like Ian, they've always been nothing but polite and friendly.

So I failed in my attempts to sign Ian Holloway but, as luck would have it, I was able to bring in a few new faces during pre-season to plug the gap left by all the retirees. First I gained an assistant by the name of Ron Hagarty, and we began to steadily rebuild the side. In came a young lad called Derek Jones, who I had actually replaced at Hanham when I came back from New Zealand. He'd been out on loan at Cadbury Heath the season before as he recovered from an injury, and he came back. Andy Lohmann and Andy Francombe also came along from Cadbury Heath, while Larry Nash and Kevin Pugsley also signed.

I managed to persuade Brian Burden to leave Oldland and he signed up too. I lost goalkeeper Steve Fey very late in pre-season, when he decided to join Paulton Rovers. It would have been much less of a headache for me had he let me know earlier in the summer! But we managed to find an experienced replacement – Roy Hamilton played in goal for Almondsbury Greenway when they reached the final of the FA Vase at Wembley Stadium in 1979, losing 4-1 to Billericay. I also picked up Micky Baker, and also called my old mate Kenny Phillips and managed to get his son Jason, a good centre-half, on board.

We got our first season underway back in the Premier Division, and we started okay with a few encouraging results. What I didn't know at that time was that all the wheeling and dealing over the pre-season had sewn the seeds for Crackers United. If they reckoned Wimbledon were crazy in the 1980s, then they should have paid a visit to Longwell Green! All the boys who came in just blended so well, and the result was utter carnage. It didn't matter where we went, what pub or club we were in, the lads were always up for a laugh. But at the same time, we were also winning games.

The one position that quickly began to prove troublesome for me was the goalkeeper. We lost the lad from Almondsbury Greenway to a serious injury fairly early on in the season – I think it eventually caused him to retire from playing football – so I gave Kenny Phillips another call. He was working with the youth set-up at Bristol City, and he let me have a young 16-year-old called Kevin Slabber who was a quality keeper and went on to play for a long time at a very good level in semi-professional football. Unbelievably, he too got injured after a few games so I had to get back on the phone to Kenny again. This time, the voice at the other end of the line recommended Dave Mogg to me.

I was startled by Kenny's suggestion. "Dave Mogg isn't going to want to come and play Somerset Prem football, he's only just been released from Bristol Rovers," I said. Kenny insisted that I should call him, because he wasn't playing for anyone at that point. Anyway, I phoned Dave's house and spoke to his father, and I arranged to go along and meet them for a chat. When I got there, I had to wait a little while for Dave to get back and I sat down in the Mogg living room which boasted a collection of England shirts hung on the walls from his schoolboy international days. That made me even more certain that I was trying to punch above my weight in trying to sign this extremely talented footballer.

Dave soon arrived and he was a lovely, very quiet, lad. We sat down and had a chat, and once I'd said my piece he just looked at me and asked: "Who are we playing on Saturday?" Dave was willing to sign the forms there and then, which was fantastic news. I told him we had an away game at Imperial at the weekend, and he said he'd be there to meet us. Saturday came along, and I arrived at Imperial around an hour-and-a-quarter before kick-off as usual, expecting to be the first one there. In those days the lads used to get out on the pitch for a quick warm-up at around 2.30pm, and then back into the changing room for a final 10-minute talk before kick-off. However, it was about 1.40pm when I got there. I looked out on to the pitch, and there was Dave Mogg warming up … on his own! His dedication was second to none, and having him in goal at times was almost like having another centre-half on the pitch. Seeing how good he was, it really made me realise what a fine line there can be between making it as a professional and not making it.

In the clubhouse after the game, I went up to Dave and asked him for his £2 match subs … his face was a picture of shock! I then offered him a drink and he asked me what the other lads would be drinking. Brian Burden was quick to let him know that Blackthorn cider was the drink of choice and, when I decided it was time for me to go home, I left poor Dave in the capable hands of Derek Jones, Andy Francombe and Jeff Meacham. I do believe he was dispatched into a taxi at around 11pm, not having a clue where he was! It was probably his first lesson in life as a non-league footballer, and I think he learned to avoid getting in a drinking pot with other players!

I don't know what it was that happened when Jones, Francombe and Meacham got together, but nine times out of ten you could be sure it would end in chaos! I remember one particular incident after a midweek training session involving the terrible trio. The three of them had somehow ended up in a nightclub on their way home from training, and the next time I saw them – it must have been at a Saturday afternoon game – both Derek and Andy were covered in bumps and bruises. Jeff Meacham? Not a mark on him, but from what I understand it was Meacham who was pinching beer from the taps that sparked an almighty flare-up! Jeff was apparently too impatient to wait for the preferred method of having a barman pour your drink, and decided to help himself when his thirst got the better of him. Unfortunately for Derek and Andy, it was those two who got caught in a tear-up with the bouncers while Jeff just quietly carried on drinking! Once Jeff had finished supping his beer, he did manage to find some time to wade in and help the other two, so they managed to get home in one piece … just!

On the pitch, the season went very well. We more than held our own in the Premier Division and were comfy in mid-table, finishing in 12th above sides like Bristol Manor Farm, Bridgwater Town and Wells City. On top of that, we managed to reach another cup final –

this time it was the Gloucester Amateur Senior Cup, which was to be played at Bristol Rovers' Eastville ground for the last time. We played a Bristol-based side called Henbury, and unfortunately we didn't play as well as we could. We went 2-0 down and I sent on Meacham as a substitute. He scored to make it 2-1, and from then on it was all us, but we just couldn't put the ball in the back of the net and lost the game 2-1.

After the game, I can remember turning round and seeing Mick Millard with a tear in his eye. I knew it was a game that Mick was desperate to win. He was getting on a bit, and he wasn't too well either – although he refused to let anyone know about it. Looking back, we had a decent season in a good league and we reached another cup final, but unfortunately we had won nothing. However I'd like to think we played an important part in helping another local side, Forest Green Rovers, reach the pinnacle of English non-league football ... the FA Vase.

During the 1981/82 season under manager Bob Mursell, Forest Green were having a phenomenal season in the Hellenic League. They were the team to beat, and not many did! In fact, they won the title that year and secured promotion to the Southern League Midland Division. It was in the FA Vase, though, that their most memorable and historic triumph came, and I'll never forget the day when Bob Mursell called me up for my help.

My boys and the Forest Green lads had struck up a pretty close friendship during the course of the season, not just because of a mutual link in Steve Millard, but also because many of the Bristol-based Forest Green players used to train in midweek with us during the winter on the all-weather pitch. When I say all-weather pitch, I don't mean Astroturf ... we used to play on a cinder surface! I was very happy with the arrangement, because Steve used to take the sessions and he was a very good coach, and it was nothing but beneficial for my lads training with such a well-drilled group of players.

Anyway, this talented Forest Green side were marching through the FA Vase rounds. They'd beaten Odd Down 3-1 at home in the last 32, and then won back-to-back away games at Shortwood United 1-0 in the last 16, and at Willenhall Town 2-1 after extra time in the quarter-finals. Bob's boys had reached the semi-finals of this wonderful competition, and he called me up one evening to request a favour. I was all ears, and Bob asked if I could bring my Abbotonians side up to Forest Green for a friendly game. What's more, he asked if we could play the exact same system he expected Newcastle Blue Star – their semi-final opponents – to play. I was more than willing to help out, so I rounded up the players and took them up to Forest Green Rovers for an evening.

As the lads were getting changed, I wandered off to find Bob and ask him exactly how he wanted us to play. "They keep the ball for as long as possible, Jeff, so that's what I want your boys to do," said Bob. "Brilliant," I thought. "My boys are going to love this … I'm forever telling them to get rid of the ball quickly, and now I'm going to be telling them to keep it!" Bob's other specific request was our shape. He wanted us to play a standard 4-4-2, with one catch – it immediately switched to 4-2-4, with the two wingers joining the attack, whenever the goalkeeper had his hands on the ball. "No problem at all, Bob, let's go and do it," I said.

I think it was 10 days before their first leg against Blue Star, and Bob put out his full-strength side that he expected to select in the big FA Vase game. If there's one thing for sure, it's that we certainly kept our end of the bargain. We kept the ball all right, in fact we did so well that we rarely let them have it and we ended up beating them 1-0! We played well, very well, and Larry Nash scored our goal to win it. On the final whistle, Bob came over and thanked me, and directed us towards the clubhouse. "There's food in there for you all, Jeff. You get in there and have a drink, and I'll see you in there shortly," he said. Well, half-an-hour later and Bob was still reading the riot act to his players in the changing room. But it must have done the trick, because 10 days later Forest Green Rovers travelled all the way to Newcastle and thumped Blue Star 4-1. The following week they won the second leg at their place 1-0, and booked their day out under the famous Twin Towers of Wembley Stadium.

Knowing how much my lads enjoyed a drink and a day out, it came as little surprise to know that Abbotonians were going to make the most of an opportunity to go to Wembley Stadium. We travelled up to London in our numbers, not only to support Forest Green but also to cheer on Steve Millard, who we still considered to be one of our own. As I've already said, Steve was a fine player and he didn't disappoint on the grand Wembley stage. A skilful midfielder with a real eye for goal, Steve was one of the main tormentors-in-chief as

Forest Green tore opponents Rainworth Miners Welfare to shreds. They won 3-0, and it was a moving moment for all of us when we saw Steve walk up those hallowed Wembley steps to raise the FA Vase and receive his winners' medal.

After such a fantastic day, it would have been criminal for Abbotonians not to make the most of their trip to the capital. Using my work contacts at the Posthouse Hotel, I'd arranged for the 14 of us to get rooms and the ale soon started to flow. We all went out for a Chinese and, as the meal was coming to a close, one of the bright sparks in our side came up with the idea of legging it without paying. Fuelled by beer, they all seemed to think it was a fine idea and, on cue, there was a mass exodus as 14 intoxicated footballers fled the restaurant and darted up the road. Unfortunately, Ron Hagarty was too busy enjoying his food and didn't hear anything about it. He was oblivious to the plan. As the rest of the boys were tearing up the road, Ron was still sat at the table looking bemused. The poor bloke had to pay the whole bill! Don't worry, though, I made sure the lads coughed up and we gave Ron the money later on at the hotel.

It wouldn't have been a Wembley trip without a visit to my old stomping ground the String of Pearls, the club based inside the Posthouse Hotel and site of many a good night. This one was no different, although not long after we'd arrived, a bouncer came up and told us it was a private function and we weren't welcome. Normally I would have just accepted this and left, but only minutes earlier the organisers of this private function had come around and sold us raffle tickets at £5 each. I decided to dig my heels in. "So they're happy to take our money for their raffle tickets, and now they want us to leave?" I asked. I think the bouncer actually saw our point, and in the end he came to a compromise. "Okay, we'll give you and your lads two drinks each on the house, and then you've got to go." I didn't need to think twice about that offer, so off we went back to the bar! A great night was had by all, although Derek Jones was in a right panic because his Sunday League side, Embletonians, were due to play the next morning in a cup final, and half his side were wrecked at the bar – himself included!

Derek was the instigator of many of the drunken escapades that happened during my time with Abbotonians. He'd also arranged for a group of the lads to go with him on a tour of Spain for the 1982 FIFA World Cup. From the stories I have heard, there were at least two of my players on that tour who would have got half-cut on a glass of water come the end! By all accounts they had a fantastic time, and saw some good football. But there was one slight problem. I had a telephone call one afternoon from Brian Burden's wife, wanting to know where he was. "He's at the World Cup," I said innocently. "No, he was meant to be back on Saturday," she replied. Brian had only told her he was going for a week, when in fact the lads had arranged to go for 15 days! Brian's missus was at the airport to meet him when he finally returned to England, and I gather it wasn't the most pleasant of homecomings for poor Brian! They went to the airport bar to talk about it, and apparently Brian's pint of beer ended up poured over his head! We never saw Brian out much after that misdemeanour. You know what they say about women though … you can take away our future, but you can't take away our past!

There weren't quite so many ins and outs over the summer before my third season in charge of Abbotonians, the 1982/83 campaign. We lost Jeff Meacham to Forest Green Rovers, while Dave Mogg went off to Bristol City, but Dave's absence was quickly filled by the return of young Kevin Slabber. I also signed on a lad called Antony Cichowski, along with Ian Elliot, the returning Larry Nash and a young lad from Kingswood called Richard 'Puppy' Iles. The nickname Puppy came from his first pre-season training session us. After the session, he was sat in the changing room when Derek Jones, in his own unique way, said: "You won't be a bad player son, when you lose your puppy fat!" Unfortunately for Richard, the name Puppy stuck with him after that, and he's still known as Puppy Iles to this day.

One of my old Bristol Rovers acquaintances, Alan Bush, also came along to assist me. With him alongside me, we managed to keep the rest of the squad together and Alan raided his Bristol Rovers contact book to bring in Nicky Martin, Nicky Showering, Paul Vassall, Kevin Bush and Glen Thomas. When he signed for us, Nicky Martin – who was a prolific goal-scorer – was still playing for Rovers' reserve team in the Combination, but they only played midweek fixtures so he was available for us on Saturdays. It goes to show what a good standard the league was back then, that we could have a Bristol Rovers player come and play for us in between reserve games for his professional club. Glen Thomas, meanwhile, was a goalkeeper who came in to replace the unfortunate Kevin Slabber, who had now gone down with glandular fever.

The 1982/83 season was another one of building, both on and off the pitch. We had some new players in to try and strengthen our position in the Premier Division, while I was building a working relationship with Alan, which went very well. Having said that, the true highlight of the season wasn't a cup final or a league game ... instead, it was the real Match of the Day with Derek Jones and his wedding to Caroline.

I can remember the wedding day vaguely, but the evening do was definitely a night to remember. Derek had a lot of rugby-playing friends too, so there were a load of top guys at the party. One of the rugby lads came up to me and suggested we all held a collection to send the happy couple down to one of the plush hotels for the night. I went around the Abbotonians lads, while he did the same with the rugby boys. Because my wife Jo didn't drink, it made sense for us to drive Derek and Caroline down to the hotel. Of course, Derek couldn't see in his wedding day without sinking a fine quantity of beer and, as we were going through Hanham, he ordered Jo to stop as he needed a leak. He must have had three or four more comfort breaks before we finally got to the hotel, just around the corner from Bristol Temple Meads train station.

It was quite a posh hotel, and there was a brand spanking new car parked outside to tie in with a motor industry conference being held inside to officially launch the gleaming vehicle. But as Derek made his way past it, he tripped up on the steps and tried desperately to regain his balance, only to tumble right over the bonnet of the car and add insult to injury by being sick all over the paintwork! A night porter at the hotel stormed out to see what was causing the commotion, and demanded to know what was going on. Trying desperately to regain his bearings, Derek stuttered: "If you were with me at 10am this morning, you'd know exactly what's happening ... I got married today!"

The porter didn't share Derek's enthusiasm, but we managed to get him into reception and checked him in. I could hear guests whispering to each other in the background: "Look at the state of him." The worrying thing was that I wasn't all that far behind him! By now Derek was staggering around all over the place like a string puppet. He was banging into things, he couldn't keep his feet, but I managed to get him up to the room while poor Caroline followed behind with Jo. When I left the happy couple in their hotel suite,

Caroline was sat on the edge of the bed, while Derek was laid flat out in the bath. That's where he stayed ... all night. It was a great wedding!

Not forgetting the action on the pitch, we actually had a pretty impressive league finish in what was our second season back in the Somerset Senior League's Premier Division. We ended up in fourth position, 12 points behind champions Backwell United with 17 wins from our 34 games. Robinsons DRG were runners-up that year, with Hengrove Athletic just two points ahead of us in third. Not bad at all for a crazy gang!

Needless to say, Derek Jones thought we deserved a little knees-up as a reward for our endeavours and he arranged a deep sea fishing trip for us. Now I'd never been on one of these boats in my life, and I can safely say I'll never go on another one again unless I had a cast-iron guarantee that the water was going to be calm and flat. Derek's brother tagged along, as did one of his rugby mates and a work colleague. The basic rule on the boat was simple. Take a rod if you want one. If not, take a pint of cider! The day started off fine, but it soon got a bit choppy and the poor bloke who had tagged along from Derek's work was soon hanging over the side of the boat making all sorts of moans and groans. He was a fair bit older than the rest of us and, before long, he was sick ... very, very sick. That wasn't the worst of it, though – while throwing up, he also lost his false teeth over the side of the boat!

"Derek, Derek, my teeth! They're in the sea," he said, in a right flap. Derek, trying not to laugh, quickly calmed him down and said he'd go to the other side of the boat and try and fish them back on board. I could tell Derek had something up his sleeve, and it turned out one of the other older guys on the trip also had a set of false teeth. "Mate, can I borrow your teeth?" had to be one of the most bizarre questions I've ever heard asked, but Derek had a plan. He tied these teeth to the line, dangled them over the side of the boat and then shouted out to the first toothless victim: "Hey look, we've caught them! We've caught your teeth!" By now the rest of us were biting our lips, tongues and anything else we could to stop ourselves from laughing. The poor guy raced over to the other side of the boat, absolutely delighted. "Thank Christ for that, I'd be lost without them," he said as he hurriedly reeled them in. He then put them in his mouth, and scowled. "Urgh, they're not my teeth," he snapped and promptly chucked them back in the sea! Derek's prank had backfired, and we now had two crew members who had to spend the day without teeth! It was a very entertaining trip, that's for sure.

Back at Abbotonians, we had earned great respect from everyone in the Somerset Senior League for what we had achieved, and we continued to play some good football and consolidate our Premier Division status over the following 12 months. We had to face up to some big changes ahead of the 1984/85 season, though. It was around this time that we merged with Longwell Green FC. Mick Millard, who had been Mr Abbotonians for so long, was very poorly by now, so much so that it really limited his involvement with the running of the club. To help out, we became Longwell Green Abbotonians which was the safest and most sensible solution to keep the club running smoothly, especially given that we already played our home games at Longwell Green Community Centre.

The merger brought Longwell Green chairman Bill Holloway on board, and the club's secretary George Threader. The only casualty of the amalgamation was Roger Tarrant. Roger had helped Mick bring Abbotonians into senior football and, with Mick no longer involved due to illness, he felt the time was right to say his farewells. We all completely understood his decision, so we wished him all the best and thanked him for everything he'd done for the club. He was a fantastic servant and had worked extremely hard.

On the pitch, we still had a good side and if anything we underachieved. If I recall correctly, we finished fourth again that season and we also reached the final of the Somerset Senior League Cup. As an added bonus, we were also presented with a memorial cup from Backwell United, who made the presentation each year to the side which had given them the most competitive game.

We had an extremely healthy rivalry with Backwell during my years at Abbotonians, and the games between the two sides were always hard-fought affairs. John Southern was the manager at Backwell, and he built a fantastic side that won the Somerset County League four years on the trot in the early 1980s – equalling a record that was then held by Paulton Rovers. John was a very nice man away from the dugout, and a fierce competitor in it. One game with them always stands out in my mind, because it was played at Bristol City's Ashton Gate stadium. John had called me up and asked me if I minded playing our away game at Backwell there instead, because he'd lined up a sponsor. There's been many a county cup final to be played at Ashton Gate over the years but, to the best of my knowledge, Backwell and Abbotonians became the first two non-league sides ever to play a league game on a professional ground in Bristol.

About two weeks before the cup final, though, I had one of the more frightening experiences of my football career involving Andy Francombe and a linesman during a game at Wellington. The two of them had words about something or other, and this linesman had called Andy some names which he clearly didn't like. Andy was furious. I'd never seen him like it before, and I think it took about eight of us to restrain him.

Straight after the game, I went into the officials' changing room and advised the referee to keep his linesman away from my player when they appeared in the clubhouse. The linesman in question, though, fancied himself as being a little bit brave in the bar and went over to Francombe to have another pop. It was a big mistake. Francombe grabbed him by the neck and pinned him up against the wall. I can remember seeing the Wellington clubhouse wall, which had recently been plastered, just crumbling into pieces when he let this linesman go. He was kicking his legs at all of us to try and get away, and they finally managed to usher him out of the clubhouse before it got any worse. I'd never seen a man lose it like Andy Francombe did that day. Andy had played a fair bit of rugby in his time and could handle himself. All I can say is, it was a bloody good job there were so many of us there to hold him back from doing any more damage. I dread to think what could have happened to the linesman had we not been there!

We picked up some great results throughout that League Cup run, and it all started when an Antony Cichowski goal helped us beat Clandown away 1-0 in the first round. Nicky Showering, Nicky Martin and Micky Baker all found the target in the 3-0 win at Burnham in round two, and that set up a quarter-final at Robinsons which we won 1-0 thanks to Andy Boulton's goal. We were finally given home advantage in our semi-final against Wells City, but there was nothing to separate the two sides in a cracking game. It ended 2-2 after extra time, with Micky Baker and Andy Lohmann scoring for us.

It all came down to a penalty shootout and, when we went 2-0 down after the first couple of kicks, I turned to Alan Bush and said: "Let's do the groundsman a favour and take down those other goalposts." I really couldn't see a way back, but as we were walking down towards the opposite goal we heard a loud roar. I turned around expecting to see a pile of Wells players celebrating, but our keeper Glen Thomas had saved their third penalty. We scored ours, and then Glen did it again … suddenly we were level at 2-2 with one kick each before sudden death.

Alan and I were quick to scuttle back to the halfway line but, as I was making my way there, my heart sank as I saw Derek Jones pick the ball up to take the deciding penalty. Derek couldn't take a penalty to save his life, but for all my hollering and screaming, his mind was set on it. Alan tried to console me. "You never know Jeff, he may even score it!" I wasn't getting my hopes up, especially when I saw Derek taking a run-up that a long-jumper would have been proud of. One wild swing later, he scuffed the ball and it somehow bounced about three times before trickling over the line – thankfully, the Wells City goalkeeper had gone the other way. There was a load of cheering and Derek turned around, confidently declaring: "I never miss penalties!" Let me assure you, he would have missed it if he'd caught it right because it would have ended up 12 miles down the road! But fair play to him, he stepped up and took it, and it put us into the final of the Somerset Senior League Cup.

I had a very tough decision to make for the final, which was against an up-and-coming side in Bishop Sutton. I had to drop our semi-final penalty hero Derek Jones. He had played for his Wednesday side the night before, and I had fully fit players in the squad who deserved to come in. Full credit to Derek, though. He obviously wasn't at all happy about the decision, but he kept quiet about it because he wanted what was best for the team. As it happened, I ended up sending him on as a substitute after about 20 minutes because Phil Baker picked up an injury. It was a like-for-like switch, full-back replacing full-back, and we went on to win the game 3-2 with goals from Nicky Martin, Andy Boulton and Antony Cichowski. Let the celebrations begin!

In the clubhouse afterwards, the League Cup was filled with alcohol and passed around in the usual fashion. But after a while, Derek climbed up on to a table to direct traffic. "Okay, the whisky is starting to taste a bit funny in this cup, so let's get into Bristol for some real drinking," he bellowed. There weren't too many objections, so we all piled onto our bus and headed down the Long Ashton bypass. The smell of beer must have been a bit too much for the driver, who asked for the roof windows to be opened. We opened them all right ... I remember Derek pushing it up, and seeing it break off and bounce across the road! It certainly made for a chilly ride as it effectively turned our bus into a convertible! "What are you going to do about it?" I asked Derek. His solution was to call up Fred Britton, who owned Chasers nightclub in Kingswood, which is where we ended another very good season. It was another great night and, although I got a lift home at a fairly respectable time, I understand the drinking went right through until the next morning for some of them.

When we returned for pre-season training ahead of the 1985/86 season, it didn't take long for the feel-good factor of that cup win to wear off. We would always warm up for pre-season by taking the side to local competitions like the Longwell Green Sixes or the Keynsham Summer Tournament. In order to get a different look at the players, I would often watch from the background and let Alan Bush take over the management reins. It was after one such game that tensions started to build between myself and the club, and it was concerning a sending-off for Andy Francombe while we were playing at Keynsham.

After the game, Longwell Green Abbotonians secretary George Threader came up to me and asked: "What are we going to do about Andy Francombe?" As far as I was concerned, we would treat it the same way as every other red card we ever got ... if I decided the sending-off wasn't deserved, then we'd appeal against it as a team. We'd won some and we'd lost some, but that's how I'd always done it and on this occasion I firmly believed that Andy didn't deserve to be shown a red card. George was angry, and he said: "There is no player who is going to hold *my* club to ransom." "Sorry George, can you repeat that?" I asked. "No player is going to hold the club to ransom," he answered. I hit back: "No George, you just said *my* club."

I'd had a feeling for a while that George was getting a little bit above himself. There's always the danger when two clubs merge that one club thinks it's better than the other, and I was worried George had always looked down on Abbotonians as mere tenants in the deal with Longwell Green. One thing's for sure, I wasn't going to stand for that and was ready to fight the Abbots' corner. I told him in no uncertain terms to remember that Abbotonians were just as much a part of the merger as Longwell Green. Of course, the conversation soon descended into a blazing row which was only ended when I told George he could keep his club.

I was an Abbotonians man, and I certainly wasn't a Longwell Green man, so there and then I decided to resign. "I'm going over the road to the pub, and I'm going to tell Alan Bush exactly what my plans are," I fumed. Naturally, Alan was disappointed and asked if there was any way peace could be restored. "No chance," I said. I went to meet the chairman, Bill Holloway, and he too tried to talk me out of leaving. I thanked Bill for his efforts, and assured him that our friendship would never be affected by what had just happened, but I'd made my mind up … I was finished with Longwell Green Abbotonians.

Years later, there's one good thing that has come out of all this. There were obviously problems with the merger going forward and, in 1998, a new arrangement was set up with Oldland at their Castle Road ground. Derek Jones and Alan Bush played a major part in carrying the Abbotonians name on, and I know they did it to remember Mick Millard. He was the man who started Abbotonians all those years ago, and he was a huge influence in my managerial career. He's still respected to this day by those who used to know him, and what he did for the club. This seems the perfect time to say a massive thanks to Derek and Alan for keeping the club's name alive with Oldland Abbotonians, and it's always one of the first results I look for on a Saturday evening.

Two men and a dog... enjoying this game between Abbotonians and Imperial! That's my good friend Derek Jones on the right, and Micky Baker in the background. I think the Imperial player on the ball is Dennis Symes.

6... A partnership is formed

DRIVING home that evening after resigning as manager of Longwell Green Abbotonians, I couldn't help but feel extremely disappointed and saddened by the whole situation. I kept going over and over it in my mind, wondering if I had made the right decision. Sure, I was very unhappy with what George Threader had said, and it confirmed what I had thought for a while – that Abbotonians were viewed as nothing more than tenants in the merger with Longwell Green. That really annoyed me. Longwell Green was the home of Abbotonians before the merger, and it was the club's home after it too. But the thing that made it really tough was walking away from a side full of great characters, and with a team spirit that was second to none.

When I got home, I sat down and stuck the television on, and told Jo what had just happened. She told me I'd made the right choice and not to worry, because something else would come up soon. I agreed and went to bed, but it was a very restless night. Waking up the next morning, it didn't feel any better. After having built up such a special bond with the players and officials over four years at Abbotonians, it just didn't seem real that I wouldn't be involved with them any more. Only a couple of months earlier, we were celebrating our Somerset Senior League Cup win in typical Abbotonians fashion. Now I had to come to terms with the idea that I wouldn't be joining in with any of their celebrations in the coming season. It hurt, and it gave me that horrible 'empty' feeling inside.

You have to crack on, though, so I went to work for the day and got that out of the way. During the day, I met a bloke I knew through football and he'd heard that I had stepped down as manager. He asked if I fancied going to watch Keynsham Town play a pre-season friendly that night, so I said I would because I thought it would help take my mind off the whole Abbotonians situation. So off to Keynsham I went, and sat myself down at the back of the little stand they had there. I'd only been there a few minutes when I felt a big paw come down on the back of my shoulder. I didn't recognise the hand but, when I turned around, I recognised the face … it was Don Gillies, the former Bristol City and Bristol Rovers player. "Is it right what I've heard about last night?" he asked me. "Yes," I answered.

"I'm not prepared to work for a club where one man thinks he owns it." To that, Don quickly replied: "Fine, that's all worked out okay then. Come on, you're coming with me! Les sent me out to see you."

Don was beckoning me over to the Keynsham clubhouse. "Les who?" I asked as we briskly walked towards the bar. When we got there, I realised it was Les Alderman, who was manager of Paulton Rovers. "Les, I'm not coming to Paulton," I told him straight away. "You've asked me before … I didn't fancy it then, and I don't fancy it now." Les started laughing, and I soon realised he had a different plan this time. "No, no, no," he said. "You're not going there, you're coming with me to Trowbridge Town." I had to ask Les to repeat what he'd just said, as I wasn't sure I'd heard him correctly. After all, Trowbridge Town were a Southern League side and, as far as I knew, Les was still in charge at Paulton. "I got the job at Trowbridge last night and I want you to come with me as assistant manager," explained Les.

I can't deny that I wasn't extremely tempted by the offer, but it had come less than 24 hours after I had resigned from Longwell Green Abbotonians. With that in mind, I didn't want to rush into making any decision. Les suggested watching the Keynsham game and having a beer that night, and then invited me to talk to him more formally about the job the next night at Warleigh Manor, which was the reform school based in an old mansion near Bath which he ran. That sounded like a plan to me, so I went home that night and told the missus about my meeting with Les. "There we go," she said. "I told you something would come up!"

I still wasn't 100 per cent sure about taking the job, given that Trowbridge was a little further away from home. However I was tempted enough to find out more, so the next evening I went along to Warleigh Manor and met Les. I jumped in his car, and he drove us to Trowbridge's Frome Road Stadium. As we arrived, I was getting more and more interested, especially when we slipped through a side door by the turnstiles and I got a first glimpse of the pitch. It was up to professional standard, and as we walked behind the goal I was very impressed. I kept my mouth shut though, and went into the club's office where I sat down with Les and we went over the list of players who were at the club. "Les, I'm going to go for a walk around the club on my own, and I'll have made my mind up by the time I've come back," I told him.

As I walked past the kit room, I saw a bloke in there and said hello to him. As I did that, I noticed a pile of around 40 new balls that hadn't even been pumped up yet, and a brand new kit that hadn't even been played in. I had a look in the changing rooms, and then walked out to the centre circle of the pitch and took a long panoramic look around the ground to take it all in. "This is lovely, and this is where I want to belong," I remember thinking to myself. I thought about my years at Abbotonians, and how much I'd enjoyed them, but this Trowbridge Town set-up was on a whole different level.

I was sold. I strolled back to the office ready to tell Les that I was on board, but before I'd even opened my mouth he said: "One more thing Jeff, you won't need to worry about your expenses, I'll make sure all of that gets sorted out." To be honest, the thought of expenses hadn't even entered my mind! I was just blown away by the whole set-up and couldn't wait to become a part of it. Everything I'd done at Abbots, I'd done for free and for the love of the game. All of a sudden, I had a well-run Southern League Southern Division side in front of me, preparing to offer expenses for my services. It was too good to be true. "Les, when do we start?" I asked. "We start now," was the reply.

With that, Les got out the player list we'd been looking at earlier and told me that, as far as he was concerned, there were only two players who he was keen on keeping. One was Marcus Bray, who had been with both Southampton and Norwich City as a youngster, and the other was Barry Thompson. Immediately my attention turned to another list pinned up on the office wall. The previous manager had kept a list of all the club's yellow and red cards, and the disciplinary points each player had racked up, and who was at the top? Marcus Bray ... I think he had more than 70 points against his name. "There's the first job," I said. "If this lad's as a good a player as it sounds, then he's got to calm his temper." Les agreed, but said there was one job that was even more pressing – we had to build an entire side in the space of a few weeks!

Les and I spent the next few months overseeing an influx of good players who we felt could play at Southern League level for the 1985/86 season. There were always a few players at Abbotonians who I felt had the talents to play at a higher level, so I got on the phone to a few of them. Jeff Meacham was one who joined up with us again, via Forest Green Rovers, while Micky Baker, Nicky Showering, Steve

Summers and goalkeeper Kevin Slabber also signed on. Les did the same with his old Paulton Rovers side, and snapped up players like Mark Hacker, Steve Strong, Dave Spencer and Steve Harding. In addition, we signed John Freegard from Chippenham, Andy Black from Mangotsfield Town, Dave Platt from Yeovil Town, Pete Hayes and Mark Taylor from Bath City, and Mark Stevens who had been with Bristol Rovers as a youngster.

We were also able to add a fair bit of professional experience to the Trowbridge Town side, starting immediately with Don Gillies who had orchestrated my initial meeting with Les. Don had come down to English football from Morton in 1973, and was part of that great Bristol City side of the mid-1970s. He played 200 league games for City, scoring 26 times, and also earned an international cap with the Scotland U23 side. Don later went across the city to join Bristol Rovers, and was with them until dropping into the non-league in 1982.

Peter Aitken was another to join us with both City and Rovers experience. In fact, I believe he was the only player ever to captain both Bristol sides. He had chalked up more than 200 appearances during eight years with Rovers, and made the switch to Bristol City in 1980. A couple of years later, Peter was one of the famous 'Ashton Gate Eight' who agreed to terminate their contracts to help save the club from folding. He'd also had brief spells at York City and Bournemouth before signing for Bath City and then Trowbridge. Meanwhile, Trevor Finnigan came to us with experience of having been at Everton, and of course we also had the aforementioned Marcus Bray. Don Gillies wasn't the only Scotsman in the side either. At the start of the season, we also had a fellow by the name of Alan McDougall, a formidable centre-half who had chalked up more than 200 appearances for Hamilton Academical and Stranraer in the Scottish Football League.

Amid all those players with impressive pedigree, I'll always remember Andy Francombe's debut for Trowbridge Town. We were due to play an away game at Dorchester Town, and we were very short of players. We needed to bring a few players in as an emergency measure, but nowhere was this emergency greater than at centre-half. When he wasn't trying to throttle linesmen and demolish clubhouse walls, Andy played centre-half a few times for me with Abbotonians – although he always preferred playing as a centre-forward. I gave him a call and told him I wanted him to play for Trowbridge at Dorchester, and he was over the moon. I made sure I didn't tell him what position he was playing, until we were on the bus and well on the way to Dorchester.

As it turned out, he didn't mind one bit. "Centre-half is fine Jeff, I'll play anywhere," he said. Andy was just grateful to be given a chance of Southern League football, although he was fully aware it was probably going to be a one-game-only deal. A couple of hours later when the final whistle went, Les pulled me to one side. "There's always one that gets away," he said after an absolutely superb performance at the back from Andy Francombe. I must admit to being a little surprised too. Andy had only come in because we were desperate for numbers, and he was outstanding. I don't think he ever missed another game at Trowbridge for as long as Les and I were there.

Performances like Francombe's at Dorchester made me feel immense pride for what we'd achieved at Abbotonians. The players who stepped up to this higher level of football – Meacham, Baker, Showering, Summers, Slabber and, later on, Steve Talboys – all did themselves proud in the Southern League.

For pre-season training, we took the players to Warleigh Manor. If any of you want to run up a hill to end all hills, then I suggest you visit there too. Even the club's fitter players were left on their hands and knees after those sessions. From the school, we sent the players up a steep embankment and across a main road, and then up an even steeper embankment to reach the fields at the top, where we would do doggies – they are stop, turn and go sprint sessions over a variety of short distances, for those who were wondering! After one such run up the hill, I remember Les suggesting that I went and looked for Nicky Showering. I soon found him … hanging over a fence just off the road, being as sick as a lord! It didn't do him any harm, though. He was an ex-pro at Bristol Rovers so he knew what pre-season training was like.

All the lads worked hard in pre-season and we were eager to get into action back at the ground. For me personally, the opening day of the season couldn't come soon enough. I was thrilled to be in the dugout for a Southern League side, and at a club with such great facilities. We didn't have to wait long to use those facilities as we were at home on the opening day of the Southern Division season, which was the August Bank Holiday Monday of 1985. Dunstable Town were the visitors, and it really couldn't have gone any better for us. We played them off the park and won 4-0, and three of our new lads – Steve Harding, Steve Strong and Jeff Meacham – all scored goals. It was a great feeling to be top of the Southern League's Southern Division that evening!

We were soon brought back down to earth the next Saturday, though, with our first away game at Hastings. The whole day was a disaster from start to finish, mainly due to a hapless coach company that turned up late and proceeded to take every wrong turning imaginable. Throw in some major traffic jams for good measure, and it was about 2.55pm when we finally arrived at the ground. I can remember leaping over the turnstiles in a panic, frantically waving the Trowbridge team sheet to try and catch the referee's eye. Kick-off was meant to be just five minutes away, but I got to the referee's changing room and he was happy to delay the game by half-an-hour. The referee was good about it. He said he'd have to report it to the league, but was sympathetic and gave us credit for keeping them informed via phone calls throughout the whole nightmare journey. The day didn't get any better on the pitch. We lost 3-0 and just couldn't get started. From then on, I made it my responsibility to personally arrange every coach trip for away games.

There were plenty of ups and downs in the early part of the season. We lost our second away game too, 2-0 at Dover Athletic, but had a great 2-1 win at home against Tonbridge. A Jeff Meacham goal and a Pete Hayes penalty got us the points, and to make it even better we had a very good crowd of nearly 400 people watching us. After that, we got a hard-earned 2-2 draw at Dorchester, which was the game Andy Francombe came in to help out.

About three or four weeks into the 1985/86 season, the most disappointing part of my time with Trowbridge Town was triggered by a phone call I received one Friday evening from Les Alderman, who informed me that the stand at the ground was on fire. The next morning I raced out to the ground at 8am to survey the damage, and it wasn't a pretty sight. The stand had gone completely, and one of the floodlights was more or less on the ground. The bizarre thing was that, as it was cooling down, it was gradually bending itself back into its normal shape – it was a very strange thing to watch. We quickly put a call into the match official who was due to take charge of our game that day, and he arranged for a local referee to come out and check to see if the ground was still fit to play. We'd blocked the damaged area off so nobody could get near it, and we were given the green light to play. But it was a bitterly disappointing blow for Trowbridge Town, and all the hard-working people behind the scenes. About six weeks earlier, I had stood in the centre circle and looked around, taken aback by the professionalism of the club and its facilities. It was at that moment that I knew I had to join. However, here we were a few weeks into our Southern League Southern Division season, and we were facing the prospect of having to get changed for games in a Portakabin.

The top two in our division that season were Cambridge City and Salisbury, and we gave them both good games on our own patch in the first half of the season. Two goals from Peter Aitken and one from Pete Hayes saw us put three past eventual champions Cambridge, only to lose 6-3 in October. A few weeks later, we held runners-up Salisbury to a 1-1 draw at Frome Road.

The return fixture against Salisbury always sticks in my mind, mainly for some team sheet shenanigans. We were players short, and I had a couple of lads on the coach who weren't officially signed on. They'd put pen to paper with us, but the forms hadn't gone off to the FA in time. Being totally honest, I'll hold my hands up to this and tell you I decided that they would play under different names. I think Richard Iles and Steve Talboys were the names we used. I knew how we would get around it. Our club secretary Pam would rarely come to away games, and I was always in charge of team sheets. Usually I would give Pam a copy of the sheets on a Monday, or call her with them if I couldn't get over to see her. She would then send the team sheet off to the FA.

At the game, John Freegard told me that the father of one of the lads who had been put under a different name on our team sheet had found out about it, and he was on the warpath. I had to change the sheet again, but by now it was different to the one we had given to the referee. So off it went, and a few days later Pam had a letter back from the FA querying the different team sheets. "This isn't like you, Jeff, what happened?" asked Pam. "I just got confused up there," I explained. "One of their committee members went down with a heart attack, and I do believe he's passed away. Our physio was helping their physio treat him while waiting for the ambulance, and I was trying to fill out the team sheet while all this was going on. My head was somewhere else, so if you could mention that in our letter back to the FA I'd be very grateful." Off the letter went, and the sympathetic reply thanked us for letting them know!

After Christmas, we put some very good results together that lifted us up into the top half of the Southern Division table. We beat Dorchester 3-0 at home, and followed that up with wins against two sides who would go on to finish the season in the top five. We got a 2-1 win away at fifth-placed Corinthian, and beat third-placed Hastings Town 3-2 at home. Draws against Canterbury City (2-2) and Waterlooville (1-1) were then followed by back-to-back wins against Chatham Town (2-1) and Poole Town (1-0). In fact, a 1-0 home defeat to Ruislip was our only loss in seven league games during March and April, and it put us in good shape for the final run-in.

Towards the end of the season, we had one away game at Canterbury City without Les, who was ill at home. I was going to take charge of the team for the day and, before we left, Les warned me to be aware of the lads and any capers they may be planning. "No problem at all Les," I said confidently as we set off from Trowbridge. We didn't have a coach that day, so instead we used one of Warleigh Manor's minibuses which Steve Harding drove. I was sat up the front, and there were a few comments and jokes which I happily let go.

When we got to the ground and all the lads sat down in the changing room, I could tell from Marcus Bray's face that something was up. I went outside to get something and, as I did, I noticed one of the windows which had a pane of glass missing. So I decided to listen to what was being said inside, and I could hear Marcus talking to Jeff Meacham about switching a tape recorder on. "You bastard, Marcus," I thought. "He thinks he's having a joke by tape-recording my team talk, so he can take the piss out of it!" I walked back in to the changing room, and focused the whole team talk around Marcus. I slated him, I went berserk at him, and at the end of the team talk I spotted the recorder hidden between him and Meacham. "Marcus, I don't mind a laugh, but as soon as we enter these changing rooms we have got to act professionally," I said as I bent over him. "I'm going to act professionally with you after the game, so go out and do a job."

Marcus played out of his skin that day, and after the game was his usual chirpy self. Straight away, I thought I'd get to the bottom of the recording prank. I asked Jeff Meacham how much he had to do with it, and he admitted that he knew it was going to happen, so I fined him a tenner. I then turned to Marcus and told him I was fining him a week's expenses. The smile soon disappeared from his face! I told him that the money would instead be going straight into the players' fund. Marcus spent the rest of the evening going around the squad and asking if he could have his money back from the pot. The answer was always an emphatic no!

On the way back from Canterbury, we were heading across Salisbury Plain – we always used to take a cross-country route because we needed to drop a couple of the players off in Warminster. Steve Harding was driving the minibus again, and he had a major moment when we got to a crossroads. There were two cars coming from one direction, and another car coming the other way. All three of them had to make emergency stops as Steve, oblivious to it all, motored over the crossing. He suddenly realised what he was doing when it was far too late to stop, but rather than put his foot down, he slammed on the brakes. All our equipment stored at the top of the bus came down, and all the stuff that was at the back of the bus ended up with Steve and I on the dashboard!

We got out to apologise to the other drivers involved, and I told Steve there and then that I was happy to take over the driving responsibilities for next season. We'd already decided that we would use the Warleigh Manor minibus for all our away games the following season as a way of cutting down on the club's expenditure. I had always enjoyed driving, and it was a nice 17-seater Volkswagen minibus which could easily do 100mph, so it was fine by me!

I say I enjoyed the driving, but there was one evening game that I certainly didn't enjoy being behind the wheel for. When we used to drive the minibus for midweek games, Les used to ask his canteen staff at the school to cook us a load of chicken that the players could eat on the way. On this occasion, I can remember driving through Bath and, just as I was about to tap the brakes to slow down for some traffic lights, dopey Mark Hacker put his hand through and yanked the handbrake up. I've never known a vehicle stop so instantly and, to make matters worse, three or four trays of chicken flew forward from the back of the minibus. There was chicken on the windscreen, on the dashboard, and all over me. I went absolutely potty at Mark, although you couldn't stay angry at him for too long as he was a very nice lad who needed to have a laugh to calm himself down before games. That was his idea of a laugh that night, but I didn't appreciate the humour!

Before finally agreeing to drive the minibus, we went through several coach companies in an attempt to find the best way of travelling to these away games. I've already mentioned that first trip of the season to Hastings, which was ridiculous – it took us six hours to get there from Trowbridge. We then found a coach company based in Bristol, which was cheap and cheerful but they had card tables on board which helped the long journeys go by a bit quicker. On another visit to Kent, I think it must have been our away game at Ashford Town, the company supplied two drivers and the first one did a great job of getting us there – especially as he had Mark Hacker to contend with!

At the start of the journey, the driver had told me that the on-board toilet was safe for number ones, but not for number twos because there was no way of flushing it away. We soon had Hacker chirping up towards the back of the bus. "You'll have to stop the bus, I need to go." We were on the M25 and there were no service stations, or anywhere we could stop for number twos! Hacker was becoming more insistent about the urgency of it all, and with it his complaints were getting louder and louder, so in the end one of the players told him to get into the bus toilet and put a carrier bag under the seat to catch it!

I was sat down near the front of the bus and, in the driver's mirror, I saw Hacker come out of the toilet with a Tesco bag full of shite! He was heading my way, and I knew exactly what was going through his mind – he was planning to put the bag in my lap. "You just walk on by, son," I told him. With that, he went straight up to the driver, held this stinking bag right under his nose and said: "Driver, what do you want me to do with this?" The poor bloke, he was motoring down the M25 at 70mph and there was Hacker waving a bag of shite in his face! "For Christ's sake hang on a minute," the driver was shouting, while the rest of the lads were in absolute hysterics at the back of the bus. He managed to pull over onto the hard shoulder and ordered Hacker to chuck it out the door. "Cheers Drive," he said, returning to the back of the bus with a big smile on his face.

The bus was sounding in a bad way throughout that trip down to Ashford, and was having real problems with overheating. When we got to the ground, the driver told me he was going to have to call someone out to have a look at it. We played the game, and afterwards I went up to the driver and asked him if everything was all right. I didn't get the answer I was hoping for. "Can't your company send another bus down here for us?" I asked. He said he was still waiting for a call back from the company and, with that, the phone went at the clubhouse. The driver answered, and I picked up the other phone nearby to hear what was happening. With that, I heard a voice on the other end of the line: "I don't give a shit what time you get them back, just bring them back with the bus in one piece so we can look at it tomorrow." "Well don't expect to be paid," I shouted down the phone to him.

The company's second driver was behind the wheel for our trip home, and he said we'd go as far as we could but that we'd need to stop as soon as it started overheating again. "We'll have to use the water from the back to cool it down," he said. "What water?" I asked. "The pee from the toilet!" We were near London when the driver requested a stop, so we pulled in at a super steak house to give the players a meal. They hadn't eaten all day – Trowbridge Town's chairman Les Doel had axed pre-match meals to help cut costs, and we decided not to hang around at Ashford's clubhouse due to the delicate situation with the bus. We had a lovely steak and, to be fair to the chairman, he paid for it all as we got back on the bus ready to see how far we'd get this time.

By now we were going through the centre of London and the driver offered us the chance to stop for a beer somewhere, because it was our last chance to get one before hitting the motorway. Needless to say, the players didn't need to be asked twice and we ended up piling in to some London jazz club! The chairman wasn't happy – it wasn't his scene and he just wanted to get home! But we all enjoyed it, and had a good laugh in there before returning to the bus. Up to this point the journey had been very slow and cautious to try and keep the bus alive. By now, though, it was really getting late and the first driver had clearly had enough. "Jeff, if it's all right with you, I'm just going to put my foot down," he said, as it was his turn to drive again. "I'm going to try and get us home as quickly as possible and, if the bus blows up, then it blows up!" That was fine by me, so we just went for it. As luck would have it, the motorway was fairly clear and we were able to get a good speed up – the wind actually helped keep the engine temperature down. I think we finally made it back to

Trowbridge at just gone 2am and we all agreed on one thing … we wouldn't be using that company again.

After that nightmare journey, Mark Hacker managed to strike up a deal with Peter Carol Travel. Peter Carol was a top executive coach company based in Bristol, and I managed to persuade the chairman to go along with paying that little bit extra because we only had five or six away games before the end of the season. We had a top-class driver who was all suited and booted, and he even represented the club in the boardroom at away games if we didn't have enough of our own directors present. The journeys with Peter Carol were hugely enjoyable. On one trip back from London, the lads had put a blue movie on the screens in the coach. Just as we reached London Bridge, the driver stopped suddenly and put on his handbrake. "I've never seen this bit of it," he said as he came back to watch the film for five minutes!

Our good league form in March and April was capped off by a superb final-day win at home, where we beat Woodford Town 4-1. It earned us a final position of 13th in the Southern Division table, which was a fantastic effort given that Les and I only had two players on board when we first visited the Frome Road Stadium some 10 months earlier. We hadn't fared too well in the two national cup competitions earlier on in the season. We lost 3-1 at home to Chippenham Town in the first qualifying round of the FA Cup, while a Jeff Meacham goal wasn't enough to save us from a 2-1 defeat away at Bideford at the same stage in the FA Trophy. However, the real highlight of our season came in the Bill Dellow Cup, which was the Southern League Cup, where we put together a fantastic run to reach the final.

We first realised we might be on to something in this competition when we knocked out Salisbury to reach the quarter-finals. At the time Salisbury were pushing for the Southern Division title, and they had a proud 14-match unbeaten home record when we travelled to their place for the second leg of the cup tie. We'd held them 0-0 at Frome Road, but ripped them apart in the replay and beat them 4-1. Jeff Meacham had given us an early lead, only for Salisbury to equalise through Tommy Paterson on the half-hour. Our lads were outstanding, though, and Mark Hacker restored our lead before goals from Meacham and Kevin Meacock finished Salisbury off. The prize for this win was a daunting quarter-final date away at Fisher Athletic, who were third in the Southern League's Premier Division.

Nobody gave us much hope, but we went there and, in front of a large and hostile crowd, we beat these promotion-chasers 3-1. It was a stunning performance, and we got the result thanks to strikes from Steve Harding, Trevor Finnigan and an own goal. Dave Regis, the younger brother of former England international Cyrille, was with Fisher at the time – it was a few years before he got his first break as a professional with Notts County – and he came up to me on the final whistle and advised me to stay close to him as we left the pitch. I didn't know where he was coming from, but I soon found out. Leaving the pitch at Fisher Athletic, you walk into a cage that goes under the main stand. The supporters in that stand wanted to kill us. They were shouting at us, threatening us, and spitting on us. It was intense hatred. Dave put his arms around me and, with him at 6ft 2in and me at 5ft 8in, I took cover and quickly headed for the safety of the changing rooms.

It was unbelievable. All we'd done was play a game of football, and beat them. There was nothing particularly bad-tempered about the game, it was actually quite an open and entertaining match. One of my first concerns was to get Marcus Bray out of the firing line. In such a hostile atmosphere, it would have been typical of Marcus to say something and fire up the baying mob even more.

We got all the lads safely into the changing room, and soon after Fisher's chairman came in to see us. "I think it will be safest if you stay in here for a bit," he said. "We've got police all around your coach, and we'll let you know when it's safe enough to leave. Whatever you do, don't wander out on your own." While he was speaking, we could hear fans on the roof of the changing room, hurling abuse and hammering away at the roof, trying to break in and get us. After a while, some Fisher officials came and escorted us to the boardroom, where we all enjoyed a steak while the tension outside eased. It just goes to show how big the support was in the Southern League in those days, and what it meant to supporters. It was quite late by the time it was safe enough for us to leave, and it was gone 2am when we got back to Trowbridge.

Having sprung a big upset on one Premier Division side, we then had to do it all over again in the two-legged semi-final, and this would prove to be an even tougher task. While Fisher finished third in the top flight that season, our semi-final opponents Chelmsford City would go on to take the runners-up spot. Also, their player-coach at the time was a young Peter Taylor, who of course went on to become an extremely experienced manager in the pro game with the likes of Gillingham, Leicester City, Hull City, Crystal Palace and Bradford City. Little did I know at the time when I first met him before our first leg at Chelmsford, but I was shaking hands with a future England manager. It was Peter Taylor who gave David Beckham the England captaincy for the first time when he took on the job as caretaker following Kevin Keegan's resignation.

We knew Taylor was a tricky winger, although on this occasion he was playing in a more centralised role in midfield. Les and I were fully aware he had the quality to do some real damage to us, so we gave Marcus Bray strict orders to mark him tight. To be fair to Marcus, he did a good and well-disciplined job. He wasn't jumping in or getting fiery, and he was all over Taylor like a rash. In fact, Marcus followed his instructions a bit too literally. I looked over at the touchline by the home dugout midway through the second half, and saw Marcus loitering about, a bit unsure of what to do. "Marcus, what the hell are you doing?" I screamed over to him. "I'm waiting for him to come back on," he replied, pointing to Taylor. "Marcus you idiot, he was substituted three minutes ago! Your man is over there!" I bellowed back, frantically pointing at Taylor's replacement. Marcus was so focused on marking a former England international for 90 minutes, he hadn't notice the Chelmsford bench call for the substitution – he thought Taylor was off to quickly treat a knock!

The game itself was just as tight as Marcus Bray's man-marking skills. In fact, it looked like we were going to hold them to a 0-0 draw, only for them to score a late winner at the death. It meant we had a 1-0 deficit to overturn back at our place, but the lads were fully confident they could do it after the hard 90-minute shift they'd just put in. That confidence was dented slightly when we realised that we would have to do it without two of our most influential players. Jeff Meacham and John Freegard were both due to serve two-match suspensions, and that ruled them out of the second leg at Frome Road. I can't remember exactly what the suspensions were for but, knowing both of them, I'd wager that it was for a load of yellow cards.

The second leg was due to be played on the following Tuesday night. That afternoon, I had a phone call from Les Alderman. "Let all the players know we're training at Yate tonight, the game is off," he said. "The showers are knackered, the whole place is flooded and there's no way we can get it sorted in time." Les then asked me to take the training session, so that he could go along to the ground and make sure the repairs were done so that we were good to go for Saturday's game. As I arrived at Yate for our hastily-arranged training session, Steve Harding was the first to greet me. "That's one game out the way then Jeff," he said, referring to Meacham and Freegard's suspensions. "What do you mean?" I asked. Steve then explained to me that the changing room leak was anything but an accident!

We played a league game on the Saturday, and then were due to play Chelmsford in the rearranged second leg on the Tuesday night. This time we got that little bit of luck we needed. Jeff and John still had to sit out another game, but our pitch had taken a real hammering through a combination of heavy rain and the Saturday game. We called up a local referee to come along and inspect the pitch. I think by the time he arrived, there may have been an added sprinkling of water on the surface too! The referee ruled it as unplayable, which was a real result … we had an away league game and we were able to wipe our suspension slate clean for the big game. Meacham and Freegard were now available for the following Tuesday night, so Chelmsford came down and we beat them 3-1. Guess who got the goals? Freegard (2) and Meacham. We had reached the final of the Bill Dellow Cup, thanks to some fantastic football, a little intervention from Les Alderman and some superb man-marking from Marcus Bray.

Our opponents in the final, which was also played over two legs, were Bromsgrove Rovers. At the end of the 1985/86 season, Bromsgrove were a club who were really on the up. They won the Southern League's Midland Division that season at a canter, and were on the verge of even greater things. A few years later, they won the Premier Division and gained promotion to the Conference. Even more amazingly, they went on to finish as runners-up to Wycombe Wanderers in their first Conference season, despite being one of the smallest sides in the league.

We knew it was going to be a tough test, so prepared as professionally as possible for the first leg in Bromsgrove. We arranged a pre-match meal for the players in a hotel at Droitwich and had a good chat about the game, which we came out of feeling positive that we could go and do a good job up there. Their manager at the time was Bobby Hope, who had made more than 300 appearances as a midfielder for West Bromwich Albion in his playing days. He was an absolute gentleman, and a lovely bloke to chat to. Bobby had also set his side up extremely well, and they beat us 2-1 in that first leg. While we were naturally disappointed to have lost the game, we weren't too despondent. After all, we'd overturned a one-goal deficit against Chelmsford in the semis, so we felt confident we could do it again with home advantage for the return encounter.

It was a massive occasion for the club. There was a brass band playing on the pitch and, when we came out of the changing rooms, we led the side out as if we were at Wembley Stadium. You had to line the players up and get introduced to all the Southern League officials. At the away game I led the side out, and Les did the duties at the home game. There was a crowd of around 4,500 at Trowbridge that evening for our second leg – it was a phenomenal experience and a fantastic night. Sadly, we just couldn't quite do enough to get our hands on the trophy. The game ended 2-2, and we had Bromsgrove pinned right back. We couldn't get that third goal, though, and the bounce of the ball just didn't go our way. We lost 4-3 on aggregate but, the disappointment of losing aside, a good night was had by all.

Looking back at that game all these years later, perhaps the most disappointing aspect is that neither club is around any more. Trowbridge went out of business in the late 1990s and had to sell off their ground, although have since reformed as a new club and are playing in the Hellenic League. Bromsgrove, meanwhile, struggled to maintain those standards set in their early Conference years and gradually slipped back down the non-league pyramid. Along the way they encountered severe financial difficulties and were eventually expelled from the Southern League just a few days before the start of the 2010/11 season.

As well as the big Bill Dellow date against Bromsgrove, we'd had another cup final to play in. This one was against Melksham Town in the final of the Wiltshire Cup, which we lost. We also played in the final of the South Western Floodlit Cup where we beat Taunton Town, so we did have some silverware to show for our endeavours.

In a roundabout way, the two-legged final with Bromsgrove also gave us one of our most memorable away games. I told a story earlier about a little team sheet misdemeanour against Salisbury. Well that was nothing compared to this one! We'd played that first leg at Bromsgrove on a Sunday, and the home leg was a week-and-a-half later on a Tuesday night at Trowbridge. The trouble was, the league fixtures were piling up and we had two games to play within 24 hours, just a couple of days before that all-important second leg.

On Saturday, three days before the cup final, we played Ashford at home. The very next day, we were due to travel to Ashford for the away game. After a tough game on the Saturday, Les and I were in agreement that there was no way we could expect our players to have two games in 24 hours, and still be in good enough shape to try and win the Bill Dellow Cup on the Tuesday night. We knew that some emergency reinforcements would need to be drafted in.

On the Saturday evening, I enlisted the help of Jeff Meacham to go down to Bristol Corn Exchange with me and see if we could find a few players to fill in. Luckily, my son Paul was in there so I went up and asked him if he knew any players around willing to come to Ashford with us the next day. Paul immediately said he'd be up for it, so that was one player added. From there on, the night took us around Bristol. We may have got a little worse for wear, but by the end of it I had rounded up 12 players to play for Trowbridge Town at Ashford! All our drunken recruits were given just one instruction – meet us at the Posthouse at Hambrook the next morning.

Sure enough, our group of hastily-enlisted misfits all turned up the next morning with varying degrees of hangovers. Bearing in mind that a lot of these lads were just Sunday League players, you should have seen the looks of amazement on some of their faces when Peter Carol's luxury coach turned up! Another thing to bear in mind is the speed in which we got these players in. There was no time for them to even sign forms, let alone get them registered with the FA! It called for some inventive thinking.

As we got going on our long trip to Ashford, I scribbled down 12 of our existing players' names on a piece of paper and put them into a hat. I then walked from the back of the bus, getting each of the lads to draw a name at random. My son Paul was the first to pick. "Paul, whatever name you pick out, that's who you are today," I said. "I'll be back down in ten minutes to ask you what name you're playing under!" To be fair to the lads, they had cracking memories – they all knew their new names off by heart by the time we reached the M25!

As luck would have it, neither the chairman or Pam the secretary were able to attend the game, so they were none the wiser about our plan to field an entire team of unregistered players under false names. Had they known, I think there would have been more than a little opposition! Remember I mentioned that our Peter Carol Coaches driver sometimes used to represent us in the boardroom at away games? Well, this turned out to be one of those days and he was more than happy to go along with our little plan. One of the blokes we roped in was Colin Bush, who was going to play in midfield. Colin was Marcus Bray's uncle, and in recent years was manager of Corsham Town when they beat Bideford to win the Western League title. Marcus played too – he had just come back from suspension and needed the match fitness, and was probably the only one playing under a legitimate name!

Les insisted that we treated the lads as we would our own side. After all, they had given up their Sunday to help us get out of a pickle, so the least we could do was give them a proper pre-match build-up. It obviously worked, because at half-time we were still on level terms at 0-0! Ashford scored a penalty in the second half to go a goal up, but we went so close to snatching an unlikely point at the end of the game. My son Paul had been a substitute for us, but I sent him on for the final 15 minutes and, with a few minutes to go, he was clean through. His shot beat the goalkeeper, but cracked the inside of the post. Paul was only an inch or two from burying the rebound too, but he just couldn't scramble there quickly enough and the ball rolled out of play.

Walking off the pitch at the end of the game, I was extremely proud of all of them. Sure, we'd lost 1-0 but each player had upped their performance levels. This group of Bristol non-league footballers didn't look out of place in the Southern League against a full-strength Ashford side, and they deserved immense credit for that. In the clubhouse afterwards, all the Ashford officials couldn't stop praising us for bringing our best side despite being only two days away from a cup final. Little did they know!

When we all boarded the coach to begin the journey home, Les brought up the subject of money. "Right, I suppose we better give these players their expenses Jeff, how much shall we give them?" I couldn't stop laughing. "We've given them a pre-match meal, we're taking them to the pub for a drink on the way home," I said. "These boys usually pay subs! What do you want to pay them for?" But that was Les for you. Out of his own pocket, he gave every player £25 and they couldn't believe it. My boy Paul was delighted, and told me that it covered his playing subs for the rest of the year. Nobody from the Southern League ever found out about it either!

At the end of a hugely enjoyable 1985/86 season, Les called me into the office and told me the club had received a notice of approach. "Which club is going after our players now?" I asked. Les proceeded to tell me that the approach wasn't for a player, but for me. I made it clear to Les straight away that I wasn't in any hurry to leave, even if it meant getting the top job and being a manager again. The approach was from Frome Town in the Western League, and Les understood that I did want to manage again, rather than being an assistant. "You want to manage and I want to manage," said Les. "You and I get on like a house on fire, so let's be joint managers. I'll tell the chairman that we are joint managers and, wherever we go in football after that, we'll be joint managers." It sounded good to me, so the deal between myself and Les was struck there and then.

Les hosted an enjoyable end-of-season bash and said some very kind words about me and how appreciated my efforts were over the previous campaign. I returned the compliment, and told the lads how much I had relished working with him. We agreed that we only needed to tinker with the side to build on our encouraging first season at Trowbridge Town, so we only brought in a couple of new players for the 1986/87 campaign.

We still had a very good squad, with a couple of promising local youngsters such as left-back Stevie Cripps also coming through, so things looked promising. I was then dealt a bit of bad news over the phone by Les, who was at his summer property in France. He told me that the Trowbridge wage bill was going to be slashed in half for the coming season. Les had been working on securing a good sponsorship deal for the club and, when I asked him how that was developing, he said the prospects for it weren't looking good. Combined with the club's cut, we were suddenly facing the prospect of going into the season with a budget that was about a third of what we had initially been planning for.

Les told me to speak to every player regarding the financial situation, and work on the basis of our budget being half of what we'd originally hoped – he assured me he would rake some extra cash in through sponsors. We'd decided to do our pre-season work at Stoke Park, which was a centre that cared for handicapped people where Jeff Meacham's wife Helen worked. There were some nice football pitches at the grounds, and they let me use one of the offices so I could speak to every player, one by one, about their expenses.

I'd sat down with our new budget, called in each player and agreed new expenses with them. It was a horrible task, having to tell them all, but I got to the end and breathed a huge sigh of relief. "Thank God that's over, and I've done it with £10 to spare," I thought as I congratulated myself. With that, there was a knock at the door and in walks Marcus Bray. "Shit, I've forgotten about him!" As I was going down the list, I must have skipped over his name by mistake. I was honest with him, and said all I could offer him was £10, but suggested that perhaps his dad, who ran his own business, may be able to sponsor him and raise some extra money that way. Full credit to Marcus, he didn't even hesitate. "If it's only a tenner then it's only a tenner," he said as he signed the forms there and then. "That will do me fine."

Stoke Park was a wonderful venue to train, and it was also a very humbling place to be. Some of the residents there were severely handicapped, but they were lovely people who were a joy to be around. When we arrived every Tuesday and Thursday, they would always be delighted to see us and were always offering to help carry any equipment for us. It was a great experience for everybody, so I suggested to Les that the club should do something for all those people at Stoke Park. I mentioned it to Jeff, and he said it would be a lovely gesture to bring them along to one of our early home games and treat them as VIP guests for the day.

Les asked one of his staff at Warleigh Manor to drive a bus over to Stoke Park and pick them all up, and bring them over to the Frome Road Stadium where we had laid on some food and reserved seats in the clubhouse for them. They all came into the ground with huge smiles on their faces, and I'll never forget a moment after the game which nearly brought tears to my eyes. I saw Jeff and Helen bringing through a chap who was mentally and physically handicapped. I'll never forget his name, it was Richard, and he was beaming from ear to ear. Richard had watched the game and had been into the clubhouse afterwards and, although he couldn't talk or make any gesture at all, you could just tell by his face how much the day had meant to him. It was a wonderful feeling, and at the same time a reminder of how lucky we all are.

When Jeff told Richard that it was time to go, the smile just disappeared so I suggested to Les that we invite him to the pub where we would have an after-match beer and a bite to eat. Jeff didn't tell Richard about it, though, so that it would be a surprise for him when he arrived at the pub. Jeff said he was as miserable as sin in the back of the motor when he thought he was going back to Stoke Park, but that his face lit up with excitement when he saw the pub. Seeing Richard's smile as he and Jeff came into the pub gave us a feeling that money couldn't buy, and it's definitely one of my fondest memories of my time in football, away from the pitch.

We started the league season pretty well, apart from an opening-day 3-2 home loss against Ashford Town. Our next game saw us beat Corinthian 4-0, and our first away game – with me now acting as our full-time minibus driver – ended in an impressive 4-1 win at Erith & Belvedere. Jeff Meacham then scored the winning goal in our 1-0 success at Chatham Town, and we were among the Southern Division's front-runners by mid-September with three wins and one defeat. Spirits were high within the camp, and they were even higher when we were presented with a chance of a weekend away in Margate.

The Southern League fixture list had thrown up two away games in Kent, and we had to play them on successive days. We were due to play at Thanet United on the Saturday, and then against Corinthian 24 hours later. Financially it made perfect sense to stay over, as we didn't fancy two round trips to Kent and back on successive days, so Les and I arranged for the team to stay in Margate on the Saturday night. We arrived there in a jovial mood after winning 4-1 at Thanet with goals from Marcus Bray, Steve Harding, John Freegard and Jeff Meacham. I was driving the minibus and, after we got to the hotel, everyone nipped up to their rooms to switch their club tracksuits for casual wear. I did the same, and got down to the hotel bar expecting to hit the town with the players. Instead, I was greeted by our chairman Les Doel, who had booked for us to go for a meal. So as all the players were scuttling off into Margate, I had to go and sit down in a restaurant with Les and the rest of the committee. I wasn't amused.

I have to say the meal was fantastic, and we did have a good laugh there. But I couldn't help but wonder what mischief the players were getting up to in the town. I was hoping to track them down and join in, but the chairman had other ideas and wanted to see us all back to the hotel bar for drinks. He had also given me a wad of notes to pay the restaurant bill. Only the next day did I realise that the cash was still in my pocket! Forgetting to pay the bill certainly wasn't deliberate, and the money came in handy for buying the players some drinks after Sunday's game.

Back at the hotel, one by one the players returned, some looking in better shape than others. Stevie Cripps had clearly got lucky in Margate and came back through reception with a young lady on his arm, which was fine – he was a young lad, free and single. Jeff Meacham and John Freegard had got back a few minutes before Crippo, and thought it would be a good idea to sneak into his room and hide in the wardrobe so they could leap out and surprise him as he was getting busy. So off they went up the stairs, giggling like a couple of schoolboys.

The unsuspecting Crippo came back soon after, and took this girl up to his room. As he sat on the bed with his arms around her, Meacham and Freegard decided it was time to spring into action but, as they tried to push the wardrobe door open, it jammed shut. The pair of them clearly tried to push too hard, and, the entire wardrobe fell forward and crashed down on to the floor – with Meacham and Freegard face down, still inside! There was all kinds of commotion. The poor girl was frightened to death, and ran out of the hotel shrieking. Other players had heard the crash, and raced into Crippo's room where they found this wardrobe flat out on the floor. A few of them managed to lift it up and, as they did, the doors opened and out flopped Meacham and Freegard with a load of coat-hangers!

This all happened at about 3am, but it was probably nearer 4am by the time they'd all calmed down and got to bed. It made Les Alderman's decision to have them up for an 8am training session all the more cruel! There were a few sore heads that morning, myself included. I was up around 7am – I've always been an early-riser, ever since my days in fruit and veg – so I cleared the cobwebs with a shower and rounded up our groggy rabble. Les and I took them down to the beach at Margate to try and freeze the hangovers out of their systems, and we gave them a good early-morning workout before heading back to the hotel for breakfast.

Our next stop was Corinthian FC, who were based at Hartley and had reached the Southern League despite being a completely amateur club from top to bottom. I was due to drive the minibus there but, after breakfast, I felt a booming headache come on – maybe the amount of beer drank the night before was catching up with me. Steve Harding took over the driving duties and, when we arrived at Corinthian, my usual pre-match spark was missing. I felt terrible, and I didn't think it was the drink. I felt weird, and spent the majority of the first half slumped on the bench in the dugout.

The action on the pitch did nothing to perk me up either, and we were 4-0 down at half-time. It was getting embarrassing, and I knew I had to snap out of it because Les Alderman was going nuts. "Jeff, let's get to work," he said to me as we were walking back to the changing rooms after a miserable first-half display. "Obviously these boys don't know how to stay away from home."

We went out for the second half and suddenly clicked into gear … 4-1, 4-2 and it started to get interesting. Then, Trevor Finnigan stormed into the box to meet a Jeff Meacham cross, and he met it all right – with his fist! Trevor punched the ball into the back of the net and ran across to the linesman at full pelt, sliding on his knees. "Pick that bastard out!" The linesman didn't know what to do, he looked terrified! Their manager was going spare in the opposite dugout, but the goal stood and it was 4-3.

John Freegard and Jeff Meacham had got the two goals before that, and Freegard struck his second to put us back on level terms with about 15 minutes to go. It was an outstanding comeback from our hungover boys, and it could have been even better. With a couple of minutes to go, Meacham ran clean through and took the ball past the goalkeeper, and had an empty goal staring at him. What did he do? Stumble and put it past the post … if it had been on the telly, it would have been the miss of the season. It ended 4-4, and we were more than happy with our weekend's work. We'd banked four more points from two tough away games, and the lads had a great night out in the process.

Those two results kept us in the top six, and we had a few games in hand over several sides around us due to some decent cup runs. We made it all the way to the fourth qualifying round of the FA Cup, beating Hungerford Town 4-0 in the preliminary round, Melksham Town 3-2, and Salisbury 2-0 in front of a crowd of 540 at Frome Road. In the third qualifying round we won away at Stourbridge 4-0 in a replay after drawing 1-1 with them at our place, but our run ended just short of the first round proper when Fareham Town beat us 4-1 in another replay. We also had a run of four home draws in the FA Trophy, beating Gloucester City 4-0, Bideford 3-1 and Maidenhead United 4-1 before losing 1-0 to Bishop's Stortford.

The victory against Maidenhead always sticks in my memory, mainly due to the antics of Marcus Bray. They were a big side, and Marcus was in one of his moods where he would dive in for tackles from about seven feet away. With football discipline the way it is today, I don't think Marcus would ever finish a game – he'd get sent off every week. In those days, though, you could always get away with the first tackle or two. Anyway, Marcus's first tackle that day unfortunately put one of the Maidenhead lads in hospital. His second, third and fourth tackles also injured players, and he was on a yellow card when we decided to take him off.

In the clubhouse after the game, Jeff Meacham came over to me and told me that Marcus needed to go to the toilet. "Why are you telling me that Jeff?" I said. "Marcus doesn't need me to hold his hand when he goes for a piss." With that, Jeff pointed over to a group of Maidenhead players. They were seething about Marcus's tackles, especially the one that hospitalised one of their team mates, and were waiting for him to go to the toilet on his own so they could follow him in and confront him. Myself, Jeff and Andy Francombe all went into the toilet with Marcus, and I told him that under no circumstance must he go anywhere on his own while the Maidenhead players were still in the clubhouse.

I went over to their manager and apologised for Marcus's behaviour, and he told me to keep Marcus well away from his players. He thanked us for our hospitality, but said it was best if the club left straight away before things turned ugly in the clubhouse. For all his bravado and toughness on the pitch, Marcus proved that day he wasn't so brave off it. I've always said that if you're going to be a hard man on the pitch, you've got to be a big man off it at times.

There was a far happier clubhouse atmosphere when we played at Ashford Town in our second game of 1987. It was a couple of days after New Year's Day, and it ended 1-1 with Jeff Meacham scoring for us. As we were all still in the festive spirit, we'd arranged a coach for the trip so we could all have a drink after the match, and we were due to leave Ashford at 6pm sharp. Just as we were preparing to leave, the Ashford manager broke into a song and was soon joined by a back-up choir of players. All of a sudden, John Freegard leaped up onto the stage and treated everybody to a rendition of his favourite Rolf Harris song, Two Little Boys. John had the whole clubhouse singing along, and was soon joined up there by Jeff Meacham doing his Guy Mitchell special. It was great fun, although our driver may not agree ... it was 8.30pm by the time we piled out of the Ashford clubhouse.

A few days later we had an away game at Aylesbury United. It must have been a cup game, although I can't remember which competition it was. We'd lost the game 3-1, and I had resumed the driving duties on board the team minibus. We hadn't had any food after the game, and the players were moaning and groaning about how hungry they all were, so they kept pestering me to stop when we saw a fish and chip shop. I took a diversion into Oxford and our coach Bill Horton, who was sat alongside me in the front seat, spotted a chippie. Bill and I were starving too, so we nipped in ahead of the players to avoid having to wait behind them all. I was expecting a large group of footballers to follow us in, but I turned around and they were nowhere to be seen.

Anyway, Bill and I finished our food and then went back out into the street, where my attention was quickly grabbed by the noise coming out of another fish and chip shop across the road. I've never heard hysterical laughter like it, and the place was erupting with noise. "I think we better go and have a look," I said to Bill, slightly worried about what I was going to find. When I stuck my head through the door, I saw Andy Black behind the counter, serving the punters!

"For God's sake Andy, try and remember that you are representing the club," I said. "Come on, get yourself out of there." The owner of the chippie had other ideas. "This is the best trade we've done in ages," she said. "This man is not leaving my counter!" With that, out came Andy's famous Norman Wisdom impression again and another load of chips were sent flying everywhere as Andy did one of those comedy trips. I've got to be honest, I laughed my socks off. But that was Andy Black. He was a real character, and his Wisdom and Frank Spencer impressions kept the lads entertained on many a coach trip.

Andy was a very good player too, mind, and I'm sure he'll never forget the role he played one of our wins against Erith & Belvedere. Andy rang me up one morning to let me know that his missus had just gone into labour. The only snag was that it was on a Saturday morning, just a few hours before we were all due to meet for our usual pre-match preparation. I suggested to Andy that I could travel to the ground via the hospital and pick him up. Then, if his good lady understood, I could drop him right back there after the game. Amazingly, she agreed to it, so off I went to get Andy. He scored the winner for us that day and, still buzzing from the game, we hurtled back to the hospital. Andy missed the birth by about ten minutes, but was the proud father of a lovely baby girl.

Sadly, we lost Steve Talboys during the season when he signed for Gloucester City. Steve always had bundles of potential as a striker, and went on to sign for another Crazy Gang when he joined Wimbledon for £11,000 in 1992. Although Steve never nailed down a regular first-team spot with the Dons, he did make 30-odd appearances in the newly-formed Premier League over four years. He played against Manchester United four times, and I can remember feeling extremely proud when I saw him score his first and only top flight goal against Tottenham Hotspur. In addition to those first-team adventures, Steve also captained Wimbledon's reserve team.

Steve came back to play the odd game for us during the 1986/87 season when he wasn't tied up with Gloucester City. I can remember him scoring a hat-trick when we beat Poole Town 6-1 on New Year's Day, and he scored another four in our 5-0 home win against Ruislip. We were playing some great football and scoring lots of goals, so it was inevitable that our players began to attract interest. However Steve wasn't the only one of our lads to make it as a professional. Jeff Meacham was in sensational goal-scoring form for us. He netted all four in our 4-1 away win at Waterlooville in December and, by the time Bristol Rovers came calling, he must have scored more than 20 goals that season for us. Jeff went on to score nine goals for Bristol Rovers in 26 appearances, which shows was a good player he was.

Shortly before Jeff left for Rovers, I remember him being part of another little weekend away we had to combine two away games. At least, that's what we thought. We'd played at Waterlooville on a Saturday, and were due to play at Poole Town on the Sunday, so we decided to stay down there for the Saturday night. To be honest it's only around 40 or 50 miles from Trowbridge, so quite a few of the local lads decided to go back home for the evening. Bill Horton, Jeff and I stayed at Trevor Finnigan's house, which was a lovely place – clearly top flight football earned you a decent few quid, even back in those days – while another four or five players were dotted around.

Les Alderman knew I was staying at Trevor's place, and called me there at around 7.30pm on the Saturday evening when he'd got back to Trowbridge. "Jeff, I've been and dropped a clanger," he said. "We're not playing at Poole tomorrow." "Who the hell are we playing then?" I asked. "We're playing Poole, it's just that we're playing them at our place!" Over the course of the evening, I was able to locate all the lads who had stayed down and let them know that we'd need to leave a bit earlier than our planned midday departure to Poole.

Anyway, the night was still there to make the most out of. After a nice meal in Bournemouth, we let Trevor decide where to take us, and he chose this club he was well involved with. Very nice it was, too. The first person we met there was Ted McDougall, the former Scottish international striker who played for, among many others, Norwich City, Manchester United, Southampton and Bournemouth. The beer was flowing, later to be replaced by champagne, and he told some great stories. Before we knew it, John Virgo had appeared and was chatting along too – there was a big snooker tournament going on in the town that weekend.

"Jimmy White will be along in a minute," Trevor told me. A few seconds later, in walked the Whirlwind. My goodness, what a character! Jimmy was fantastic company, and had us in stitches all evening … so much so that, before we knew it, it was 2.30am. I have to say that these well-known sportsman do have it hard when they go out to places, because they get pestered all the time. There we were, all sat down, and there was a constant stream of people coming up to them and asking for autographs, asking questions. Most were respectful, but some were jackasses, asking Jimmy why he didn't get a better break and obnoxious questions like that. It was a very interesting insight into how top-class sportsmen deal with the attention on a night out, and I have to say Virgo and White were brilliant with it.

Speaking of our coach Bill Horton, who enjoyed that night with us, I can remember at one point during the 1986/87 season when he made some national headlines for Trowbridge Town. Yet again, we were desperately short of available players, so we needed to call Bill up for a one-off appearance. Bill was probably in his mid to late-40s by then, and hadn't played for 15 years. We also drafted in Bill's lad Phil for the game, and *Shoot! Magazine* ran a feature asking whether it was the highest standard of football in England where a father and son had played in the same team. I know Phil was particularly thrilled to get a chance to show what he could do at Southern League level. However, he probably wasn't quite so delighted when we dropped him for the next game… and kept his dad in! To be fair, Bill was a pretty decent player in his day, having turned out for Bath City among others, and he ended up playing about 20 games that season!

On the pitch at Trowbridge, things were going well … but it wouldn't last. After one away game, I can't remember where, Les Alderman had a big row with the chairman Les Doel. I was called to a meeting at the chairman's house with Les and Bill Horton. He told us that Trowbridge Town were effectively bankrupt. Les Doel told us that there was no money whatsoever left, and that we wouldn't be able to pay anyone from now on. A new chairman did come in, but the budget was slashed in half again and Les Alderman said he'd had enough. After another argument about the money situation – it's the root of all evil at any football club – Les Alderman called me up and told me that he'd handed in his resignation.

I was called to the committee room at Trowbridge where I met Les Doel and the new chairman, and they told me that they were more than happy to let me take sole charge. "I'm very sorry," I said. "I came here with Les Alderman, and I'll leave with Les Alderman." That was exactly how I felt, especially after the agreement we'd made when we became joint managers at the end of our first season. "If Les is unhappy about something, then I know I'll be unhappy about the same thing." We'd had loads of hiccups during the season due to money not being there, and I felt the club had gone from being a promising Southern League outfit to a Wiltshire League side behind the scenes. It had been an enjoyable and rewarding 20 months in many ways, but all good things have to end and my loyalties were with Les. Trowbridge Town closed the 1986/87 season in 12th place, but they finished it without Jeff Evans and Les Alderman.

I lead Trowbridge Town into battle in the Southern League. Pictured (back row from left) are me, Steve Harding, John Freegard, Jeff Meacham, Kevin Slabber, Andy Francombe, ???, Mark Taylor and (front from left) Marcus Bray, Dave Mitchell, Pete Hayes, Barry Thompson and Charlie Aitken.

7... A great honour, and money to spend!

WHEN my phone rang just a day after Les Alderman and I had walked away from Trowbridge Town, it was little surprise to hear it was about football, and it was a very familiar voice that greeted me on the other end of the line. Ralph Miller, who had been my manager for a short time when I played at Cadbury Heath, was calling up to ask if it was true that we'd left Trowbridge. By now Ralph was in charge at Mangotsfield United in the Western League, and he was keen to get myself and Les along to take the reins from him. It must have been around February-time in the 1986/87 season, so we said we'd take up his offer on a trial basis for the three-and-a-half months that would take us up to the end of the campaign.

Mangotsfield weren't having the best of seasons at the time, but several of the lads at Trowbridge decided to follow Les and I over to Cossham Street. Steve Harding, Don Gillies, Andy Black, Alan McDougall and Dave Spencer are just a few players who spring to mind, who signed on for us at Mangotsfield. In addition, there were three or four quality players already there. Striker Steve Price was one such lad who caught my eye. Nearly eight years earlier, I was in the crowd at Wembley Stadium to see a 19-year-old Price score in the 1979 FA Vase Final for Almondsbury-Greenway in their 4-1 loss to Billericay. Now, at Mangotsfield, Price had developed, matured, and was a very good striker at Western League level.

There was a lad from Cirencester called Chris Smith, and he could catch pigeons, such was his unbelievable pace. Up front we had Ian Foster, who was a man-mountain known as Fozzie who would go through a brick wall for you. There were also a lot of familiar faces, and several of the lads who I had played with at Mangotsfield some ten years earlier were still there – only they were committee men now, rather than players. It was good to see Pat McKeown, Chopper Hill, Steve Frith, and Mike Hamilton, better known as the Womble, who was club physio.

We saw the season out and got Mangotsfield to tenth in the final Western League table, although we were only four points off Bideford who had finished sixth. We ended the campaign with 17 wins, eight draws and 17 losses from our 42 games, and finished level on 42 points with Barnstaple Town and Chippenham Town. The icing on the cake was another two cup finals. We reached the Les Phillips Cup Final – the Western League Cup – where we lost to league champions Saltash United 1-0 in a game that was played at Barnstaple's Mill Road ground. We also got through to the final of the Gloucester Senior Trophy against fifth-placed Bristol Manor Farm, which we won at Forest Green Rovers. I believe the score was 3-1.

All in all it was a fairly successful trial run so, at the end of the season, we got down to the nitty-gritty of talking with the club about a longer-term arrangement. When we first arrived at Cossham Street, Ralph had asked us if we had any objections about working with Clive Hall, who had been his assistant. I certainly had no qualms, because I knew Clive to be a wonderful character and a gentleman. He was also an excellent motivator, and he could get the players buzzing in those final crucial minutes before the team left the changing room.

Before we met with the club to officially discuss the 1987/88 season, Les and I held our own meeting to share our thoughts on the situation. Les asked me again if I was happy working with Clive, and I reiterated my previous thoughts that I had no problem with it whatsoever. Les then asked if I would have any problem with Ralph Miller taking over as vice-chairman, and admitted that he had serious doubts about it. I could see where Les was coming from. He was concerned that Ralph would interfere with team selection and management issues due to his long background as a manager.

Anyway, I said to Les that I would chat to Ralph about our concerns before we went for the full meeting. Ralph was very good about it, and admitted that becoming a vice-chairman was a very hard thing for him to do after being a No.1 for so long. He assured us that Les and I were there at his invitation, and that he had no intention of interfering with any team selection. To be fair to Ralph, I could understand it if he did do that. After all, if I was in the same position, and had switched from managing the side to being a committee member behind the scenes, I too would always be thinking I could build a better side than the man in charge. I guess football management stays there, once it's in your blood.

After reporting back to Les, we agreed to take the job on when we met with the committee formally. We said we'd see them back at the start of pre-season training, and that we'd have a side ready to challenge in the Western League for the 1987/88 campaign. That summer, we found out what Mangotsfield United was all about. When we returned to Cossham Street, we were taken aback by the amount of work the committee had done. The ground had been painted, the pitch was immaculate, fencing had gone up, there was a new training area – I pulled Les to one side and told him that this would be a different ball game. This was a family-orientated club, with man, wife and children all helping out with the work that had to be done.

You noticed it even more on match days. There were a crew of ladies, married to players or committee members, going around selling raffle tickets, running the tea hut and then cooking all the food for the players after the match. All of this was done on a purely voluntary basis, and it was magnificent seeing the effort and dedication that everybody put in. I don't know what it's like at Mangotsfield today but, if it's anything like it was 20 or so years ago, I'm sure it is still a fantastic family-friendly club.

We had a very encouraging pre-season, and hit the ground running in the Western League very quickly. The work off the pitch was mirrored by hard work on the pitch and, by the time Christmas 1987 rolled around, we had established ourselves in a top-three Western League spot. In the FA Cup, we had beaten Yate Town 1-0 and then held Conference side Cheltenham Town to a 1-1 draw at Cossham Street. We lost the replay 2-0. We also made it to the third round of the FA Vase, knocking out Wellington and Exmouth Town before losing 2-0 to Falmouth Town at home. The player atmosphere was great, and there were still some good characters about. Andy Black was still performing like he always did at Trowbridge, while Clive Hall's quick wit always ensured a lot of laughter in and around the Mangotsfield changing room.

As we cruised towards the Easter period, I remember us preparing for a tough away game at Radstock Town. We would have probably settled for a point away from home at this stage of the season, but disaster struck when some simmering tensions between Les Alderman and Ralph Miller threatened to boil over soon after kick-off. A frustrated Ralph, watching from the stand, had shouted out and called one of the players a chicken. The player in question was carrying an injury, and was not on the field for his tackling ability. He was selected for his footballing know-how, and to lay the ball on for Fozzie to stick it in the back of the net.

Les was livid, and wanted to storm up there and have it out with Ralph over what he'd just heard. I calmed Les down, and advised him to take the team into the changing room at half-time while I had a quiet chat with Ralph. I told him that those comments weren't helping, and asked him to keep a bit quieter during the second half. Ralph was a very strong character, though, and he certainly wouldn't give in to my requests. In the second half, the same thing happened two or three times and when you hear one of your players being called a cheat or a chicken, you have to do something about it. After the game, Les marched over to Ralph and said there was no way he or the players would put up with his mouth any more. "You were asked to be quiet, and you wouldn't listen," he fumed. "You clearly still want to run this side, so you run it ... I'm off!"

My heart sank when I saw the argument erupt, purely from a selfish point of view. "Please no, not again," I was saying to myself under my breath. The managerial job at Mangotsfield United was ideal for me. It was a club just a few minutes down the road from me, and one that I had played for earlier in my career. In the bar afterwards, I told a few of the committee members that I would have a word with Les when he'd calmed down a bit and see if there was any way we could resolve the situation. I drove over to Warleigh Manor to meet Les, and we had a long talk about it. During the course of the conversation, he highlighted several other aspects of the job that were niggling him, that I'd probably glossed over due to the fact that I was enjoying it so much there. But one thing was for sure, there was no chance of a ceasefire between Les Alderman and Ralph Miller.

One thing I did get from Les, though, was his blessing to take the job on myself if I wanted to. Driving back from Warleigh Manor to Mangotsfield, I weighed up the idea. Part of me really wanted to take it. As I'd said, it was the perfect club for me and a great chance to establish myself as a No.1, rather than one half of a management duo. But I couldn't help but think back to the conversation we had back at Trowbridge when we first became joint managers. We made a vow then to be a team and, if one of us left, we both left. As much as I wanted the Mangotsfield job, in my heart I felt I would be doing the dirty on Les if I took it – even though he had given me the green light to go for it.

I explained my position to the committee members, and with a heavy heart I said I couldn't carry on. It was a crying shame. I was walking away from a club who were second in the Western League and still in two cup competitions. But the damage between Ralph and Les had been done, and my conscience enabled me to leave Cossham Street with my head held high. I thanked the committee for everything they had done, and told them it was a pleasure not only managing their side, but playing with them too. However I stressed that Les and I arrived together, and we would have to leave together.

Several of the players urged me to stay on until the end of the season and think about it again then, but my mind was made up. After we left, Mangotsfield got knocked out of both cup competitions but still finished third in the Western League with 25 wins and 10 draws among their 42 games. It left them level on points with runners-up Saltash United and fourth-placed Plymouth Argyle Reserves, which shows how far we'd come in 12 short months. From a mid-table side at best, Mangotsfield were suddenly competing on an even keel with the league champions and a professional club's second team. However I firmly believe that the heart of the side vanished after Les and I left, because the players still wanted to be playing for us. The following year the club only just avoided relegation and finished 18th.

I'd been kicking my heels for about a month – my longest spell away from football for many a year – when Les called me up one afternoon to tell me that Bobby Jones had been sacked as manager of Bath City. Bath had started the 1987/88 season with high hopes of becoming a Football League club, with the newly-named GM Vauxhall Conference being granted an automatic promotion to Division Four. A great FA Cup run and the added financial boost of getting Bristol Rovers in as tenants at their Twerton Park ground left Bath feeling very optimistic about a title challenge. It never panned out that way, though, and Jones was soon under pressure after just two wins in their opening 17 games. Jones also lost top-scorer Paul Bodin to Newport County for £15,000 – although the club never saw that money, because Newport folded a while later – and he was given the boot in April.

"Do you fancy it Jeff?" Les asked me. Obviously the answer was yes, so we went to see their penultimate home game of the season against champions Lincoln City. The papers reported that it was the biggest crowd of the season, and that was mostly down to the main stand being full of managers interested in taking the job for next year! Les and I were among them, and we knew immediately that this was a big club. Despite being at opposite ends of the table, Bath City actually won the game, beating Lincoln 2-1 thanks to an own goal and a Ricky Chandler goal. A crowd of 1,336 saw it, but it was too little, too late in the battle to avoid the drop and Bath City were relegated. I was desperate to be part of any rebuilding process though!

Our applications went in, we were interviewed for the job and I believe I made it all the way down to the final shortlist of two. In the end, though, we just missed out to Harold Jarman. Fair play to Harold, he had a decent managerial pedigree. A few years earlier he had returned to Bristol Rovers, where he made more than 400 appearances as a player, and saved them from relegation during the 1979/80 season. He was also a First Class cricketer in his day with Gloucestershire. Harold's gain was our loss, though, and we were left with nothing to do football-wise during the summer of 1988.

About six or seven weeks into the 1988/89 season, with Bath misfiring again in the Beazer Homes Southern League, Les called me up to tell me he'd heard a fairly reliable whisper that Harold was far from happy at Twerton Park. A few days later, Les rang again to tell me we were in at Bath City! What an opportunity for us both. We had clearly impressed in our interviews at the end of the previous season, and we were Bath's first port of call when Harold left.

Les and I used the first couple of games to assess the side, see what players we had and identify the areas we wanted to strengthen. There were a lot of good players there already, including a certain John Freegard who had done so well for us at Trowbridge Town a few years earlier. But throughout the side there were players with professional experience. Phil Barton, Keith Brown, Tony Ricketts, Gary Smart and captain Dave Palmer were all ex-Bristol Rovers players, while Paul Stevens and Gary Fulbrook had been at Bristol City. Former Weymouth and Forest Green Rovers player Dave Singleton was also an important part of the side, and we knew him well too – he was part of the Forest Green side who used to train with our Abbotonians lads.

We quickly decided that the first area to strengthen was between the sticks, so we made goalkeeper Jim Preston our first signing as he had recently moved down south with his family. Jim had played Scottish professional football with Queen's Park. Another important addition came behind the scenes, when we brought Mike Ford in. Mike had managerial experience at Radstock Town, but had also been an assistant at Welton Rovers and had an impressive array of coaching qualifications. Mike had the time to work closely with Bath's YTS players on a day-to-day basis, and the biggest success story was young defender Jason Dodd. He made his first-team debut for Bath during the season, and played 16 times for us before being snapped up by Southampton. He went on to become one of their most popular players, racking up more than 400 appearances over the next 15 years. He was an incredible servant for the Saints, and I believe he's back there now overseeing the club's youth academy.

It was also a pleasure to work with the Bath City physio Dave Monks. Dave was an absolute gentleman, who worked tirelessly for the club and who backed Les and I from the first minute we arrived at Twerton Park. I know Dave was also working hard in other areas behind the scenes at the club, and he was a delight to be around.

We had a particularly memorable week in November that saw us go to Ninian Park to play Cardiff City in the third round of the Welsh Cup. We had police escorts to and from the ground, and played virtually a full-strength Cardiff side. We lost the game 3-0 but our lads had performed admirably, although Les had made his mind up about our next position to strengthen. We were desperate to sign another centre-half to play alongside Tony Ricketts so, with no game on the Saturday, we decided to plan a scouting mission.

This was a big difference to how we had done things before. At my other clubs, I was usually able to pluck a player out of thin air and he would fit into the side without a hitch. But because of the standard of football we were involved in now, we couldn't leave anything to chance. Potential players had to be watched and studied, otherwise you're wasting your time and at risk of making yourself look like an idiot! At that time we were one league below Conference football. In today's terms it would be Conference South, and I'm sure all the sides in that division act in the most professional manner. It was no different for us.

The next day, Les called me at work to tell me we were going to Newcastle! Les had been given a tip-off about a player, and he'd arranged for us to stay up there on the Saturday night. I had to go home and explain to my wife what we were planning. She knew we didn't have a game on the Saturday, but suddenly I had to tell her that I needed to go to the other end of the country for the weekend to look at players. You can guess her reaction!

I went to watch Bryan Robson's brother Justin at Newcastle Blue Star, while Les went along to Vauxhall Motors to watch Micky Smith. We ended up signing Micky, who had been a pro with Wimbledon and I believe played in all four divisions for them. He had picked up an injury and had left the pro game shortly after the Crazy Gang reached the top flight but, under the terms of his injury insurance, he was still allowed to play for us as it wouldn't be a professional deal. Les gave him a job at Warleigh Manor along with some accommodation there, and he was a massive signing for us – exactly the colossal centre-half we needed.

Our squad was beginning to show some encouraging signs. We brought Chris Smith and Darren Tilley over from Mangotsfield, and former Manchester City trainee Dave Wiffill came on board, as well Steve Bailey and Bruce Halliday, formerly of Bristol Rovers and City respectively. Les and I felt confident we had a team that could compete, not only at Southern League level, but also back in the Conference. We suddenly sprang into life in December, and put together three back-to-back wins at Twerton Park that gave everybody a real shot in the arm.

We beat Dartford 4-2 with goals from Dave Payne, Micky Smith, Dave Singleton and Gary Smart in our first December match, and that took us from 14th to 10th. Two games later, we found ourselves up to fourth in the table after hammering Redditch United 5-0 and Bedworth United 6-0. Even more encouraging was the number of different goal-scorers – in those three wins, we had no fewer than nine different players on the scoresheet. Darren Tilley caught the eye in particular, netting a hat-trick against Bedworth. Tilley also scored in our 3-1 Boxing Day defeat at Merthyr Tydfil, watched by a crowd of 1,362. That loss in Wales was our only defeat in eight games over Christmas and New Year. Singleton scored twice in a 2-1 win at Wealdstone on New Year's Eve, and we then drew 0-0 with Crawley Town and 1-1 with Worcester City – John Freegard getting that one.

We also got tantalisingly close to the FA Cup Third Round and the possibility of drawing one of the country's biggest clubs. Sadly, it wasn't to be. We'd beaten Grays Athletic 2-0 in the first round thanks to another Singleton double, and we had a huge attendance of 1,361 cheering us on at Twerton Park when we hosted Welling United in the second round on December 10. Despite Welling comfortably being a mid-table Conference side, we fancied our chances but just couldn't get the goal we needed. They came and did the job they set out to do, got the 0-0 draw and took us back to their place for a replay the following Tuesday.

The game was televised, but sadly the referee that day wasn't up to the same standard as the football played. He sent John Freegard off for two yellow cards, even though the first yellow was actually shown to Tony Ricketts. Okay, if you put them side by side they look fairly similar, but for pity's sake, they had different numbers on their backs! We screamed and shouted from the dugout to try and make the referee aware of his blunder, but what can you do? He'd made his mind up, and Freegard was sent off. We had been 2-0 up through Dave Payne and Micky Smith, but lost the game 3-2. The game was also held up for ten minutes when part of a wall collapsed due to the size of the crowd behind one of the goals. Welling's ground was filled to capacity that evening. Officially the club said there were 3,117 people in there ... I was convinced the actual figure was double that. But to go out in such a frustrating manner was very hard to take. What made it even worse was hearing the third round draw – Welling's reward was a home tie with Blackburn Rovers.

Heading into February, we were still well positioned for a promotion push back to the GM Vauxhall Conference despite dropping a few points. A 3-1 home defeat to Gosport Borough on February 11 was sandwiched between two away draws at Moor Green and Cambridge City, both 1-1, that had seen us slip to tenth but still well in touch. However, February 25, 1989, was to provide me with one of my biggest shocks in football. It was a Saturday morning, and we were due to play a home game against Bromsgrove Rovers at Twerton Park. It was a game Les and I were particularly looking forward to, as we'd had two fantastic games against them in that Bill Dellow Cup Final while in charge at Trowbridge Town.

I remember the weather overnight had been terrible. It absolutely tipped it down most of Friday, and then all through the night. Les called me up first thing next morning and suggested we get to the ground and check it out. He was certain the game was going to be off. When I arrived at Twerton Park, the secretary Paul Britton said Les was out on the pitch, so I wandered down the tunnel and hooked up with him. We had a look at the pitch, and then the pair of us walked around the ground to have a chat. I didn't have any idea at all that anything was up – I honestly can't remember what we were discussing, but there was nothing said that gave me any cause for concern whatsoever.

While this was going on, a local referee had come along and surprisingly given the pitch the green light to play. With that, Les told me that he needed to pop back to Warleigh Manor and that he'd see me back at the ground later. "No problem at all," I said as I strolled back to the office to have a cup of tea with Paul Britton. Bath City's chairman Paul Richards, a very nice bloke indeed, came in soon after and asked for a brew, and for his post which Paul Britton had gathered. I saw the chairman's expression change as he started reading his first letter. He glanced at me, then back to the letter, and then looked at me again when he'd finished reading it. I sensed something wasn't quite right. "I think we need to pop out for a bit of lunch," said the chairman. We jumped in his car, and went along to a coffee shop, where he presented the letter to me. "Have you read this?" he asked. To my utter amazement, I cast my eye over the first few lines and my heart sank as I quickly realised I was reading Les Alderman's resignation letter. There was no reason in the letter, no justification … it was simply informing Bath City that he was resigning as manager. I immediately told Paul that I knew nothing about this, and that just half-an-hour earlier we had been walking around the pitch together where he'd given no indication at all that he was thinking of leaving.

I assured Paul not to worry about that afternoon's game against Bromsgrove, because we had already selected the team and everything was in place. I put in an urgent call to Don Gillies and asked him to come in early and help me out, but in truth I was shellshocked. To this day, I've never found out what drove Les to hand in his resignation that day. He's never spoken about it with me, and I really can't think of anything that had happened to upset him. I know from time to time he was questioned on his sense of dress by the club's committee – Les had his beloved duffle coat that he wore everywhere – and I know some committee members weren't happy that we let a couple of the players go to Brian Godfrey at Gloucester City. The chairman had never expressed any concerns about it, but there were a few grumbles from other committee members. Ultimately, though, we were the managers and the players we shipped out didn't fit in with our plans. Whether this had anything to do with Les's decision, I really don't know.

As it worked out, the match against Bromsgrove was postponed as the rain just kept hammering down. It gave Don Gillies and I the chance to have a chat about Les's exit, and what we were going to do next. On the previous two occasions when Les had decided enough was enough, I had no hesitation in going with him. However, this situation was different. Don said he would be happy to be my assistant and coach if I took over as manager so, with that in mind, I approached the chairman. He told us to stay at the ground while the directors had an emergency meeting. He said he would call us in when they were ready to speak to us.

A good hour went by with us sat around twiddling our thumbs, so it was clear the committee members had a lot to talk about. Although, knowing the board at Bath, they were probably having a good drink before they called me up! When I went in, they asked me the reasons why I wanted to take the job on myself. That was an easy answer to give. I told them I'd always wanted to improve myself in life, and in the back of my mind I had that Dear John letter from Bristol Rovers niggling away at me. I didn't want another chance like this taken away from me.

I put a few other thoughts on the table, but then they asked me a very good question. "Why haven't you gone with Les?" the chairman asked. "You've always gone with him before." I answered as honestly, and as thoroughly, as I could. I told them what a fantastic club Bath City was, and explained that I had no idea why Les had decided to quit. When he wanted to leave Mangotsfield United and Trowbridge Town, I knew what problems were upsetting him and I agreed with them. This time, though, I couldn't see any problem whatsoever – we were still in a good position in the league, we were still in the Somerset Premier Cup, and I didn't understand it.

After thrashing out some financial issues, I agreed to sign a contract until the end of the season. If we got on well in those final few months of the season, we agreed there would be scope for taking things further, especially if I could accommodate my work commitments around the Bath City job. To bolster the squad I brought in Andy Black from Mangotsfield and Richard Iles, who had just been released by Bristol Rovers. I also drafted in Duncan Fear and Mike Keen from the reserves, and got a little bit of luck in that I was able to reunite with Jeff Meacham at Bath. Jeff had just gone out on loan to Weymouth from Bristol Rovers, but something went wrong with the deal so I dived in and brought him to Twerton Park.

All that was missing was one quality centre-forward. If we could find that missing link, I felt confident we could deliver what I had promised the chairman in the boardroom when they offered me the job. I had told Paul Richards that I could give Bath City a top-ten finish in the Beazer Homes Southern League, and that we would lift the Somerset Premier Cup. To be fair to the chairman, he backed me and gave me £3,000 to bring in the striker I so desperately wanted. It was a massive moment for me, to be given money to use as a transfer fee to bring in a top-class player. Paul Richards was only a small chap, but I remember him looking deep into my eyes. "Do not waste the club's money," he told me, sternly.

I do not think I wasted one penny of the club's money. I signed Paul Randall for a full £3,000 from Yeovil Town, and a lot of people have said it was one of the club's greatest ever signings. Paul had originally turned pro with Bristol Rovers in 1977 after joining from Frome Town. He was Rovers' top-scorer for the next two seasons, scoring 33 goals in 52 games which earned him a £180,000 move Stoke City. After being used largely as a winger in the Potteries, he played his part in the Stoke side that won promotion to the First Division, before returning to Rovers in December 1981 for £50,000. Over the next five seasons he was top-scorer at Rovers on three separate occasions, adding another 61 goals to his tally. In 1986 he signed for Yeovil, which was where I picked him up.

Paul made an instant impact in our side, and was just what we needed up front. He scored six goals in eight games at the end of the season, including strikes in two back-to-back away wins at Fareham Town (2-0) and VS Rugby (2-1) that sealed us a finish of ninth in the final Southern League table. Paul went on to become a goal-scoring legend for Bath City, and I feel an immense amount of pride that I was the manager who signed him. The following season, he scored an incredible 51 goals as the club won promotion back to the GM Vauxhall Conference. At the highest tier in non-league football, Paul enjoyed two 20-goal seasons and scored 112 goals in just 210 appearances for club. I think it's safe to say I spent that £3,000 wisely!

I'd achieved my first target of a top-ten finish, but what about the Somerset Premier Cup? Well, that went pretty well too. We started the competition with two easy games, walloping Watchet 9-0 in a game that saw John Freegard score six of them, before following it up with a 2-0 win at Minehead. It set up a semi-final against Taunton Town, which would prove to be a far tougher proposition. We drew 2-2 at their place thanks to goals from Gary Smart and Freegard, but brought them back to Twerton Park for the replay and hammered them 4-0. Freegard got another two, Keith Brown scored one and the returning Jeff Meacham got his name on the scoresheet too.

The final of the Somerset Premier Cup was a two-legged affair against Mangotsfield United, of all teams. We played the first of those matches at a snow-covered Cossham Street on a Tuesday night in early April. Gary Smart and Micky Smith were both on target in a narrow 2-1 win, but we saved our best for the return leg at Twerton Park. Jeff Meacham and Darren Tilley helped themselves to two goals each, and Smart got the other in a 5-1 win. We'd won 7-2 on aggregate, and I can still feel the hairs on the back of my neck stand up when I recall walking off the pitch that evening hearing the crowd chanting 'Evans for manager'. It was a proud moment, and I couldn't wait to get to the boardroom and say my piece to Ralph Miller who, for once, was very quiet! Before he had a chance to open his mouth, I steamed in and said: "There you go Ralph, that is for the way you treated Les Alderman!" It was a sweet moment.

During those final few games of the season, I was getting an increasing amount of grief from my managing director at work for the amount of time I was having off due to football. He was grumbling about the time I was arriving in the morning, not to mention the number of afternoons off. I told him that I would definitely be seeing the season out, but I felt duty-bound to talk to the chairman Paul Richards about my situation. I pulled him to one side after our last home game against Waterlooville, which we lost 2-0, and it was one of the toughest things I've ever had to do. I loved the job, and I was desperate to stay at Twerton Park. But managing Bath City in 1989 was the same as managing Bath City today. It's a full-time job. Bobby Jones was a full-time manager before Les and I got there. I just couldn't risk losing my job in chemicals to do the Bath City job permanently, mainly because you never can tell how long you're going to be in a football management job! I had a family to provide for, and I couldn't take the risk.

I've already mentioned our final two away games in passing, but let me just go into a bit more detail about that very last game away at Rugby. If they could have beaten us that day, they would have finished as runners-up in the Beazer Homes Southern League, so they had everything to play for. It needed a magnificent performance from us to stop them, and that's exactly what we produced. The players knew it was the last time we were all going to be together as a group, and they made sure it was a display to remember. I had arranged to take the team down the motorway to Clive Hall's pub in Gloucester, and it was a fitting end to a hugely enjoyable season. Andy Black was performing to his usual standard on the bus, Clive laid on a load of food and the pub and we had a proper sing-song. After that, we piled into Bristol and it was a great night out.

If I had been able to see into the future, I would have never chosen work over Bath City. With the benefit of hindsight, it's a decision I regret because I left the company the following February anyway. As I mentioned in a previous chapter, I had made the switch into chemicals when I sold my fruit and veg shops in the late 1970s. Although I knew nothing about chemicals, I always had the gift of the gab when it came to selling and I soon climbed the ladder within the industry to become a manager, and then special account sales which took me all over the country.

In the early 1980s, I'd guess around 1982, my sales manager Ken Willetts opened up his own company and I went over to work for him. He made me a director of the company about a year later, and it kept me extremely busy away from football. This was the key factor in me not pursuing a full-time role with Bath City. However Ken and I fell out over wages, so that was when I left and decided to go my own way. If only it had happened a few months earlier, it would have definitely made me look at the Bath City opportunity in a different light. But they say it's better to have loved and lost, and all that. I got the chance to manage Bath City, even if it was just for one season, and it was a huge honour that nobody can take away from me. I'd like to use this book to publicly thank Paul Richards and his committee for giving me the opportunity. I'll never forget it, and it was an absolute pleasure.

After a year working on my own, I had quite a decent turnover and I took over a company in North Devon which I've still got today. It goes by the name of PAC Chemical & Paper Products – PAC stands for Paul, Amanda and Clive, my three children. I run that alongside a lot of mobile toilet companies that I deal with, selling a product called Sani Flush. I'm still doing this now, and I've got no intentions of jacking it in at the moment.

The business took up a lot of my time, and that was without all the time and effort I was putting in to football. To be fair to my wife Jo, she did most of the bringing-up of the kids. I had a pretty easy time of it! Paul went to Pucklechurch School and then on to Mangotsfield Senior School. He played football for both of them, and also played for me a few times at my various clubs including Abbotonians and Trowbridge Town. He finished playing football when he moved to Dawlish on the South Devon coast, with his wife Vicky. They still live there, and they have given Jo and I two lovely grandchildren, Amy and Luke.

Amanda, known as Mandy, also went to Pucklechurch School before going on to Downend School. At school she was very competitive in athletics, but her main love has always been horses. It started off with local shows, but as she grew up she became really involved in eventing. She was sponsored by Ken Willetts' company, and later PAC Chemical, and competed at a decent level. Mandy's eventing became a real Evans family affair during the summer months when the football season finished, and we'd travel all over the place, sleeping in the horse box at two-day events. She still has three horses and is a veterinary nurse, and her life revolves around animals.

Like his brother Paul, Clive went to school at Pucklechurch and Mangotsfield, and has always been football-mad. He loved playing the game, but developed asthma in his early teens and he had to pack it in. It did give him the opportunity to be my permanent partner on Saturdays and, no matter what club I was managing, Clive has always been there too. He also deals with horses for a living. He worked very hard through a five-year apprenticeship to become a farrier, and now works for himself. He deals with several of Great Britain's international riders, including Mary King down in Devon. Clive lives with his wife Penny, son Gabi and daughter Alyssa. Like his dad, Clive still loves his football too.

Sweet success! Bath City celebrate winning the 1989 Somerset Premier Cup after a two-legged final against my former side Mangotsfield United. Pictured (back row from left) are me, Dave Wiffill, Jeff Meacham, Mike Keen, Keith Brown, Micky Smith, Tony Ricketts, Darren Tilley, physio Dave Monks, assistant manager Don Gillies and (front row from left) Andy Black, Richard Iles, Jim Preston, Gary Smart, Duncan Fear and Paul Stevens.

Away from the dugout... my daughter Mandy's eventing kept me busy during my brief spells away from football.

8... I'm in charge, Ossie!

B Y THE time the summer of 1989 came around, I knew I'd taken charge of my last Bath City game, and I had no new club lined up. So, with no pre-season to organise or players to find, I was able to put my heart and soul into my daughter Mandy's eventing. We spent a few weekends away and, during one of them, I received a message from John Evans who was manager of the newly-formed Stroud side – he wanted to know if I was interested in going up there to be his assistant. Stroud were effectively Forest Green Rovers in all but name. After the high of that FA Vase win in 1982, and subsequent promotion from the Hellenic League into the Southern League's Midland Division, the 1980s went a bit stale for Forest Green. It was hoped that, by rebranding as Stroud FC for the 1989/90 season, it would breathe new life into the club.

I told John I'd call him to discuss his offer in greater depth when I got home from the eventing. During the day, I kept mulling it over and I really struggled to get my head around the idea of being an assistant manager again. After all, I'd mainly been the top man in the previous jobs I'd had ... even with Les Alderman at Trowbridge, I'd only spent those early months as his assistant before we realised we were both the top men and became joint managers. The more I considered it, the more I thought that there was probably no real point in even calling John back. But out of courtesy, I got on the phone that night and returned the call.

I told John all about my thoughts and concerns, and he suggested I travelled up there for a meeting, so we could discuss things face-to-face. I still wasn't sure, but thought there was no harm in it so I said I'd go up and watch a training session, and we could chat afterwards. The next training session was being held at the Forest Green Rovers stadium, The Lawn, so I headed up there to cast my eye over things. A couple of directors were there, and both of them said all the right things to me, and the chat with John went well too. From being very sceptical about the offer, the visit there had done enough to change my mind and I thought I would just take the plunge and get involved.

Because I was dipping in towards the end of pre-season, I spent those final few weeks getting to know the players, and the side's strengths and weaknesses. My initial gut feeling about the new-look

Stroud FC was that the players and management may not be taking things quite as seriously as they should. After all, they would be playing at a decent standard, in the Southern League's Midland Division, and they had a good set-up at The Lawn. Obviously, I'd just come from a Bath City outfit that was highly focused and professional in every manner possible, but my eyes were really opened to the Stroud situation when I arrived at the coach for our first away game of the season.

The game itself wasn't that great, and we didn't play particularly well. But before a ball had been kicked in anger, I couldn't believe what I saw when I got on to the bus that morning. The players were scattered about the bus – some at the front, some at the back – and there were wives and girlfriends all on board, as well as directors and supporters all over the place. After we'd got home, I voiced my concerns to John. I told him that it wasn't good enough. We were travelling to what should have been a professional non-league game, but instead it resembled more of a family coach trip to the seaside. Sometimes, what you don't or can't say to the players in the changing room during or immediately after the game, has to be said on the coach on the way home. Even at Western League level, the players will all sit together at the back of the bus and, if the management have issues that need to be discussed, it can be done at the back. "There was no chance of doing that today," I said to John. "What you've got here is more like one big kids' party."

John agreed and said he would try and initiate some change, but he didn't convince me. He basically said that this was the way the club had travelled when he arrived, and this is how it would probably carry on. To my utter shock, John didn't get much time to even try and enforce these changes. Out of the blue he was given the sack, probably just a month or so into the season, and it left me not knowing whether to stay or go. I went along to a committee meeting, and I was asked if I wanted the job. I told them, honestly, that I didn't know, but I agreed to take charge initially on a short-term basis to see how things went. Straight away I laid down some new ground rules, and said that we would not be having wives and girlfriends on the team bus from now on. That new rule applied to supporters too, although I didn't want to discriminate against those loyal fans who had come all their lives. I came up with a little loophole, which allowed the club's directors to bring one invited guest on the coach.

Stroud's officials agreed and, when it came to the next away game at Bromsgrove Rovers, it was like being with a professional club again when I got on the coach. With the backing of the players, I took the job and made Bobby Jones my assistant, and brought Mike Ford in as my eyes and ears. There were a lot of things to alter and a lot to change within the club, and a lot of the people there were adverse to too much change, so we knew it was going to be a tough task that lied ahead.

I signed a hard-tackling midfielder in Nigel Gillard to toughen us up in the centre of the park, and also snapped up Martin Wheeler, a class forward from Bath City. Martin was an integral part of Bath's Southern League championship-winning side in 1977/78, and also turned down a pro contract with Alan Mullery at Brighton & Hove Albion. I also signed Martyn Grimshaw from Weymouth and Mike Kilgour from Trowbridge Town. Mike was a commanding centre-half and his nickname, 'Killer' Kilgour, said it all about his style of play! In addition, I persuaded Shaun Penny and Chris Smith to stay at the club and we started to see an improvement in team spirit – away trips were now something to look forward to, rather than a chore.

Before away games, the Bristol-based players would always wait for the team bus at the Posthouse Hotel in Hambrook. On one occasion we arrived there to see Shaun Penny armed with a full cutlery dinner set. Knives, forks, spoons ... he had the lot in this case, and he asked me if he could auction them off on the coach. "How much did you pay for them?" I asked, and he told me £30. "It's just market tat! You've been done," I said. "I know that and you know that," said Shaun. "But there's a director here who will tear his hands off to get them, we just need to get the bidding up." I remember the director in question was a northern bloke called Terry, and Shaun was adamant that he could get a good offer out of him with a bit of back-up, so I agreed.

About 30 minutes into the trip, I heard a bit of a din at the back of the bus and saw that Shaun had got out this case of cutlery for the auction. I shouted back to him and asked him how much his highest bid was so far, making sure that Terry heard at the same time. "£220," said Shaun. I went straight in with an offer of £250, to which one of the players quickly upped to £275. "I tell you what Shaun, £300 and you can have the money when we get back to the hotel," I said. By now the directors were starting to get interested and one –

who I later found out was also in on it – offered £350. Terry couldn't keep quiet any longer, and jumped out of his seat to examine the knives, forks and spoons. He asked Shaun what the highest bid was, and Shaun told him £375 – even though it was actually only £350! Terry had heard enough. "I will give you £400, in cash, now!" The rest of the players all had to turn their backs on the auction, they didn't want to give the game away by bursting into laughter. But Shaun had heard enough … sold, to the brash northerner! A lot of the £400 was spent back at the Posthouse Hotel bar that evening, and I can assure you we had a very good night's drinking!

Not long after that trip, I received a call from Gloucester City manager Brian Godfrey, who asked if we could take a Stroud side over there to play in a charity match for a chap called Dougie Foxwell. Dougie was a midfielder who had played for both Gloucester and Forest Green Rovers, and he'd recently suffered a broken leg. The club were looking to raise a bit of money for the lad, and Brian said we could play as many guests as we wanted … "the bigger the better," in his own words. I put a call in to Don Gillies, who had been with me at Trowbridge Town and Bath City, and he was a big name following his successful career with Bristol City. Don was more than happy to get involved, and he also suggested that I called up Chic Bates, the assistant manager at Swindon Town – Don knew Chic well from their brief spell at Bristol Rovers together in the early 1980s.

Chic and I had a very good chat and he was well up for coming along. He asked me if I'd like him to bring the manager along as well and, after a quick gasp of breath, I answered with an emphatic yes. After all, we weren't talking about any old manager here – this was Ossie Ardiles, the former Argentina international and Tottenham Hotspur legend who had recently taken over at the County Ground. A couple of days later I received the call from Chic I had been waiting for, and he confirmed that Ardiles would be at the game. It was wonderful news.

On the day of the game, I spotted Ossie arriving at Gloucester's ground so I went over and introduced myself. He was an absolute gentleman right from the word go but, to my amazement, about five minutes later I caught him smoking in the changing room toilet! "You know the rules," I said with a smile on my face. "No smoking in the changing rooms, you're one of my players now and you will have to be fined!" He took it in good spirit, and said he'd buy the first round of drinks in the bar after the game. As the players were getting changed, Ossie came back over to me and asked if I could look after something for him. I opened my hands, and he gave me the biggest Rolex watch I've ever seen. "Whatever you do, don't lose it Jeff," he said. "It's worth about £10,000!"

Ossie played the entire first half for our Stroud side, and at half-time he said he was more than happy to come off if someone else wanted a run-out. "I tell you what Ossie," I said. "You go out there and start the second half, and I'll take you off once you've scored a goal." Ossie obliged, and jokingly told the lads he'd be taking any penalties should we win one. He kept up his end of the bargain, and duly scored a goal in that second half, so I indicated to the referee that I was ready to make a substitution. I think there were only about ten minutes of the game left, but I shouted over to Ardiles and off he came, to a standing ovation. It was a special moment for me – what other non-league manager would get the chance to manage a player of the calibre of Ossie Ardiles, a World Cup winner with the 1978 Argentina team? And not only that, I got to haul him off with ten minutes to go!

Back at Stroud, we were pushing on in the league, but I was never really happy with the directors and the set-up there. Without about a month or so left in the season, we were lying around about fourth place in the Southern League Midland Division and I was trying my best to get a little bit more money out of them to bring in another centre-forward and make one final surge for promotion. I waited on a call to tell me whether this was going to be possible or not and, when the phone finally rang, it wasn't with the news I was expecting. One of the directors was on the other end of the line, informing me that my contract would not be renewed for the next season. I wasn't at all impressed. "If the chairman can't be bothered to speak to me himself about this, then I can't be bothered to be at Stroud next season," I said. "I wish you all the best, but I'll be on my way this week." I made sure all the loose ends were tied up, said my farewells to the players and left the club with three games of the season left. It really did all happen that quickly.

In the end, they finished the 1989/90 season in tenth. It would turn out to be the best finish they achieved during a largely unsuccessful three-year spell as Stroud. In the following two seasons they finished 18th and 19th, and it wasn't a popular time as lots of long-time fans and committee members turned their backs on the club for abandoning the Forest Green Rovers name. In 1992, they dropped the Stroud title and Forest Green were back. Frank Gregan took over soon after, and took them all the way to the Conference and the FA Trophy Final.

During the summer, I had a call from my old mate Steve Millard, who was ringing to let me know that he'd passed on my name and telephone number to a bloke by the name of Phil Rogers, who was a committee member with a team called Stapleton in the Gloucestershire County League. "Steve, I've just spent five or six years managing in the Southern League," I said to him. "I don't know any players at that level these days, so I don't think it's a good idea for me to go there." Steve was very persuasive, though, and he advised me to have a word with Mike Ford about it. Steve knew Mike and I had got on well over the years, and he also knew that Mike had some good contacts with players at Gloucestershire County League level. I still wasn't keen enough to chase up this job, but I thought I'd bide my time and see if anyone from Stapleton got in touch with me.

Sure enough, the phone call soon came from Stapleton chairman Trevor Lewis, and he was requesting a meeting so we could have a chat. Out of politeness I agreed, and I also took Steve's advice and spoke to Mike about the position. We went along for the meeting with the chairman and, after a bit of bartering from both sides, Mike and I agreed to take charge. Trevor was fully aware that I'd come from Southern League football, and we had an understanding that, if a job offer came up back at that higher level, then I would be leaving.

I can remember that first training session at Stapleton's Carsons Road ground, which is where they were based at that time. Mike and I looked at each other and we were both thinking the same thing. The group of players there were simply not good enough and, if we were going to do anything at all that season, then we had to rebuild the entire squad first. The negotiating quickly started, and a new wave of players began to arrive at Stapleton. Former Bristol City youngster Colston Gwyther came in having also played for Paulton Rovers and a few games for Les Alderman and I at Trowbridge Town. Steve Bailey, who was with me at Bath City, came along, as did ex-Paulton player Ricky Murphy.

After bringing in those slightly more experienced heads, we then decided to look around at some promising youngsters to complete the squad. We brought in James Hewlett, whose brother Matt had a good pro career with Bristol City, Swindon Town and Torquay United. Neil Britton was a young full-back who had come up through the divisions, Paul Waring was a much-travelled but still very young midfielder, and Rob Shepherd was a strong centre-half.

As the season started, I found it extremely hard to get used to the lower level of football associated with the Gloucestershire County League. Mike Ford knew how I felt, which probably explains why he was completely baffled when I informed him that I had turned down an offer to go and manage Western League side Frome Town not long into the season. He couldn't believe I turned the opportunity down, which came after I received a call from Frome's chairman one evening. The trouble was, it just didn't feel right for me. I can't really explain it in any other way. Over the past few years I had gradually worked my way up through the leagues, and at one point with Bath City I was only about three or four places away from the Conference. It was about as close as I could possibly get to being a professional manager. However I was enjoying the challenge of finding youngsters at Stapleton, and I explained to Mike that I'd love to do what I did at Abbotonians – bring a squad of talented players together, and then get a job at a higher level and take five or six players with me. We needed to go out and watch midweek games, and try and uncover more players like Hewlett, Britton, Waring and Shepherd.

Mike still couldn't believe I'd turned it down, but he understood my reasoning. Soon after, though, another Western League job came up at Welton Rovers, and that seemed like a better move for us. We knew a couple of Welton committee members quite well, so we got in touch with them and enquired about the vacancy. We went and had an interview with the chairman, which I later found out was secretly recorded. I wasn't impressed when I found that out. If the interviewing panel needed a recording of the interview because they couldn't remember what was said, then that's a pretty poor show. Another person interviewed for the job was Steve Millard, and he was offered the position only to turn it down a couple of days later. Welton's chairman then got on the phone to me and offered Mike and I the job. I didn't hesitate in telling him that we weren't prepared to be second choice to anyone, and turned it down too! So it was back to Stapleton.

We finished the season in 11th, but I was becoming more and more disillusioned at Stapleton – not just because of the standard of football, but also because of the childish attitude of certain committee members there. There was no professionalism whatsoever, and in trying to introduce it just seemed like we were banging our heads against a brick wall. No job opportunities came up over the summer so Mike and I carried on into our second season at Stapleton, but after a while we held a meeting with the players to let them know what was on our minds. I told them that we were going to have a rest from the dugout for the remainder of the season, and instead we'd go around the grounds making notes on any exciting young players we saw. With the 1992/93 season approaching its conclusion, another vacancy came up that was too good to ignore. Western League side Chippenham Town were looking for a new management team. Needless to say, my application was in the post …

Brief encounter! Me (back row, left) during my short time as manager of Stroud, formerly known as Forest Green Rovers. Among the players I signed were **Mike Kilgour (back row, second left)** and **Martyn Grimshaw (front row, right).**

9... From the dugout to the boardroom

I T WASN'T long before I heard back from Chippenham Town and, after being invited in for an initial meeting with the Western League club's committee, they let me know that I was on their final shortlist of three or four to be interviewed in full for the job. As soon as I heard this news, my first phone call was to Mike Ford. With Les Alderman and I having gone our separate ways after our time together at Bath City, I had built up a fantastic working relationship with Mike and, if I was going to go to Chippenham, I wanted him there with me. On the phone, I suggested that it would be a good idea for Mike to come with me to the second interview, which he was happy to do. I wanted him to give the club a little bit more insight into what we were all about, especially in areas such as his training methods and procedures.

The interview process at Hardenhuish Park was certainly thorough. We gave a pretty good account of ourselves in that second interview with the chairman Doug Webb, and then we were invited back for a third one. After about 15 minutes of talking in that third interview, I felt pretty confident that we had got the job, just by the way Doug was speaking to us, and phrasing his questions. When the conversation had finished, I just went for a straight answer. "You've invited us out for a third time, Doug, so have we got the job?" Sure enough, the answer was yes and Doug said he'd like us to go along and meet the managers of Chippenham's second and third teams as soon as possible.

So off we went to Hardenhuish Park, where we also met the club's physio Paul Christopher, his wife June who was on the committee, and Doug's wife, along with the rest of the committee. Doug also introduced us to the second and third team managers and, when we had a quiet moment to chat, said he was willing to back me if I wanted them to stand down and reappoint my own men for those jobs. It was an encouraging show of backing from my new chairman, but I didn't think I needed to take him up on it just yet. "Let's just see how we go in training," I answered. "If I feel that they're not doing a good enough job, then we'll talk about it then."

On the way home from that meeting, Mike and I stopped off at a pub to have a quick pint and talk over our new job at Chippenham Town. We knew the club had great potential and drew decent crowds. They had finished the previous season, 1992/93, fifth from bottom in the Western League's Premier Division, so we knew it was going to be a hard job and there was plenty to start building on. The key thing we stressed during that pub chat was the need for professionalism. Mike and I both agreed that we needed to go back to the way we worked at Bath City, and treat the Chippenham job as if we were at a professional outfit. If we went into it half-hearted, there was the danger of the club slipping down the leagues rather than charging up through them. Having seen what life was like at a lower level with Stapleton, I definitely didn't want to experience that again in a hurry.

As always, building the side was our first priority. Chippenham already had a quality forward in Robbie Lardner, a great midfield player in Jeremy Christopher and a solid goalkeeper in Mark Batters. Immediately we had inherited a fairly decent spine for the side, with a few other good players to work with like winger Frankie Coleman. Mike and I wasted no time in bolstering the rest of the squad with several new additions. We signed centre-forward Geoff Britton to play up front alongside Lardner, and gave the midfield another attacking option by bringing in Timmy Mayes. A useful defensive addition came in the form of the versatile Paul Lindo, who could play anywhere across the back four if needed. Last but not least, I made a phone call to my old favourite, Andy Black, who came complete with his Norman Wisdom impressions to join me at yet another club! All of these players had vast Western League experience, and were important additions.

During our brief time at Stapleton, Mike and I had identified several young players around the local area who we felt might possess the tools to be able to step up to play at Western League level. We had also promised several of the Stapleton lads that, if we felt they could make the step up, we would give them a chance should we get a job at a bigger club. With Chippenham Town, that job had arrived. So in came James Hewlett, Neil Britton and Rob Shepherd from Stapleton, and I challenged them to prove their quality in pre-season training if they wanted to make their Western League debuts and fit into the side. At the same time, I had a telephone call from an old mate of mine, who told me his 16-year-old son had just left Bristol Rovers and would like a chance at Western League football. I was happy to oblige and, at our next training session, a fresh-faced and very young Lee Gitson turned up.

Inevitably, it took time for this new team to gel. I didn't expect anything else, having hurriedly put new teams together at other clubs I'd managed. About a month or six weeks into the 1993/94 season, a very worried chairman pulled me to one side and expressed his concerns. Mind you, we were in the bottom four at the time, but I told Doug not to panic. "Rome wasn't built in a day," I said to him. I had faith that the team would blossom, and I had already seen signs that the team were starting to blend together. We had beaten Bideford 3-0 in a preliminary round replay in the FA Cup, having drawn 2-2 down at their place, but the first qualifying round draw wasn't kind to us and we lost 5-0 at Weymouth. In the FA Vase, we forced two replays, with mixed results. In the preliminary round, a 2-2 draw at Odd Down brought them back to Hardenhuish Park, where we knocked them out 2-1. But we were unable to finish off Torpoint Athletic at home in the first qualifying round. We drew it 2-2, and then lost the replay 3-0 down in Cornwall. However we fared rather better in the Wiltshire Premier Shield, which was the county's main cup competition.

We took Chippenham all the way to the final, which was to be played at Swindon Town's County Ground against none other than Trowbridge Town. We lost it, but had a very good game, and a very tight game for the best part of 70 minutes. In the bar afterwards, it was good catching up again with John Freegard, who was back playing for Trowbridge Town and still finishing the night off with his rendition of the Rolf Harris song Two Little Boys. In the league, although there were worrying times for the chairman earlier on, we managed to get well clear of the bottom four and actually finished the season in eighth place. A comfortable top-half finish with one of the league's smaller playing budgets gave us plenty of positives to build on.

I started my second season with the signing of John Freegard, plus Paul Rose and Stevie Cripps from Melksham Town, and Bristol-based players Tim Banks and Adie Stag from Manor Farm. I arranged a meeting with Doug Webb to discuss the playing budget for the 1994/95 campaign – mainly to see if there was any more money! I've never been the sort of manager to ask for more money just so my players could earn a bit more. It was down to being able to attract a better type of player to Chippenham Town. The lads Mike and I had brought in were doing well, but to bring in those players who add that little bit extra quality to the side, then you have to pay extra for it… it's a fact of life. In those days we were competing in the Western League against the likes of Tiverton Town, Taunton Town and Weston-super-Mare. To be able to keep up with them, we needed to have a little bit more about us. "If the money's not there, that's fine," I told the chairman. "Just don't expect any miracles from this side."

Unfortunately, the club couldn't find any extra cash to add to the budget. What we had was our lot, and it just had to stay where it was – Doug said he couldn't risk making the club skint, which of course you understand. However it did lead me to make one of the hardest and most horrible decisions I've ever had to make in football. I'd already decided that I wasn't 100 per cent happy with our goalkeeper from the first year, Mark Batters, so I'd signed Paul Weekes, who I felt was a talented up-and-coming goalkeeper from Bristol. Soon after, the chance to sign Steve Perrin came up. In terms of goalkeepers, Perrin was the bee's knees in and around Wiltshire and I knew I wanted the best keeper I could possibly get for my side. I'd only signed Paul a couple of weeks earlier and, with the start of the season still well away, I had to call in the young lad and tell him I was signing Steve Perrin. Of course, I gave him the option of staying and fighting for a first-team place, but he and I both knew that was a pretty tall order when you're going up against Steve Perrin.

I hated having to tell Paul this news, but it was still relatively early in pre-season so he had time to find himself a new club, which he did do. Understandably, he wasn't at all happy about it, but I just couldn't turn down the chance of signing Steve Perrin. As it happens, Paul Weekes went on to have a good career in the Southern League as a goalkeeper, and he's now a pretty good manager as well with Cinderford Town. If he's ever found himself in a similar situation during his managerial career, hopefully he'll understand the position I was in when I had to release him.

As for Perrin, well, what can you say about him? In the past 20 years he's been one of the finest goalkeepers outside of the Football League, and he also captained Wiltshire Cricket Club. He had seven years with Forest Green Rovers in the Conference – earning a call-up to the England non-league side in the process – and more recently helped Bath City win promotion from the Conference South before finally hanging up his gloves in the summer of 2010.

Despite the tight purse strings, I was able to shuffle the squad a little bit and bring in a few extra new faces, including Paul Waring, Ian Mullery and Richard Bryant, and we felt we'd put together a decent squad capable of competing with the top sides in the Premier Division and we managed to repeat our eighth-place finish of the previous season. Not only that, but we brought in some valuable income – not to mention some great memories – when we went on a great run in the FA Vase during the 1995/96 season. It all began with a 2-0 win over Clyst Rovers in the first qualifying round, and that earned us an away tie down in Cornwall at St Blazey.

In my Southern League days with Trowbridge Town, I saw how good weekends away could be for building a team spirit, so the tie at St Blazey gave us the perfect chance to try a similar thing with Chippenham. It was a long trek down into the depths of Cornwall for the game, which we won 3-0 after a fantastic all-round performance. That evening, we'd booked in at a hotel in Newquay, so all the players could have a night out. Mike and I pottered off to find a bar somewhere, and we left the players to go and find whatever nightclubs or discos they wanted to keep themselves amused for the evening. After some beer in a few pubs, Mike and I made it back safely back to the hotel, only to learn later that the landlord had locked up soon after! Come the morning, we had no idea where most of the players were, but thankfully Andy Black was around. Blackie always had a talent for rounding everybody up, and we sent him out with his Wisdom to find out where all the missing players were.

In the Vase run, that earlier Clyst Rovers game turned out to be our only game at home. After the win at St Blazey, we headed down to Tiverton for a game against Elmore in the first round proper, which we won 4-1. We then travelled to Sussex in the second round to meet Wick, and beat them 1-0. It got us to the last 32 of the competition but, of all the teams we could be drawn against, it was Taunton Town away. To make matters worse, we had a couple of players suspended.

You have to remember that suspensions were dealt out in days rather than matches back in those days and, with impeccable timing, the Wiltshire FA had decided that our players would miss a fortnight when this Taunton game was due to be played. We also had a couple out with injuries, but to this day I still believe we could have given Taunton a real game with our full side. In the league earlier that season, we had drawn 2-2 with them at our place after fighting back from 2-0 down. However this Vase tie turned out to be one game too many for our depleted side, and we lost it 4-0. Fair play to Taunton, under Russell Musker they were a quality side and they won the Western League title that season. In the FA Vase, they reached the quarter-finals the following season, and were then twice losing semi-finalists in 1998 and 1999, before finally raising the trophy at Villa Park in 2001.

We managed to sneak in a couple of other weekends away, mainly due to the bad winter weather that caused a load of postponements and gave us quite a major fixture headache. Our secretary Arthur Wimble arranged a couple of weekend double-headers to try and get some games out of the way, and the first saw us travel down to Exmouth Town on the Saturday, before heading to Liskeard Athletic on the Sunday. Our Saturday stop-over destination was Looe, down on the south coast of Cornwall.

It started excellently, and we won 4-0 at Exmouth. When we arrived at the hotel in Looe, I sat the players down and stressed to them the importance of professionalism. "By all means go out and have a good time," I told them. "Just be professional, remember you've got an important game at Liskeard tomorrow, and be here at 9.30am for breakfast."

Mike and I stayed at the hotel and watched all the players head off into town, and down to the sea front in Looe where most of the liveliest bars were. Next morning at 9.30am, we all gathered in the breakfast room at the hotel and a quick headcount showed there were three players missing. "Oh no, what are we going to do?" I asked Mike. The clock was ticking, and we were starting to panic when, out of nowhere, one of the missing trio, Adie Stag, appeared. "Is breakfast ready gaffer?" "Where the hell have you been?" I asked. "No need to worry, I've just been out for a walk around the grounds," said Adie. "Yeah, I bet you have!" I thought.

No sooner had we finished the conversation, I glanced out the window and saw Timmy Mayes strolling across the bridge at Looe with a newspaper under his arm. As he was walking across, I watched him roll his paper up, take a swipe at a seagull perched on the side of the bridge before skipping into the breakfast room with a grin on his face. "Morning guv, is breakfast nice? You told me 9.30am, here I am!" Two of the three missing cases were solved, but the worst was to come. We still had no idea where Timmy Banks was, so somebody went up to check his room. There he was, crashed out on the floor in a right state. We made him have a shower, got him downstairs, and Mike took the team out for a brisk walk and some fresh air.

The game at Liskeard kicked off at 3pm and, on the way to the game, Banksy was sick three times. When we got to Lux Park, Liskeard's ground, Banksy had to have two more showers before being in a good enough state to go out and warm up! It was clear he was in no condition to play though, and our physio confirmed it: "There's no way at all that he'll be able to play this afternoon Jeff." We were still half-an-hour away from kick-off, so the referee was perfectly happy to let me change the team sheet and withdraw Banks. We won the game 1-0, and my favourite memory from the game is Mike and I singing 'handbag handbag give us a wave' to the home stand in the 89th minute. Liskeard's manager Jimmy Hargreaves was not our biggest fan – we'd had a bit of a touchline disagreement during a league game at our place, and he had never forgotten it. Such was his dislike for us, I think he chose to watch the game from the stand opposite rather than be in the dugout next to us. We'd nicknamed him 'Handbag' Hargreaves as a result, and it was a sweet moment to get that win!

A month or so later, Arthur's next double-header saw us play Taunton Town on the Saturday and then Saltash United on the Sunday. As at Looe a few weeks earlier, the same rules applied to the lads for their Saturday night out in Plymouth, although I can remember finding Steve Perrin curled up fast asleep in the corner of the lounge bar where we were staying, at 10am the next morning! The results of the two games? We drew at Saltash, and lost at Taunton. Had we played the games in our usual fashion on Saturdays, a point from those two tough away games wouldn't have been considered a disaster, so we couldn't complain too much.

Those weekends away only helped to increase the team spirit within the Chippenham squad and, although we had to settle for tenth place in the Premier Division, we also got through to another Wiltshire Premier Shield final. This time we had to play at Westbury, which was a little disappointing because it wasn't the greatest pitch in the world. Salisbury City were our opponents, and we lost 3-1. After the game, one of the local newspaper reporters came up and asked me if I was all okay for a fourth season with Chippenham Town. "Yes fine," I said. "I've already had words with Doug Webb, we've had meetings about it and everything's been sorted out."

In one of those meetings with Doug and Malcolm Lyas, who was due to take over as chairman at Chippenham, it was even suggested that Mike and I sign a contract for the 1996/97 season. It was left at that, until we were asked to come along to the club's annual general meeting. Having already verbally agreed terms for the next season with Doug and Malcolm, I couldn't see any point why Mike and I needed to be there. But we went along, and we were staggered to hear Doug suggest that the pair of us stood down from our managerial positions, and reapply to the new chairman. "I have nothing to prove," I told them bluntly. "You've seen what I can do in three years on a very restricted budget and if that's not good enough for you, then I've just got one thing to say ... goodbye."

I believe our playing budget was one of the lowest in the Western League's Premier Division at that time, and yet we'd just taken the club to eighth, eighth and tenth in successive seasons. It was the club's best league performance in ten years – the last time they had finished in the top ten of the Western League was back in the 1986/87 campaign, when they were ninth. I got up and, without hesitation, made my way to the door. As I was storming out, I could hear Doug telling me to come back and talk about it, but it was too late. A long time ago, I had vowed never to work for people who go back on their word and, in my opinion, this is what had just happened at Chippenham. I had been verbally offered a deal only a few weeks earlier, and here I was being told to stand down and reapply. Mike stayed behind, and was asked where he stood on the matter. Mike told them he'd come with Jeff Evans, and he'd leave with Jeff Evans. I was told that Malcolm Lyas kept quiet throughout and, for me, it was a very disappointing way to end things. I've never spoken to Doug Webb or Malcolm Lyas since.

Through the summer months, the manager up the road at Calne Town, Tommy Saunders, was constantly on my back, and on the phone, trying to get me up there. At first I declined. I didn't think Tommy was the greatest manager around, and I'd had the odd ruck with him in the dugout before – not that I ever hold any malice to opposing managers who I've clashed with in the heat of battle on a touchline. In the end I asked him what he wanted me to do there and, to my complete surprise, he suggested I take over as Calne Town's chairman. I'd never been a chairman in my life, but Tommy said there were a few Chippenham players he was trying to sign. He felt he'd have a better chance of signing them if I was on board, because apparently they weren't too happy at the way I was treated there.

It suddenly hit me that, by going to Calne, it gave me a perfect chance of getting my own back on Doug Webb and Chippenham Town, for going back on their word to me. I went to meet the board at Calne Town, and I have to say they were very nice people. That helped me decide to take the job on, although I did so on condition that I was free to leave should a manager's job come up. Mike Ford came in as vice-chairman, and away we went.

I have to admit that it was a position that I didn't really enjoy, and I would never ever take on a chairman's role again. Having experienced it, I can understand and sympathise with Ralph Miller at Mangotsfield United. Although he annoyed Les Alderman and I when he was our chairman there, by taking a similar position at Calne I saw first-hand how difficult it was to oversee footballing matters and not get involved yourself. Having said that, I was chairman of Calne Town and I had to do the job as professionally as I could, and to the best of my ability. I've got a business myself and at Calne, much like with my own company, you don't go into it to lose money. After two or three meetings at Calne, however, it soon became clear that the club had no money.

The first thing I had to do was pull in Tommy Saunders and tell him there was going to be a cut in budget, by 75 per cent. Tommy quickly told me he was on contract, but I reminded him that this contract wouldn't be worth the paper it was written on if the club went bankrupt. There was not enough money in the budget to allow Tommy to have an assistant manager, although I did suggest to him that he used some of his contracted money to pay for a number two. He asked me if I'd tell the players, which I was happy to do. I've got no problem at all in revealing what the financial situation at Calne Town was like after these budget cuts. It worked out at £10 per player. Nothing more. When the players were told the news, they reacted magnificently. I remember one of them standing up and saying: "£10 each then, no problem. We're here to play football, so let's get on with it."

Being chairman enabled me to take a step back and see how all aspects of the club was run – something I wasn't able to do as manager. I was able to look at who was giving the tactical talks, and who was taking the warm-ups. It was Colin Bush, who was Tommy's assistant. I was impressed with the way Colin conducted himself, and I suggested to Mike Ford that, if we were offered another Southern League job, that we should headhunt Colin to join our management team. He was definitely worth his weight in gold at Calne Town, he was a lovely bloke and tactically he was very switched on. That Southern League job offer never came for Mike and I, but Colin proved what a good manager he was in his own right by taking Corsham Town to the Western League title a few years ago.

Calne Town finished the 1996/97 season in seventh place in the Western League, two places behind Chippenham Town. It was a great finish for a small side with no money, but I decided to tell the committee that they should start searching for a new chairman and vice-chairman. Mike and I found it extremely hard to adjust to being away from the dugout and changing rooms on a Saturday afternoon, and we were desperate to get back into football at managerial level. If a job came up, it was a safe bet to say we'd accept it, and I just felt it wasn't fair to keep Calne in limbo like that. I also wouldn't have wanted to leave them in the lurch, and without a chairman, midway through a season, so we all decided it was for the best to stand down at the end of that season.

The club found a new chairman, and also had to look for a new manager. Ironically, Tommy Saunders was given the job at Chippenham Town and, with a much healthier budget in place, he had the resources to build a team that reached the final of the 2000 FA Vase – losing to Deal Town 1-0 – and won promotion to the Southern League the following year. As for me, I had to start keeping an eye out for another managerial vacancy. An unexpected visitor to my PAC Chemical & Paper Products office in North Devon that summer meant I didn't have to wait long…

10... Torrington? Are you serious?

YOU always tend to worry when you see a smartly-dressed man in a suit loitering around outside your office, so I was pretty concerned when it happened to me while I was sat in my North Devon office one Thursday morning going over some paperwork. You immediately assume it's the taxman, or an inspector of some sort. On this occasion, thankfully, it was neither. "Can I help you?" I asked him. He introduced himself as Dave Priscott, the secretary of Western League side Torrington who had been one of Calne Town's main rivals the previous season in the Premier Division. In fact, Calne had just got their noses ahead of them on the last day of the season. Torrington finished one point behind, in eighth place.

"I hope you can help me," Dave said in reply to my question. "But is it okay if I come in and we sit down for a chat?" We went back into the office, pulled up a couple of chairs and, to my great surprise, he offered me the Torrington job there and then. I couldn't quite believe what I'd just heard. "Are you serious?" I asked. Dave obviously knew I was in North Devon fairly regularly for my PAC Chemical & Paper Products company, and he was also aware that I was without a club after bidding Calne farewell. "I'm serious," he said. "We've got a team at Torrington, we just need a manager." I just couldn't see how it would work. Okay, so I was down in North Devon one day a week for work, but most of the time I was in Bristol. It was a two-hour drive away, and a lot of miles. Torrington isn't the easiest place to get to from other parts of Devon, let alone Bristol.

Mike Ford was down with me in North Devon that day, and was out doing some deliveries when Dave had made his unexpected visit. I said I'd need to mention it to Mike when he got back to the office, and Dave was happy for me to do that. When Mike got back, I told him about the offer and asked him the same thing I'd been asking myself ... how could we possibly make it work? Credit to Mike, he looked at all the positives and spoke very enthusiastically about the offer. Calmly and sensibly, he talked me through our situation and suggested we simply reverse the way we look at things. "If we take over at Torrington, our home games will just take the place of the away games that we have always travelled to," he said. "And for

Torrington's away games, they will be like home games for us." He made a good point.

"We're down here on a Thursday anyway Jeff, so we can take training sessions on Thursday," he added. "We will need to bring someone in who can take training on Tuesdays, although there'll be games on Tuesdays so we'd need to come down for those." I could tell Mike was confident it could work, so I said I'd give Dave a call and arrange a meeting for that evening, while we were in the area. Dave said that would be fine, so Mike and I made the short drive over to Torrington once we'd done everything at work.

The last time I'd been at Torrington's Vicarage Field ground as a manager had been with Chippenham Town, and I'd been sent off from the dugout by the referee. As soon as we arrived, I recognised the chairman Winston Martin, as it was him who'd tried his best to calm me down following my dismissal. He clearly didn't hold that against me though, and they were all very professional. After greeting us, Winston showed us into the committee room where Dave was sitting alongside the club's treasurer Graham Avery and three hard-working committee members, Brian Sussex, Albert Williams and John Bright. We all sat down and talked things through, and I explained to the committee that the expenses for fuel to bring players down to Torrington wouldn't come cheap. They all agreed with everything that was discussed, and were very keen to make the appointment and get things rolling … at this point, the opening day of the season was only a few weeks away. We shook on it, and I asked Dave to arrange for all the club's players to be at the ground for training the following Thursday evening, so Mike and I could meet them.

Seven days later, Mike and I drove out to Torrington early to cast our eye over the squad before starting training. We weren't expecting what we saw. No players. Not one. Eventually three players put in an appearance, but only to tell us that they were unhappy about an incident at the previous season's club presentation evening and that, after careful consideration, they felt they couldn't play for Torrington again. While we were having this chat, I'd missed a call from another player, with a message to call him back. The player in question was goalkeeper Dave Penberthy, who everybody knew as Denzil. I called him back, and he told me that he too was unhappy, but was willing to meet me and have a chat. Denzil said he'd come along to the following Thursday's training session so we could talk about things face to face.

It was around about this point that I turned to Dave Priscott in amazement. "You've been dreaming," I said. "This club has no players. How on earth do you expect us to bring a whole new team of players from Bristol all the way down to North Devon?" Mike and I had been so enthusiastic about the job, because we knew Torrington had a fairly decent side the season before. We thought we'd be able to bring a few quality players in from Bristol to complement the existing players and make a push into the top two or three places in the Premier Division of the Western League. In reality, it looked impossible. The new season was almost upon us, and we had not one player – well, unless you count a 'maybe' from Denzil Penberthy if we could talk him around. It was virtually impossible.

Winston pulled me to one side and offered his apologies. He said he had no idea the situation was as bad as it was and, like me, had been led to believe that many of the players had in fact signed on for the 1997/98 season. "Please accept my apologies," he said. "Now, how can we get out of this mess?" My immediate answer was to call up one of my old mates, so I went into the club office and got on the phone to Steve Fey, who was then manager of Clevedon Town in the Southern League. The main reason for the call was to see, just on the off-chance, that he may have a couple of left-over players in his squad that he could give us to help us out. "I've got some good youngsters for you Jeff, but I haven't got any experience I can give you," Steve said. "I'll take anything," I said.

Straight away, we took six players from Clevedon's youth team including Geoff Stevens, Damien Bromley and Matthew Duncan. Knowing that they were all based around Clevedon and Weston-super-Mare, it meant arranging transport for them all to get them down to North Devon for training and matches. We also signed on a young defender called Karl Baggaley, who was a very gifted footballer indeed. But Mike and I knew we needed to get some North Devon-based lads in urgently so we could get a full quota of players. Sat in the Barnstaple Hotel on a Thursday night, a lot of names were thrown about.

One of them was Matthew Chugg, a kid from Barnstaple who had already played for Torrington a couple of years earlier. Ian Rowe was another one who signed up, but we tried and tried to get others without any joy. Local players were just not interested in joining a losing side. And I'm afraid to say that's exactly what we were ... a losing side. The 1997/98 season was a complete disaster. We were being forced to scrape eleven players together each week, and we were suffering badly for it. It ended up being my first experience of relegation as a manager, and I didn't enjoy it one bit. We only picked up two wins all season, along with eight draws and 28 losses, and finished rock bottom of the Premier Division with 14 points.

I couldn't have asked for a better chairman than Winston Martin. He knew what the situation was at the club, he hadn't expected any miracles and he had braced himself for the worst. At the end of a miserable season, he agreed with me that the whole side needed rebuilding, and he told me he had complete faith in me. He said he would leave it completely in my hands, and that I had his full backing. It was superb to hear such kind words from a chairman, but that was Winston – he was a lovely man and a true gentleman. It was also the perfect tonic after the disappointment of the season, and I was really fired up to turn the club around.

Mike and I worked our socks off that summer to try and build for life in Division One and transform Torrington's fortunes. We signed Karl Madge from Weston-super-Mare, Lee Gitson from Chippenham Town and Alan Chapman from Barnstaple Town. All three were very good players who added a lot to the side and, after losing our opening three league games of the 1998/99 season, we finally got that all-important first three points when we beat Frome Town 2-0 at Vicarage Field at the end of August. Our goal-scorers that day were Craig McConachie and Mark Billitteri. Craig was a local lad from North Devon, while Mark was another one of our Bristol recruits who came down with us.

The season was only a couple of weeks old when we learned we'd need to search for a new goalkeeper. Taunton Town came in for Denzil Penberthy, and I've never liked to stand in the way of a player who has a chance to play at a higher standard. Like it or not, Torrington were now a Division One side whereas Taunton were Premier Division title-chasers. I told Denzil he could also have a chance of playing in an FA Vase Final if he signed for Taunton, and gave him my blessing to go.

At Torrington, Karl Madge and Karl Baggaley were very good mates and always travelled down from Weston-super-Mare together.

They recommended that I spoke to a young lad named Peter Trego, who was Weston's young starlet of a goalkeeper. At the same time, he was also a top starlet in the cricketing world with Somerset. He was just starting his first year as a professional cricketer so, even though the cricket season was about to finish, Peter still needed to get permission from Somerset to play football. Permission was granted, and off we went with a professional cricketer between the sticks.

Other signings we made for our Division One baptism included Trevor Haslett and Dave Powell from Weston-super-Mare. Trevor was a player with vast experience, while Dave also had a decent amount of experience despite being relatively young. Striker Hector Christie also joined us, and I remember him scoring two goals to help us complete the double over Frome Town in mid-February. We had been 2-0 down before a Hector double and an own goal gave us the points. Our other new signings had also played crucial roles in getting us vital wins. Madge (2), Haslett and Powell all scored in a 4-3 thriller at Chard Town, while Madge, Stevens and McConachie got on the scoresheet in a 3-1 win over Heavitree United.

We weren't pulling up any trees in Division One, but we were doing more than enough to stay away from the bottom group of teams. There were also plenty of promising signs for the season ahead, even if Mike and I did have a major disagreement one cider-filled evening. With both of us being as stubborn as each other, neither one of us would back down and admit we were in the wrong. The argument got out of hand, and our managerial partnership that had lasted seven years was terminated. It was certainly one of the low points of the season. I will say that, since that night, the disagreement has been resolved and everything has been forgiven and forgotten … Mike and I are still the best of friends, and always will be.

Anyway, it left me without an assistant for the final five or six games of the season. Craig McConachie's dad came in to help me out, and he also did a bit of physio work for us. The aforementioned committee man Albert Williams had been doing the physio job as well, but he had an ever-increasing list of important jobs to do in the clubhouse and bar. On the pitch, the season really started to peter out around this time. We beat Corsham Town 4-0 at home in March, and also had back-to-back away wins at Pewsey Vale (3-1) and Glastonbury (3-2) in early April. However our last six games ended with five defeats – the only win was a 2-0 home win against

Warminster Town. We finished the season in 14th with 13 wins and 23 losses – not a single draw! Another positive was finishing ten points ahead of Chard Town, who were the other team to drop down from the Premier Division with us.

For my third season in charge of Torrington, I decided to fly solo. Rather than start looking for another assistant, I thought I could do the job on my own and that my time would be better spent looking to build the squad. A goalkeeper was once again at the top of my wish list. Peter Trego went back to Somerset for the start of the cricket season and, with his stock on the increase up there, I knew the chances of him being allowed to play football were slim. I found the solution to my goalkeeping problem in the unlikeliest of places, namely Hanham Athletic's third team in the local Bristol league.

It was a young Richard Fey, who always fancied himself as a midfield maestro. You can tell by the fact that he was plying his trade for Hanham 3rds that he never quite made it as a star midfielder! I knew, though, that he was a quality keeper who had lost his way. He needed to be picked up and brought back in at a decent level of football. I also knew Richard as a person – I'd been good mates with his dad Steve since our Abbotonians days together – and I was fully aware of how much he enjoyed a laugh. For me, that was almost as important as his goalkeeping skills. I had no doubt that his presence within the side would provide a massive boost to our team spirit. He was an entertaining and likeable lad, and it was impossible not to get on with him and have a laugh with him.

A year or so earlier, I'd encountered real difficulty in trying to attract any local North Devon-based players to Torrington. By now, it seemed the hoodoo surrounding the club was starting to lift and I was able to sign a trio of players from Barnstaple. Lee Langmead was an extremely athletic and versatile striker, Mark Barrow gave us another strong option in midfield, and Barry Yeo came on board to bolster the defence. Dave Newsome and Steve Burns signed from Ilfracombe Town, and I also went further afield to sign Paul Terry from Weston-super-Mare. It was another busy pre-season, but I thought we looked a much stronger side as the 1999/2000 season got under way.

Early results certainly backed up my gut feeling and we won our first four games. We won 5-2 at Larkhall Athletic on the opening day of the season, and a week later beat Pewsey Vale 3-1 at home. Goals from Langmead and Powell helped us beat Wellington 2-0, while

Langmead and McConachie scored in a 2-1 win at my old club Calne Town. But before we could get too carried away with ourselves, we lost four of the next five – only a 4-1 win at Corsham Town broke up the mini-run of defeats. The addition of Richard Fey to the ranks was certainly having a positive effect on our team spirit, though – not to mention our many long drives down to Devon with all the Bristol-based players. There was never a dull moment with him around.

Feyer's favourite trick was to bring a copy of the *Western Daily Press* with him, turn to the classified adverts and try to find the most bizarre and random items for sale. He'd then phone up the seller and, for a laugh, try to barter a deal! One particularly entertaining phone call always sticks in my mind, and that was to an old woman who was selling three suitcases. She was getting completely confused when Feyer kept stressing to her that he only wanted to buy one or, as he put it, the middle-sized one. "I'll pay the full price," he kept saying. "But I just want the one medium-sized case." The lady couldn't get her head around it. "But if you're paying full price, you may as well take all three," she insisted. Feyer was like a dog with a bone and, with the conversation broadcast to us all on speakerphone, it was almost impossible not to burst out into fits of laughter. In the end, she put the phone down. "I can't get any sense out of you whatsoever," she ranted just before we heard the clunk of the phone being put down.

Another occasion, Feyer called up some bloke who had advertised the sale a set of metal gates. By a set, I mean two. That wasn't enough for Feyer, though, who called this chap up and asked him what condition the one on the right was in! "Why do you ask that?" asked the voice on the other end of the line. "Well I only want the right one," said Feyer. "I've got the left one at home!" The bloke was baffled. "But I'm selling them together!" Listening to the man's voice suggested to me that he wasn't someone to be messed with, but Feyer kept on pushing him. He was getting more and more irate at this clown on the phone trying to negotiate a deal for a right-handed gate, and in the end told him exactly where to go before slamming the phone down.

There were other times when I was laughing so hard, I had to pull the motor over on the hard shoulder. We were darting down the M5 when these pranks were being pulled, and sometimes I just couldn't hold it in any longer. One particularly unlucky bloke was a person who I would guess was in his late 20s, and he was selling his fish pond. An advert with this scope for comedy was like gold dust for Feyer. "How much water does this pond hold?" he asked after introducing himself on the phone. The lad on the phone didn't know how to answer, but Feyer didn't give him much time. "I'd like to know how many fish will fit in this pond please," he added. The guy was trying his best to answer, to be fair to him, and even said he would deliver it when Feyer asked how the pond would arrive at his place. But Feyer kept going. "How many fish will come with it?" The bloke apologised, and said the fish had all died, which is why he was selling the pond. "What?" said Feyer. "You can't sell a fish pond without any fish!" Then came the question that finished me off. "Mate, how are you going to get the water over to us?" That was it for me. I was gone, and the tears were rolling down my face. I had no choice but to pull over. The bloke on the phone had realised by now that he was being taken for a ride, and was ranting and raving about his time being wasted. It was hilarious.

As you can no doubt tell, Richard Fey had instantly become a character within the changing room on his arrival at the club. There were other top lads in the group as well, and was fast becoming more of a pleasure than a challenge, being manager of Torrington. The results were picking up as well, and among the more memorable ones were a 2-1 derby win at Ilfracombe Town during the Christmas holidays, and a 5-1 triumph at Warminster Town in mid-January. At Easter, we completed the double over Ilfracombe with a fantastic 3-2 win. Steve Burns scored against his former side, and Craig McConachie also scored. A lad by the name of Paul Hutchings got the other goal. Paul was a local lad, and a marvellous player, having been a professional on Aston Villa's books in his younger years. We closed our home campaign with a good 4-0 defeat of Larkhall Athletic, and finished seventh in Division One – just three points off fourth spot. It was a fantastic improvement on the previous season, and it showed that we weren't far away from having a promotion-winning side.

The following season, 2000/01, would prove to be one of the toughest Division One campaigns in many years. Team Bath had won promotion into the Western League, and they were joined by the likes of Bath City Reserves, Frome Town, Exmouth Town and a very strong Keynsham Town side. Team Bath were the most well-equipped side of the lot. As a university side, they targeted young professionals who had just been released by pro clubs, and offered them the chance to combine full-time training and competitive playing with studying for a qualification. The manager at the time was Paul Tisdale, who of course went on to greater things by taking Exeter City from the Conference up to League One. Team Bath stormed through the leagues and, in the space of just ten years from their formation in 1999 to 2009, they went all the way to the Conference South. The journey ended there, though – due to their university status, the FA ruled that they were not eligible to compete in a national division, so the club folded.

I still needed another centre-half, so I signed Jeff Parish from Appledore, and also brought in Carl Armstrong from the same side. The squad blended well, but we were unable to better our finish of the previous season and we had to settle for a final position of 10th. We still felt we had a good season and, although I was a little disappointed to drop a few positions, I suppose when you factor in the strength of the division in general, it wasn't a bad achievement at all. We played some good stuff, though, and we started the season on fire. Lee Langmead scored four goals on the opening day when we beat Pewsey Vale 5-1 at their place. Paul Terry got the other one that day. Langmead and Trevor Haslett got two each in our next game, a 4-1 home victory against Bath City Reserves, and a 3-0 win over Bitton saw us finish August as leaders of Division One.

We weren't quite strong enough to hold onto it though, especially when we came up against the likes of the aforementioned top sides. We lost 5-0 at both Team Bath and Exmouth, although we gave Keynsham a hell of a game before losing 4-3 there. They did us 4-1 at Vicarage Field, though, and Team Bath went one better and beat us 5-1. But that was where we were. We had a good, well-organised side with character and an ever-increasing spirit about them, but we just lacked the real quality to match teams like Keynsham and Team Bath. With Torrington's location, and our inability to offer big-time expenses, it was to be expected. Those two sides ran away with the league and both got promoted to the Premier. Team Bath went up as champions – one of four promotions for Paul Tisdale there before he was snapped up by Exeter City in 2006 – and runners-up Keynsham were only two points behind.

On paper, there doesn't appear to be anything particularly memorable about a 1-1 draw at Bitton on January 20, midway through the 2000/01 season. However it's one game I'll never forget, thanks in no small part due to the referee Guy Beale. It's a name that will probably be familiar to most football fans, as he went on to be a regular linesman – sorry, assistant referee – in the Premier League. On this cold winter's day at Bitton, Beale sent off three of my players in the opening 30 minutes as all hell threatened to break loose.

We were 1-0 up at half-time, and during the break I went over to the referee's changing room to ask him what he had sent the third player off for. He told me it was for swearing. I accepted it, but asked him where we stood for the second half in terms of rules. "What do you mean?" Beale asked. "Well, I do believe that if we go down to seven men, you'll have to call the game off," I said. "Yes, that's correct," he replied, with a look of concern. "But you're not going to take that path, are you?" I could see he was worried. "I'm going to go and talk to my players now, and I'll see what they have got to say about it," I told him. I then went into the changing room, and gave the players the choice. They didn't even give me the chance to finish my sentence, and I was given an emphatic no. The players completely rubbished the idea, and told me they were going to go out to try and win the game with eight men. I was proud of their attitude.

We started talking about how we should approach the second half in terms of a system, so I told them we would play a 4-3-0 formation. Without any thought or hesitation, a baffled Karl Baggaley looked at me. "Who's going to play up front?" he asked. I looked at him, gobsmacked, and all the other players were in hysterics. "What are you laughing at?" he asked. After explaining the finer mathematical points of playing with eight men to Karl, we came up with a strategy. When we got the ball, we would keep it as long as we possibly could. Of the three midfielders, only Karl Madge had permission to run the wings so, when the opportunities arose, the players were instructed to send the ball down the flank for Madge.

Out on the pitch, the Bitton management didn't have a clue how to break us down. They scored with a heavy deflection about six or seven minutes from the end, and we were denied what really would have been an against-all-odds win. I couldn't help myself at the end of the game and, as I walked past the Bitton dugout, I shouted over to Richard Fey. "No wonder they're tapping you up Richard," I yelled, making sure the dugout could hear. "But why on earth would you want to go and play for a management team who haven't got the brains to break down eight men?"

As the season wore on, we became hungrier and hungrier on our journeys back to Bristol. Not for wins, but for food. I lost count of the fish and chip shops we weren't allowed to go back to. I'll give you one chance to name the cause of the problem. You guessed it … Richard Fey. It didn't matter what chippie we stopped off at, Feyer would always head straight for the salt and vinegar and undo the lids. He just couldn't help himself. He'd then sit there, waiting for the next unsuspecting customer to come along. Time and time again, we had to try and keep a straight face as some poor guy ranted and raved about the fact that his supper had just been ruined by a pint of vinegar and a pot full of salt! After a while the owners would cotton on that it was us causing the mischief. I guess we weren't the most inconspicuous customers … a car or minibus load of footballers. "Not you again," we would hear as we all piled in. "Sorry, you're barred." It ended with us having to wait until we got home to have our supper. But, much like the trips down to Torrington, Feyer always ensured that the journeys home were one hell of a laugh.

Even those journeys, though, paled in comparison to Torrington's infamous end-of-season tours. Our first was to the Isle of Wight at the end of my second season in charge and it was the chance for all the players to have a laugh and a joke together. Thinking he needed it to get into the Isle of Wight, Karl Baggaley was the only one who brought his passport with him! He also called me up when they were on the ferry, because I had to do a last-minute delivery and missed the boat. "We're at sea Jeff," he shouted down the phone. I think Baggaley thought he was on a cruise, rather than a little shunt across the English Channel from Portsmouth to the Isle of Wight!

Poor old Albert Williams ran out of money, and ended up having to eat a box of chocolates that had been bought for Penny Avery back at the club because he was so hungry. At our hotel, some of the players thought it was a good idea to jump out of a window onto a flat roof below. They were able to run along the roof to Albert's window, which he'd foolishly left open, snuck in and nicked all his clothes! They were duly returned to him on the ferry back to Portsmouth.

We had a young lad with us called Danny Bell, who never got involved with any of the drinking or nightclub escapades. He just had this little football, and it went everywhere with him. He was kicking it about all over the place and doing keepie uppies with it from the

Friday right through to our Sunday ferry home. It was then that Matthew Chugg decided he'd had enough, snatching the ball from Danny and giving the bloody thing an almighty punt into the English Channel. The ball was seen last floating down the Solent, and Danny Bell was nearly crying in his soup!

The following year, we'd arranged a trip to Dublin for our end-of-season celebrations. It was a three-hour crossing on the boat, and beer was £1 a pint, so you can imagine how well it was going down. I remember one of our single committee members, Dave Bright, thought he'd been chatted up a young lady at the ferry bar. He came back to the table looking very pleased with himself. "I think I've pulled," he laughed, before admitting that he didn't really know what to say to her next. "Don't you worry at all David," I said. "You just come with me." We marched over to this woman near the bar, and I asked her outright: "How much do you charge, love?" Dave almost collapsed, he couldn't believe what I'd just asked her. The lady in question wasn't offended, though, and she even gave me an answer including the cost of a cabin! Dave hadn't realised that she was one of the boat's prostitutes! Needless to say, that earned him a fair bit of teasing during the course of the weekend.

Dublin was a fantastic city. There was plenty of drinking, and some great laughs. However the main thing I remember from the trip was when we left Dublin on the coach back to catch the ferry at Rosslare. We took every wrong turning possible, and I lost count of the number of roads where we got lost. At one point we ended up in the forecourt of a mansion house, trying to do a three-point turn with the mansion's owner going absolutely potty and telling us to get the coach off his property. When we finally pulled into the car park at Rosslare, we had arrived just in time to see the ferry sailing over the horizon. It cost the coach company a lot of money, because it meant they had to put us up in a hotel overnight – there wasn't another boat back to England until Monday morning.

The lads just saw it as a bonus night to tag on to the end of their tour and, when we booked in to the hotel, all I could hear was a bunch of lads shouting and bawling while I was trying to phone the missus and explain why I wasn't going to be at home! She found the explanation very hard to believe with all the laughter and nonsense going on in the background, but it honestly was the truth Jo! As a result of us getting lost, the main thing I remember about that Dublin holiday was what a prick that driver was.

We knew we wanted to go back to Dublin for our third end-of-season trip, but this time we made sure to avoid the problems of the previous year and travelled by air from Bristol. There were Bacardi and cokes all round for breakfast on the flight over, and it steadily went downhill from there … largely because our tour organiser was none other than Richard Fey. On arrival at Dublin, our first stop was Temple Bar which is the city's liveliest area. Feyer led the way with a whistle in hand and, every time he blew it, a new challenge was set. One such challenge ordered every player to bring a woman's bra back to him. To be fair to the lads, nobody failed! The most memorable sight for me was Feyer trying to return the bras to their rightful owners after the challenge. He was walking around the bar with his arm outstretched, with all these bras hanging off. Feyer encountered some difficulties with bras that looked the same and, the gentleman that he was, he offered to measure up the ladies in question. Needless to say, they didn't take him up on that particular gesture!

Dave Newsome was driving everybody insane with the My Garden Shed chant that he would sing what seemed like every other minute. In the end we were so sick and tired of Dave's bloody singing that Barry Yeo and Feyer picked him up and bundled him into one of Dublin's giant commercial dustbins. Dave was only a small lad, so it didn't take much work! Down went the lid, and off we went in fits of laughter. Dave did turn up a little bit later, but we had to explain to him that he smelt a little bit.

At night, myself, Winston and a couple of other committee members would go out for a meal and a couple of drinks, before returning to the little pub that was just around the corner from our hotel. As we were walking down the road after our first night's meal, Winston stopped me and pointed across the road. "Is that one of our players Jeff?" I looked over to see a horse and cart, and one of the lads sat in the back with a woman on his arm, being taken down the cobbled street as if he was William the Conqueror. Little did she know that his usual mode of transport was a bicycle around North Devon!

The next night, we were walking back to the hotel to get changed ahead of the evening's festivities. We walked past a place where a big crowd had gathered, and I recognised the loud music blaring out as a

Stevie Wonder song. "That bloke in there hasn't got a bad voice," I said to Winston. We thought we'd stick our heads in and have a look, and to my utter amazement, it was none other than my player and assistant manager Paul Hutchings! Hutch was up there on stage, singing his heart out, and he wasn't half bad! Later on that evening, he explained that he was running a little short of beer money to see him through the rest of the tour but, after a dazzling performance on stage, he had more than enough cash to see him through!

As good as Dublin was, we decided on a change of location for the 2001/02 end-of-season tour, and decided to go to Jersey. The original plan to go over there by boat changed at late notice, and we had to fly over there from London City Airport. We were flying late at night but our coach still got caught in traffic heading in to the capital. A few of the lads couldn't understand why the roads were so busy. I had to explain to them that people in Torrington may all be asleep at midnight, but up here in London, they were just getting ready to go out. Anyway, I wasn't particularly happy about having to fly from London City Airport. To me, it didn't seem to be much more than a slab of concrete down the middle of the airport. I was quietly worried about the flight home ... I knew that we either had to land on this little bit of Tarmac, or in the River Thames. I didn't fancy it at all.

The beer was great, and no doubt after several pints my nerves concerning the flight home had eased sufficiently. However one grumble I do have about Jersey was the bouncers at the bars – they were just too fussy. I found myself being chucked out of one of the sports clubs there, and felt very hard done-by.

Back at Vicarage Field, I had managed to get a few more local lads on board for that 2001/02 season, including Paul Leach, Danny Robinson, Jon Vooght and Neil Bettiss, to mix in with the experienced players I already had there. Peter Trego also returned when his cricketing commitments allowed, and that season he proved he was just as capable outfield as he was with the goalkeeping gloves on. Looking back, I firmly believe that this was the season when Torrington truly arrived, and that we under-achieved to 'only' finish in fourth position. We were banging in goals left, right and centre, starting as we meant to go on with an opening-day 4-1 win over Cadbury Heath with efforts from Damien Bromley, Lee Langmead, Dave Newsome and Vooght.

When we scored goals, you could guarantee Langmead wasn't far from the action. He was as lethal in the air as he was with the ball on the floor, and I remember him scoring a wonderful hat-trick when we beat Division One's new boys Willand Rovers 6-0 at Vicarage Field in September. Barry Yeo, Leach and Trego also scored that day. Those four scorers also netted a goal apiece when we won 4-1 at Minehead a few days later. Our downfall was ultimately a few silly defeats in games we never should have lost. We ended up losing ten that season, while Frome Town, Bath City Reserves and Exmouth Town – the three teams above us – lost just four, two and four matches respectively. It meant we were eight points shy of the second promotion spot that season, despite a flying end to the season that saw us take five wins and a draw in our last seven games. On the penultimate weekend of the season, we had two away matches on successive days and scored 11 goals. We won 6-1 at Weston St Johns on the Saturday, and 5-1 at Warminster Town on the Sunday, but by then it was too late to trouble champions Frome and runners-up Bath City.

With those two sides winning promotion to the Premier Division, I was adamant that Division One would not be as strong for the 2002/03 season. The two relegated sides were Westbury United and Bristol Manor Farm, and I didn't think either side would be as tough as the previous season's top two. With that in mind, I didn't really want to make many changes to the squad. It just needed the slightest bit of tweaking and spicing up, and that came in the form of midfielder Darren Polhill from Bideford and the very experienced striker Andy Stevens from Taunton Town.

We made a tremendous start, winning seven out of our first eight in the league, and ten out of our first 12 if you include our FA Cup and FA Vase wins. We started with a 5-1 demolition of Minehead, with goals from Langmead (2), Stevens, Karl Madge and a Barry Yeo penalty, and it continued from there. Wins against Chard Town (4-3), Corsham Town (2-1), Willand Rovers (5-3 and 1-0), and Weston St Johns (2-1) saw us top of the table with a maximum 18 points by the end of September.

The Chard game really was a memorable one. It was our first league away game of the season, on August 24, and anyone who's been to Chard's ground will know exactly why they are always 'games of two halves' there. The sloping pitch has to be seen to be believed.

You could probably let go of a football in one goalmouth, and watch it roll unaided all the way down into the net at the other end. I seem to remember someone telling me once that the bottom goalmouth was about nine feet lower than the top one. I don't know if that's accurate, but I wouldn't bet against it.

On this occasion, we played down the slope in the first half and went back into the changing rooms with a 4-0 lead at half-time. Straight away I reminded the players that this game was far from over. We had to defend the slope, and I told them to do that by putting the ball over and beyond their full-backs. With our two fast wingers in Karl Madge and Danny Robinson, I could easily see us nicking another goal or two in the process. Chard changed their tactics too, though, and with ten minutes to go they had pulled it back to 4-3. It was around that time that the referee ran over to our dugout to speak to me. "Where's your goalie?" he asked. "Ref, he's gone to get the ball in the hedge behind the goal," I said. The referee quickly sent on another ball, but then ran down to our penalty area to have an argument with Richard Fey when he appeared from out of the bushes. He gave Richard a rollicking for leaving the field. "I'm only trying to help out, ref," said Feyer in reply.

By this time, the increasingly impatient Chard management team had also booted another ball onto the pitch. We now had two balls on there, so Feyer nipped over and gathered up both of them. "Which one would you like me to use, ref?" he asked, trying to waste even more time. "Just pick one and get on with it," ordered the referee. Feyer took the first ball and walloped it back to the Chard dugout. Unfortunately, he over-hit it and the ball bounced over the fence and out into the road. The members of the home dugout were seething with rage by now but, for us, they were all valuable seconds being wasted. After that, Feyer made sure the ball was kicked out of the ground every time he got his hands on it. In the end, he was booked for it. But amazingly, the referee still blew his full-time whistle bang on 90 minutes. He didn't even add one minute of stoppage time! The Chard bench were beside themselves, but fair play to Richard Fey. His goalkeeping skills had won us many points in the past but, on this occasion, it was his antics and resourcefulness that got them for us!

We weren't just flying high in the league – we were also through to the second round proper of the FA Vase. But I felt something just wasn't right. There was something missing inside me. I'd had an extremely hard challenge over the last five years, one that even seemed impossible at times. But here we were, flying high at the top of the division, with a fantastic team. It was almost as if the challenge had gone, because I was watching football that was easy. We were winning games easily. Maybe I was a glutton for punishment, but I just couldn't ignore the vacancy up the road at Barnstaple Town. They were in a right mess, rock bottom of the Premier Division with just one point on the board. They'd got rid of manager John Hore after just one game, although his dismissal was largely down to a disastrous pre-season that included a humiliating 14-1 thrashing at the hands of their biggest rivals Bideford. They had very few senior players there and were having to pull in players from their reserve team every Saturday, and it almost looked like they were sinking without trace. Now that's what I call a challenge ...

I got in touch with Barnstaple Town and went for an interview with Noel White, who was the chairman there at that time. Soon after, the job offer came and I just couldn't turn it down. Not only was it the challenge I was hungry for, but Barnstaple Town were also a very big club. The ground and facilities were good, and I firmly believed that, if I could turn things around, there would be the perfect foundations for a push towards Southern League football there. I said yes to Barnstaple, but before I could take the reins there, I had to do the hardest thing I've ever had to do in my football career.

Torrington were playing Shepton Mallet away on Saturday, October 12, and I had to tell my chairman Winston Martin that I was resigning. He was speechless, and said he couldn't understand why I would want to leave. Winston had told me before that he'd never ever sack me, and he reiterated that before we left for Shepton Mallet. "I've supported you through thick and thin, and I always will do," he added. I knew he meant it too, but I just pleaded with him to understand why I wanted to accept this new challenge with Barnstaple Town. I explained that I'd given Torrington more than five years of my life, and that I'd enjoyed it thoroughly. There were bits I hadn't been so fond of, particularly some abuse to Lee Gitson from one of the 'fans' in the crowd the previous season. Just because the lad was having a bad game, it was no excuse to shout: "Gitson, just break your leg and piss off back to Bristol." Lee was upset by it too, and he did in fact leave the club not long after that. I told Winston I'd got over that, but I desperately needed this new challenge. Winston did understand, and we parted company on good terms. I remain very friendly with Winston to this day, and we get on just as well now as we did back then.

It proved to be a winning send-off at Shepton Mallet. We won 4-2 with goals from Lee Langmead, Danny Robinson, Andy Stevens and Barry Yeo. After the game, I had to tell the lads in the changing room about my decision to take the Barnstaple Town job. A lot of them couldn't believe it, and they said I was absolutely crazy to leave a side who had just won seven out of eight league games – for a side who couldn't buy a win. I sat down with them and told them the same thing that I'd explained to Winston earlier in the day.

Paul Hutchings took over the side and, sure enough, they went on to win the Division One title that season, which I can assure you made me very proud. It was also a great honour to manage a side that, at one point, had no fewer than five internationals among the ranks. Karl Baggaley and Paul Terry had been England youth internationals while at Stoke City and Bristol City respectively, while Hutchings had played for England Schoolboys and Karl Madge had been a non-league international. You're probably wondering who the fifth player is. Don't forget Peter Trego … he played cricket for England U19s!

While I was chatting with a very sombre group of lads, an hour or two up the road in Wiltshire, a chap by the name of Lee Barrow was talking to an equally dejected group. Lee was the caretaker manager in charge of a Barnstaple Town side in disarray, and they'd just lost 3-1 at Melksham Town. It was their fifth loss in six Premier Division games – their only point was from a scrappy 0-0 draw at Keynsham Town – and they had plummeted out of all cup competitions at the first stage. This Barnstaple team needed serious and urgent attention, and it was the challenge I'd been yearning for.

Samba football at Torrington! Karl Baggaley and I welcomed a Brazilian youth side to Vicarage Field for a friendly. It was quite a sight, seeing Brazil's top young footballers heading into Torrie for fish and chips!

11... The big challenge I'd been looking for

THE drive down to North Devon for my first game in charge of Barnstaple Town provided a sharp reminder of how different things were going to be from now on. It was October 19, 2002, and I was motoring down the M5 ready to take control of a home game against an Odd Down side who just so happened to now be managed by my old assistant Mike Ford and another good friend, Chris Mountford. As I was driving, I kept thinking about the banter and the atmosphere on the Odd Down team bus. I knew there would be joking, laughter and all sorts of things going on, but there was none of that for me on this particular morning. There was no Richard Fey and the Bristol boys with me, as there had been for all the other Saturday journeys down to Devon for Torrington duty. The only laughter I heard, and the only company I had, was from the radio, because I had nobody else to speak to.

I travel to North Devon at least once or twice a week for work, along with hundreds of Torrington matches over the past five years, but the drive to Barnstaple's Mill Road ground on that morning felt like one of the longest journeys I've ever experienced. When I finally got there, I was greeted by Lee Barrow, who had been put in caretaker charge of the club while they were looking for a manager to replace John Hore. Lee was a good coach – he ran the Plymouth Argyle Youth Development centre at Chivenor, and his true forte was coaching kids. He's had a number of success stories to come out of that Chivenor centre, including the midfielder Joe Broad who won two Championship medals with Plymouth Argyle. As good a coach as Lee was, he wasn't a Western League manager and the club was struggling. They were rooted to the bottom of the Premier Division table, with just a point to their name after they scrapped to a 0-0 draw at Keynsham Town in mid-September. However I knew Lee's coaching ability was second to none, so I had no qualms about keeping him on as part of my management set-up at Mill Road.

I told Lee to name the team to take on Odd Down that day, and I also asked him to take the team talk. I just wanted to take a step back, take some notes, assess the team and generally see how the afternoon went. If at any point I wanted to make a point or say something, then I was fully prepared to, but the main purpose for me that day was to observe and assess. I sat down in the changing room and watched as the players trickled in, one by one. They all looked at me with a little bit of apprehension, and sat themselves down on the benches. Straight away I could tell there was no team spirit or atmosphere within this team. Most of the players had just sat down quietly with their heads down, staring at the floor. They didn't even talk to each other as mates, so it was no surprise that they weren't able to play as a team. But this was the reason why the club had employed me. My job was not to just build a team, but also a team spirit.

I was asked to keep a close eye on two players in particular, Karl Curtis and Darren Edwards, who were both making their Barnstaple debuts. Lee had a very good relationship with Argyle's youth development officer John James, and he'd brought these two lads up from Plymouth to try and bolster the side a little bit. They both started the game, and I took up a position just behind the bench to oversee proceedings, with Lee controlling things from the dugout. It didn't take long before I was itching to get involved. It got to half-time and we were 1-0 down, so I decided to voice my opinion on a few things that I thought were going wrong out on the pitch. It got a little better in the second half, but we could only score the one goal from several goalmouth scrambles and we lost the game 3-1.

In the changing room immediately after the game, Barnstaple Town quickly found out about Jeff Evans. A few players had already stepped into the shower, so I ordered Lee to get them out and sit them down. I looked around the changing room at the team – some of them were dripping wet with towels around their waists, while others were still in kit – and I told them a few home truths. I told them in no uncertain terms that there would be new rules in place, and that nobody was to go for a shower until I had finished talking to them after a game. If anyone objected to what I was saying, then I let them know they were welcome to get in the shower, but they wouldn't be welcome in my team any more. To be fair to the lads, nobody moved. I wasn't finished though. They were told that they had no passion, and that they had got used to losing. "Don't make a habit of that," I said to them. "I don't accept losing." The players were then all told to report back to Mill Road on the Tuesday evening, as we had a Devon St Luke's Bowl game against a young Plymouth Argyle side, which we also lost.

In the clubhouse after that Odd Down defeat, a lot of the supporters were very worried about the situation at the club, and I understood their fears. The Christmas period wasn't far off, and we had just one point on the board. Again, I had to explain that Rome wasn't built in a day, but that I would be working my hardest to try and build it by the end of the season and keep Barnstaple Town in the Premier Division. On the evidence of what I'd just seen on the pitch, though, I knew it was going to be one massive task.

I made a point of speaking to every player individually, and assured one or two of them that things would be changing. I also felt I needed to apologise to a few of them for the situation and football that they had been brought in to, particularly the two lads from Plymouth I'd been introduced to, Edwards and Curtis. Putting it bluntly, I felt embarrassed putting them into that team with some of the players they had to play with on that first Saturday. I didn't mean that disrespectfully to some of the lads who were there – they had been chucked into first-team action from the youth and reserve teams, and they were simply out of their depth in the Western League.

Ten days after taking over, I got my first point as Barnstaple Town manager when Edwards and Keith Shapland got a goal each to snatch a 2-2 draw against a very poor Elmore side, but I wasn't getting carried away. I knew I was going to have to make a lot of signings in a short space of time. Shapland was a hard-working midfielder, and was one of the early players to come in from local football and show he could cut it at Western League level. There were also a few other players there who gave me a decent base to work with. The two Plymouth lads fitted in well, Curtis in midfield and Edwards at centre-half, and had good pedigree from their Argyle coaching. Simon Ovey was another local lad who was a good midfielder, although he'd been playing out of position at centre-half at the start of the season. We also had a good young goalkeeper in Jon Vaughan, who had recently been released as a pro at Peterborough United. He was a local lad too, another one who had come through Lee Barrow's youth coaching set-up, and at 6ft 7in he was a giant between the sticks.

The new faces soon started rolling in. I signed a young lad from Dawlish Town called Tom Barwell, who played out wide for us, and full-back Ashley Cole came in from Elmore. I also brought in a couple of local players, midfielder Richard Bray and striker Tom Marsh. As Christmas approached, we managed to bring in two young lads on loan from Plymouth Argyle. Jake Barwick and Rob Guppy were both North Devon lads who had been snapped up by Argyle, and had also been coached by Lee in their younger years.

Christmas came and went, and we were still waiting for our first win of the season. We had just the two points from those two draws earlier in the season, and we were in real danger of being left behind at the foot of the table. The sides immediately above us – Welton Rovers, Devizes Town and Elmore – had all won games, and a worrying gap was opening up. I think we were about six or seven points adrift at the bottom when the scheduled Boxing Day derby with Bideford was called off due to a frozen pitch.

In the New Year, though, things suddenly began to click into place and we got our first win of the season at Mill Road on January 4 when two of our new signings, Cole and Guppy, scored to beat Frome Town 2-1. It kick-started a run of three wins in five games, which was as much as we could have hoped for considering that the two losses were both against Team Bath. Much like in Division One the previous year, the university side were battering their way through the Premier and had even reached the first round of the FA Cup earlier in the season, losing to Mansfield Town in front of the live Sky Sports cameras. We lost 3-0 against them in both games. Considering that they went on to win the league by eleven points, scoring 109 goals and posting a goal difference of +81, the fact that they could only put six past us showed signs that we were moving in the right direction.

Keith Shapland scored the only goal of the game at Twerton Park to see us beat Bath City Reserves 1-0, while Richard Bray, Ashley Cole and Tom Marsh were all on target in a 3-0 win that saw us do the double over Frome Town on February 1. We took our new-found form and confidence on the road with us in February, aided by what were probably my two most important signings of the season from local rivals Ilfracombe Town. Striker Kevin Squire was a natural goal-scorer and had already established himself as a fans' favourite at Mill Road the previous season. He had gone to Ilfracombe in the summer, but I managed to persuade him to step back up to the Premier Division and rejoin us. A while later, I pulled off a coup by signing Combe's highly-rated centre-half Lee-Roy Cochrane, who was an outstanding centre-half and clearly had the potential to play at a higher level.

Squire scored twice in our 3-3 draw at Odd Down, and that was followed three days later by my first taste of a North Devon derby against Bideford. These games were always the highlight of the Barnstaple Town calendar for many fans, and they always drew massive gates – this one was no different, despite being played on a freezing cold February night after the original Boxing Day encounter had been frozen off. We were very much the underdogs. We were still bottom of the league, while Bideford were the reigning Western League champions and only Team Bath's charge was going to deny them back-to-back titles.

Bideford's previous visit to Mill Road – for a charity pre-season game back in July – had seen them humiliate Town 14-1, but there was to be no humiliation this time around. We were 2-0 down with about 15 minutes to go, but my hastily-built side dug in and Tom Marsh pulled one back before Squire netted a dramatic late equaliser. The atmosphere was electric. There was a crowd of around 750 in that night, and it was fantastic to see the scenes of celebration in the main stand at Mill Road when that goal went in. I was even more pleased with the reaction of my players. I remember seeing Keith Shapland going ballistic celebrating that equaliser in front of the stand, and again at the final whistle. There was pride in the result, and they were proud to be playing for Barnstaple Town. It was exactly the sort of spirit I had wanted to create.

Beating relegation had seemed almost impossible a couple of months earlier, but here we were in March and it was looking like we might just do it. I made a couple of extra signings for the final push, starting with defender Nick Bowrah from Willand Rovers. A while later, Russell Jee also joined from Willand to give us another attacking option down the left wing, and we managed to put together an eight-match unbeaten run. Kevin Squire led the way with a load of goals, including two in a 3-0 win down at Dawlish Town. At the end of March, we faced probably our two biggest games of the season – back-to-back six-pointers against our relegation rivals Welton Rovers and Devizes Town. We were still bottom of the table at this point, but I knew the importance of winning these two games. I asked for six points, and that's what I got. Squire hit a hat-trick in our 3-1 win at Welton, and he added two more alongside strikes from Tom Marsh and another local lad, midfielder Ross Middleton, when we thrashed Devizes 4-0 at Mill Road a week later.

It was an amazing turnaround. From the opening day of the season on August 17, through to January 3, Barnstaple Town had gained just two points. But from January 4 through to our final game on April 27, we gained 30 points. The push was enough to take us out of the bottom two, and we actually finished the season fourth from bottom. Even if I do say so myself, Barnstaple Town had got their money's worth from appointing me that season. Relegation had looked a certainty, but through a lot of hard work we had hauled ourselves to safety.

Ironically, during the summer we learned that there would be no relegation that season. My old side Torrington, now managed by Paul Hutchings, had stormed to the Division One title, and won promotion along with runners-up Exmouth Town. But with Premier Division champions Team Bath taking promotion to the Southern League, and Bath City deciding to withdraw their reserve team from the Western League, it was ruled that Devizes and Elmore – they finished in those bottom two places – would be spared relegation. It didn't take away anything from our achievement, though. We had pulled away from the drop zone on merit, and the Barnstaple Town clubhouse was a much happier place to be now than it was when I first walked into it back in October.

The pre-season build-up to the 2003/04 season was just as busy in terms of player ins and outs, and I made several summer signings. Getting striker Ryan Trudgian in was a particularly exciting capture. He had been on the fringes of the Plymouth Argyle first team over the previous year or two, and had made one substitute appearance in a 0-0 draw against Rochdale in Paul Sturrock's first season as manager. Pairing Trudgian up front with Kevin Squire would give me a strikeforce as strong as any in the Western League, and I felt very confident of making real progress. We also signed Jake Barwick and Rob Guppy on a permanent basis after they were released by Argyle. I felt it was important to draft in players with Western League experience too, bringing in centre-half Simon Hill, right-back Mark Thomas and Steve Rowland from Elmore, and Luke Vinnicombe from Tiverton Town in the Southern League. Young midfielders Ross Middleton and Craig Holman also committed themselves to Barnstaple, and all of a sudden I felt we had a very useful side capable of competing with the Premier Division's top sides.

Behind the scenes, the club's president John Brend was fantastic with his backing for the club. John's Brend Hotels group were the main club sponsors, and they offered the lads free use of the hotel on a Saturday night. Barnstaple was out on a limb, geographically speaking, and I was aware that it may be tough to build a feeling of togetherness in the squad with the lads coming from all corners of Devon to play for us. John's offer of accommodation was invaluable, because it brought all the lads together and enabled us to go out as a team and have a few beers in Barnstaple. As a result, the team spirit within the camp blossomed. John also provided me with a free room so I could stay down in Barnstaple on a Tuesday and a Thursday after training and midweek matches. Not only did that gesture help to ease the burden of travelling from Bristol all the time, but it also helped me get on with my business work in North Devon too.

We started the season fantastically well, and won our first four league games without conceding a goal. Ryan Trudgian and Kevin Squire quickly formed a lethal partnership up front, and we scored nine goals in those first four games. We also put in a couple of good performances in the early rounds of the FA Vase, beating Ilfracombe Town 2-1 to set up an away tie at South Western League side Newquay. The lads had all arranged a night out in Newquay after the game, but I decided to head down there on the Friday evening with Lee Barrow, Barnstaple's club secretary Dave Cooke and our physio Dave Griffiths. We decided to stick our heads in Newquay's clubhouse on the Friday night, where the barman was all too keen to tell me about their game the next day.

"This Barnstaple Town side are a professional outfit," he told me, completely oblivious to who he was talking to. "It's going to be a massive game for us, and it should bring in a big crowd." In the end, he asked if I was staying down for the weekend and offered me complimentary tickets to watch the game! I politely accepted without letting on, and the chap's face was a picture when I returned to the club the next day at around 1pm. "Blimey you're here early," he said. "Not really," I replied. "The manager of the away team usually gets here around this time!" Realising his error, he had a good laugh about it.

He may have been expecting 'a professional outfit', but I'm sure he would have been impressed with the second goal in our 2-0 win there. Trudgian had already put us 1-0 up, and we then put together a passing move that probably involved every player on the pitch. Luke Vinnicombe finished it off by lobbing the goalkeeper from 25 yards, and the lads' celebrations were a joy to watch. The only shame is that it wasn't scored at Mill Road, so all our fans could have seen it. It was as good a team goal as I've ever seen from one of my sides, and they all thoroughly deserved their night out in the pubs and clubs of Newquay that evening.

Back in the league, our winning run was halted by my old side Torrington in a Wednesday night derby at Mill Road that attracted a crowd of more than 500. It was being billed in the local newspaper as Master versus Pupil, because my former player and assistant Paul Hutchings was managing the Torrie side. On that evening, Hutch very nearly got one up on me because Torrington were leading 2-1 going into the last minute, only for Simon Ovey to head home a last-gasp equaliser for us. It preserved our unbeaten record, but only for a few days – we went down 2-0 at Backwell United the next Saturday.

I really do feel the team under-achieved that season. We had a strong side, but we just weren't able to put a really dominant winning run together. There were some great performances in there – I can remember Squire (3) and Trudgian (2) dismantling Keynsham Town 5-1 at Mill Road – but some disappointments too. We should have taken more than just the one point against a newly-promoted Torrington side. We were particularly poor when we lost 3-0 at Vicarage Field in early January. On a positive note, we took four points off Bideford which meant that season's league champions were unable to beat us.

Our win came on Boxing Day at Bideford's Sports Ground, and it was especially sweet as they'd beaten us convincingly 4-0 there on Good Friday at the end of the previous season. I managed to play a trump card on the morning of the game by including an extremely talented player by the name of Marcus Gross in my starting line-up. Marcus was a big lad and had recently been released by Exeter City. He'd won a scholarship to go and play college soccer in the USA, but was back visiting his family in North Devon for Christmas while the American season had its winter break. Being a Barnstaple lad, Marcus particularly enjoyed putting us 1-0 up against the old enemy from the penalty spot. In celebration, he ran the length of the pitch swinging his shirt over his head like a cowboy with a lasso. I don't think it went down too well with the 700 or so Bideford fans!

Anyway, Bideford came back at us and equalised, although they did have former Barnstaple Town player Alan Chapman sent off for a nasty-looking lunge on Lee-Roy Cochrane. That only served to fire us up and, although it looked like things were heading for a draw, Kevin Squire popped up with an 87th minute winner. Just like he'd done at Mill Road back in February of the previous season, Squire had silenced Bideford. Only this time, he'd earned us three points as well. It was a very satisfying result for everybody connected with Barnstaple Town.

The return encounter at Mill Road on Good Friday was even more incident-packed and, even though it ended all square in a 1-1 draw, Bideford were seething with our goal. Their manager Sean Joyce and his dugout were absolutely livid with the officials, the club's committee members were going potty and the mass of Robins supporters behind our dugout were baying for blood. Why? Because we played to the whistle and they didn't!

Bideford's defence were pushing forward as they launched an attack, but we managed to grab possession in our own half and ping a ball back across the halfway line. It was Craig Holman and Ashley Cole who ran on to it, by which time the entire Bideford back line were stood still with their arms in the air, appealing to the linesman. I don't think there was even an issue about Holman and Cole being offside, because they'd chased the loose ball from inside our half. I think the Bideford players were looking at Kevin Squire, who was jogging back into an onside position over the far end of the pitch when the move started.

Bideford's centre-halves Darren Hawkings and Matt Hare were howling at the linesman for a flag, but it never came. The referee that day was Andy Bennett from Hatherleigh in Devon, who is now a top official in the Championship and Football League. With no flag, Bennett was frantically waving play on but Bideford ignored this and carried on protesting. Even the goalkeeper Ryan Draper had stopped. Holman could hardly believe his luck. He actually stopped, stood next to Draper and looked around to see what the fuss was all about, before rolling the ball into the net. I don't think he knew if it was a goal or not, and nobody knew whether to celebrate. Every one of the 800-strong crowd were baffled, and all eyes were locked on the referee. He gave the goal, rightly so in my opinion, and the fireworks began!

Even before that decision, there was a highly-charged atmosphere inside Mill Road. Lots of supporters had travelled over from Bideford and had toured the town's pubs prior to kick-off and, half-an-hour or so into the game, it was all threatening to boil over. I think it took a good few minutes before play resumed as Bideford's players surrounded the referee and fans hurled abuse from the touchline. For a moment it took me back to the atmosphere in that cup tie at Fisher Athletic, although at least this time we didn't have to get locked in our dressing rooms for our own safety! That said, though, there were some pretty fiery scenes outside the changing rooms at the end of the game as the Bideford players and officials continued their protests with the referee. Several fans climbed over the fence too, in a bid to try and confront the officials. In the next edition of the *North Devon Journal*, Bideford's chairman Paul Mitchell said his club were writing a letter of protest to the FA and described it as 'the most unfair and disgraceful decision I have witnessed in 40 years' connection with the game'.

Tough luck! That was my initial response. We'd played to the whistle, taken the goal and earned ourselves a home draw. Everyone at Barnstaple Town enjoyed the result, and we were all happy. The same couldn't be said for the so-called 'fans' from Bideford who thought it was a good idea to vandalise my van outside the ground after the game. When I left the clubhouse, I arrived at my van to find a load of graffiti scrawled all over the bonnet and sides. I won't repeat what they wrote on it, but it was filthy and vile abuse focusing on us being 'cheats' because of that goal. It was very offensive stuff and I had to get it scrubbed off my van as quickly as possible. Clearly there are a few children in Bideford, so let them play with their toys.

After that Bideford game, we only managed to pick up a point from our final four matches when Barwick and Squire scored in a 2-2 draw at Welton Rovers. We ended up with a comfortable mid-table finish of tenth, a point ahead of Torrington. It was a major improvement on the previous season, but I still felt we should have done better. We also missed out on a cup final in the cruelest fashion possible, losing in the semi-final of the Les Phillips Cup to Paulton Rovers on penalties at Mill Road.

Although Paulton didn't win the league that season, they were still promoted to the Southern League as runners-up because champions Bideford chose not to apply. They were a very strong side and we knew we were going to have to work hard. For 120 minutes, we did just that. We battered them, and I'm not exaggerating. Simon Ovey was outstanding in midfield, and we saw chance after chance whistle inches past the post or centimetres over the crossbar. Karl Curtis got a free-kick on target in stoppage time and it looked a certain goal, but Paulton's keeper John Rendall somehow got his fingertips to it. It went down to a penalty shootout and, sadly, we were blown away. Karl Curtis and Jake Barwick both missed, and then Rendall saved from Squire to knock us out 3-0 on spot-kicks. Two hours of tireless work in what was arguably our best performance of the season and, in the space of about two or three minutes, it was all for nothing. The lads were gutted afterwards, and the nature of the defeat knocked the stuffing out of them. But it showed how far we'd come that we were able to push a strong side like Paulton to the limit.

I think one of the main reasons the side struggled to come to terms with defeats like that was because there was a lack of a big character in the changing room who to lift them up. I needed a Derek Jones, an Andy Black or a Richard Fey sat in the dressing room – someone who could come in and raise spirits just with their personality. With that in mind, during the 2004/05 pre-season I signed Alan Chapman, known to many as Chipper, and winger Danny Robinson from Torrington. Chipper was a well-known character in North Devon footballing circles and young Robinson, in his own way, reminded me a little of Andy Black.

The major blow of the summer came with the loss of two quality players in Ryan Trudgian and Lee-Roy Cochrane. Trudgian had been offered a soccer scholarship out in the USA, while Cochrane had to move up north and is still playing football at a decent level to this day for Brigg Town. Although the team spirit was generally quite good, there was still something wrong with the side and I couldn't quite put my finger on it. Later that summer I learned that three more players would not be signing on for us for the 2004/05 season. Simon Hill, Russell Jee and Nick Bowrah all decided to go back to Willand Rovers, and this got to me a little bit. I didn't think I had done anything wrong, and there was no sign of them being upset or disillusioned with things when we'd had the club's end-of-season presentation night.

A while later, I saw them all at a pre-season charity match and I thought I'd ask them the reasons why they decided to leave. They all had the same answer, and told me they were fed up of being spoken to like children. "What?" I said. "I've never treated you like children. I may have acted like a child myself after a few ciders, but I've never spoken to you like one!" They explained that they were just not getting on with Lee Barrow, and weren't enjoying his methods of training and speaking to them.

I thought about their criticisms of Lee as I was driving home and pondered over what I should do. Okay, so a few players had got in a bit of a tizz and left, but there was more to Lee Barrow than his coaching. He worked tirelessly in the community, trying to bring money into the club through sponsorship and fund-raising. All credit to him, he did a great job. He also arranged some cracking nights, including a memorable Elvis night at the Barnstaple Hotel and an evening with Plymouth Argyle manager Paul Sturrock in the clubhouse at Mill Road. Lee had organised all the food and catering, and arranged for Sturrock and his coaching team of Kevin Summerfield, Geoff Crudgington and youth development officer John James to come up for an evening of questions and answers. The clubhouse was packed, and it was a thoroughly enjoyable evening. A good night of drinking ended with us all heading to the Chicago Rock nightclub in Barnstaple, before returning to the hotel and drinking into the early hours of Sunday morning.

I took note of what the Willand lads had said, and reduced the need for Lee to talk to the players in the changing room before and during games. Instead, I'd make sure we would sit down and talk in length about the team after the Thursday night training sessions so I knew exactly what his thoughts were. I also had a problem of filling the gap left by the departing players, so I signed another promising local striker in Mike Symons from Ilfracombe Town. He was brought in to replace Trudgian. A few other Torrington lads came over to join up with me again, including centre-half Jeff Parish, Mike Hedden and striker Andy Stevens. Young right-back Darren Parish also joined us after being released by Plymouth Argyle, and a young 17-year-old midfielder by the name of Aaron Harper-Penman also broke into the first team after impressing me with some excellent performances in pre-season – notably against Barry Town at Mill Road.

The 2004/05 season started disastrously with a 5-0 tanking at Frome Town, but we responded well and won 4-1 at Clyst Rovers on the Tuesday night. Danny Robinson scored his first two goals for the club, while Darren Parish and Mike Symons also opened their Town accounts. Later in August we had a good 4-1 win at Torrington, and we also earned the club a few quid with a good little FA Cup run, beating Tuffley Rovers 3-0, Torrie 3-0 and Bournemouth Poppies 3-1, before losing 5-0 at a very good Eastleigh side. It was clear that there was still a lot of work that needed to be done, though. We hadn't improved on the previous season's foundations, and we saw out the season in 12th place. We'd even suffered a double defeat to Bideford. We were 2-0 up after five minutes at Mill Road on Boxing Day through Darren Parish and Andy Stevens, but lost 5-2, and then went down 2-1 at the Sports Ground on Good Friday.

One positive to come out of the closing weeks of the 2004/05 season was the arrival of Shane Tolley. He was another lad who had graduated through Lee Barrow's coaching set-up and, along with goalkeeper Jon Vaughan, had earned himself a contract with Peterborough United. Tolley was released by the Posh towards the end of the season, and came in to play a couple of games for us at the end of the season. He was only a little lad, but he was quick, he had a great touch and he knew where the goal was. He came back on board for the 2005/06 season, which I knew had the potential to be a very exciting campaign for Barnstaple Town. There were whispers of a new chairman coming in to take over, and we had an excellent pre-season, including a 3-0 win at Welsh Premier League side Haverfordwest.

Being a proud Welshman, Lee had set the game up for us and I can remember him getting all flustered when we arrived at the game late, and with a squad that was short of a few players. "This is a top side Jeff," he kept telling me. "We need to be more professional and treat this warm-up properly, or they'll embarrass us." Walking off the pitch after our dominant win, I told Lee there was nothing to worry about as they were 'only a Welsh League side' with a grin on my face! We actually had a pretty good weekend up there. Lee had arranged with Haverfordwest for the players to stay at the ground, free of charge, so they could all have a night out. The last I saw of them must have been at around 2am when they were heading back to their sleeping bags in the away team changing room! I'm pleased to say that the management didn't have to slum it, and we all stayed in a hotel for the night.

Our 2005/06 Western League programme started with two draws. Our new 'SAS' strikeforce of Squire and Symons both found the net in a 2-2 draw at Backwell United on the opening day, and Squire scored again when we were held 1-1 at home against Devizes Town seven days later. It wasn't exactly the flying start we had hoped for, but it was solid. It actually took us until September 24 to win our first Premier Division game, and I remember the game well because it saw two more of the club's youth team players make their mark at first-team level. Aaron Harper-Penman was by now a regular fixture in the team and, in the 3-1 win against Brislington, both Richard Hevingham and Ricky Marinaro scored their first Barnstaple Town goals.

That game was also the last game before our new chairman was officially announced. Steve James was a well-respected North Devon businessman who had been keen to get involved in the local football scene for a while, and it was quite a coup for the club when he took over on September 27, 2005. Sadly, we couldn't get a win on the pitch that night and lost 2-0 at Torrington. With a new man in charge at the top, I was in no doubt that we were going to have to improve, and fast.

Around the same time, Elmore's long-serving manager Pete Buckingham had stood down from his job at the Tiverton club. I had known Pete for a long time in the Western League, as he'd managed Bideford in the 1990s before taking over down at Elmore. We'd also been appointed as joint managers of the Devon FA's county side, which I'll talk about in more detail the next chapter. I spoke to Pete and expressed my interest at bringing him to Barnstaple Town as my assistant. We had worked well together with Devon over the past few seasons, and I wanted to bring that working relationship to Mill Road as well.

Pete accepted the offer and his first game alongside me in the dugout was a midweek away trip to Exmouth Town. Of course, bringing Pete in meant a change in role for Lee Barrow, who was my current assistant. After finalising the agreement to bring Pete in, I specifically asked the committee not to mention anything to Lee because I wanted him to hear it from me, face to face. My plan was for Pete to be my assistant, and for Lee to be first-team coach while also overseeing the club's youth development. We'd already seen encouraging signs with Harper-Penman, Hevingham and Marinaro coming through, and I felt Lee's Argyle youth experience made him perfect for that type of job. I firmly believed Barnstaple Town could push for the Southern League with the right infrastructure in place, and with an ambitious chairman. After all, Barnstaple is one of the biggest towns in Devon and, when you look at all the other towns within a 30-mile radius, I still believe Mill Road could be packed out each week if they were playing at a higher level of football.

Anyway, my request to the committee not to tell Lee about Pete's appointment was ignored. Unfortunately Lee found out before I could meet with him. As for who told him, I have my suspicions, but it was a furious Lee Barrow who called me up to have it out with me when he found out. I was driving down the A34 to Southampton at the time for work, and my wife was with me in the van, so I took the call on speakerphone. Lee was livid and I had to tell him that my wife was with me and, unless he toned it down, I would end the conversation there and then. I could see the situation from his point of view and understood why he was angry. Perhaps I should have made more of an effort to meet him face to face before he heard it elsewhere. Perhaps I could have discussed my idea with him before speaking to Pete. But 'perhaps' is a big word, and I made the decision purely with the intention of taking Barnstaple Town forward.

That first game together, down at Exmouth Town, ended in a 3-2 win with another goal for Ricky Marinaro, one for Darren Parish and a winner from Steve Blurton, my newest signing. Blurts was soon joined by several other new signings, with Pete using his Mid Devon contacts well. Danny Tapp came in from Willand Rovers and could play either up front or in defence, and we signed defender Steve Avery and midfielders Perry Carpenter and Gavin Meecham from Elmore. The most high-profile signing was winger Shaun Goff, the former Exeter City pro who had been a first-team regular for Tiverton Town in the Southern League's Premier Division before being hit by injury.

We started scoring a lot of goals and, more importantly, we were putting a good run of results together. Shane Tolley was in great form for us, scoring a hat-trick in the 5-2 home win over Radstock Town, backed up by goals from Kevin Squire and Perry Carpenter. Squire (2) and Tapp scored in a 3-0 win over Keynsham Town and, a week later, we walloped Melksham Town 4-1 with goals from Mark Thomas, Blurts, Meecham and Squire. Sadly, though, that good form came crashing to a halt with an absolute disaster on Boxing Day. It was the eagerly-anticipated derby with leaders Bideford, and we were trounced 7-0. It was a horrible day, made worse by a blazing row in the changing room afterwards between myself and goalkeeper Jon Vaughan about what had just happened. There was no coming back from that, and Jon never played for me again at Barnstaple Town.

We could afford to waste no time in finding a replacement for Vaughan, and we signed another Mid Devon player, Steve Johns. The pain of that Bideford drubbing was eased slightly by a 5-1 home win over Torrington on January 2, and we didn't have to wait long for a chance of revenge against Sean Joyce and his Robins. We beat Dawlish Town in an absolute cracker in the quarter-final of the Devon St Luke's Bowl at Mill Road, when two late goals from Jake Barwick turned a 2-1 deficit into a 3-2 win. The reward for that comeback was a semi-final with, you guessed it, Bideford.

We had a point to prove at the Sports Ground after the humiliation there about six weeks earlier, and we won the game 1-0 when Perry Carpenter struck the winner with about ten minutes to go. It was a bitterly cold February night, and our new keeper Steve Johns was fantastic. He'd picked up an injury on the Saturday and could hardly move, let alone kick a ball. But he managed to stop everything Bideford's potent attack of Andy Watkins, Mike Southgate and Ellis Laight could throw at him. Avery, Thomas and Carpenter helped him out too, making three goal-line clearances in less than a minute! It was backs-to-the-wall stuff, admittedly, but we showed tremendous grit and character to beat Bideford that night. It meant we had a cup final to look forward to and, thanks to our connections with the Devon FA, Pete and I were able to arrange the final on our home ground at Mill Road, where we would face Martyn Rogers and his Tiverton Town side.

It was a fantastic day for the club, and a good way to end the season. We'd already finished our league programme, and we were a little disappointed with our final position of 13th. But we could forget about that, and put all our energy into the Devon St Luke's Bowl Final. The game was being played on the Bank Holiday Monday in May, there was a crowd of 1,000 and BBC Radio Devon were broadcasting live commentary of the game. In addition, the Devon FA representatives were out in force, and it all made for a day of bumper takings for the club – not just in gate receipts, but also at the food hut and behind the bar. We knew we were the underdogs, because Tiverton were an established Southern League Premier Division side with some very good players. But with home advantage, I was confident we could cause a shock if we played to our full potential.

Sadly, it wasn't to be, and we were beaten 2-1 after extra-time. To be fair, we really couldn't have got off to a worse start, and we were a goal down inside 30 seconds. Tiverton's striker Jamie Mudge and Steve Johns were both distracted by an offside flag as Mudge raced clean through. Both players stopped, but the referee said the ball had come off a Barnstaple player and waved play on. A hesitant Mudge tapped it away, and it was 1-0 to Tiverton. It didn't take us long to equalise, and Shaun Goff got one over on his old club when he nodded home a Carpenter cross, with a little help from a Steve Blurton flick. Steve Johns had a great game in goal again, and made two phenomenal saves to deny Mudge and Chris Holloway, but he could do nothing about substitute Tom Beddow's winner in the 108th minute. We tried our hardest to pull back an equaliser and force a shootout, but it just wasn't to be.

As we were preparing for the 2006/07 season, I started to sense that something wasn't right. I wasn't thinking about the team this time either. At the end of the previous campaign I had got the impression that something was amiss behind the scenes, but I couldn't quite put my finger on it. At first I kept trying to dismiss it as paranoia, but I couldn't help but think there were people on the committee who didn't want me there. I had no facts or evidence to suggest this, it was simply a gut feeling. Little things niggled me. When Pete had first joined as my assistant manager, a report in the *Western Morning News* said that he had taken over as manager of Barnstaple Town. I wasn't sure whether someone from the club had told the paper this, or whether the journalist had simply made a mistake. During the summer we had a pre-season friendly at Elmore where the club had arranged to have their official team picture taken. A photographer turned up from the *Sunday Independent* and he'd been given the name of Barnstaple Town manager Pete Buckingham as the contact for the job. I explained that I was the manager and he apologised, and said he clearly had some duff information.

Other than a 5-0 collapse up at Devizes Town in mid-August – I still don't know how we managed that – we had started excellently in the league. We had two new strikers in Lee Langmead and Steve

Ebdy, who joined Kevin Squire in an exciting three-man attack, and we scored 18 goals in our first seven games that put us in the top four. However we'd just lost a disappointing FA Cup replay, 1-0 at home to Saltash United on a Tuesday evening, and things started to become a bit clearer a few days later at Almondsbury, where we had been drawn to play an FA Vase game. We were trailing 2-1 in the first half up at Almondsbury, and I was sat up in the grandstand because I had a bad back that day. I remember seeing the club's general manager Doug Green running up the touchline shouting to Pete to sort it out at half-time. I told him that I was the manager, and that I'd be sorting it out at half-time. We eventually won the game 3-2.

After the game at Almondsbury, one of the player's dads pulled me to one side and asked me if the rumour he'd heard was true. "What rumour is this?" I asked. He then told me he'd heard that I would have been sacked had we lost the game. It was the first I'd heard of it, but I knew I had signed a contract a couple of years earlier which still had eight months to run. Throughout my managerial career, my son Clive has been my eyes and ears at games, and he also told me he thought something was up at Almondsbury, and that there seemed to be a lot of private conversations taking place outside the clubhouse. I told him that I wasn't overly worried, because I was under contract until May and the club could do what they liked then. I also had a five-day holiday booked to go to Guernsey with my wife, her cousin and her cousin's husband Bob, and we were due to leave the next morning.

When we were in Guernsey, we were just about to sit down and have a spot of lunch when my phone rang. I looked at the screen, and it was the chairman Steve James calling. I answered, and Steve informed me that I was sacked as manager of Barnstaple Town. I got the impression that Steve hadn't had to make this type of phone call before. He was apologetic, his voice was a little shaky, but he informed me that an extraordinary general meeting had been called for the Monday night, where it had been proposed that I was sacked. This proposal was then backed by other members of the committee. I reminded Steve that I still had eight months left to run on my contract, and that I would also expect to receive the £500 I had loaned the club a few months earlier to help pay some expenses. He said he would sort it, and would write to me.

I walked back to the table, and my wife Jo could tell something was up. I told her about the call, and she told me not to worry and that I should be used to leaving clubs by now! Bob said we should enjoy the rest of our holiday, but that he would help me sort out my contract issues when we got back to Bristol. I was able to put the issue to the back of my mind for the next few days and we enjoyed our Guernsey break, but when we got back to my house, Bob asked if he could take a copy of my contract to look over.

During my time at the club, there had been a few different chairmen. Noel White was there when I first took over in 2002, but he was really only holding the fort and his main interest lay with the club's youth section. His assistant chairman was John Cann, who took care of most football-related matters on match-days but couldn't put as much time into the club as he would have liked due to deteriorating health. John was a complete gentleman, but eventually passed away after suffering from cancer, which was a very sad day for the club and everyone who knew John.

By the time John died, Noel had stood down and a chap by the name of Roy Lucas had taken on the position. I knew Roy fairly well. He had done some work for me in the past, and he was a district councillor. John had been helping him out as well but, after he died, the club looked to bring someone else in to assist with the chairmanship. That man was Doug Green, who was given the title of general manager. I had no idea who Doug was, as I had not met him before or seen him at any of the games. It's safe to say we never really got on. He questioned a few of my footballing decisions during meetings, so I asked him what level of football he'd played at or managed at. I never did get an answer.

Back around the time of the St Luke's Bowl final, I had gone down to the clubhouse at Mill Road to watch Dave Cooke play a skittles game one evening. Cookey was one of the best secretaries I've ever worked with, and I'd go as far as to say he was the best in the Western League. As a result, I got on very well with him as a friend, as well as a club colleague. It was a night when I was due to stay over in Barnstaple, so I thought I'd go along and watch Cookey's game while having a few pints. At the clubhouse, I spotted a left-over sheet of paper that looked like an agenda for a meeting. I picked it up to see what it was, and I noticed it was a copy of the minutes from a Monday night committee meeting. I saw on this sheet that a proposal had been made that I should be sacked as manager of Barnstaple Town. Nobody at the club knew I had seen this piece of literature, but I folded it up and shoved it in my pocket. To this day, I've still got it in my file at home. On that occasion, the proposal was thrown out, but I knew from that day on that there was at least one person on the committee who I wouldn't be able to trust.

At the second meeting in September, though, a similar proposal was carried through. Of course, I was away at the time when this proposal was carried, and I know at least one other committee member, Dave Cooke, wasn't at the meeting either. But it didn't make a difference. The committee had voted, and I had been sacked. I felt very bitter about the whole situation, and I still do. I wasn't given a reason why I was sacked, and I've never been told the exact reason. All the club did was release a brief statement to the press, which also didn't include any specific reasons.

The statement, published in that week's *North Devon Journal*, reads: "It was felt that, in order to achieve the club's aims and ambitions, it was in the club's best interest that Jeff Evans be relieved of his managerial duties. Following a discussion between the chairman and Mr Evans, it was decided he should stand down with immediate effect." Chairman Steve James added: "I want to place on record our sincere thanks for all that Jeff has done for the club. He joined us when we were bottom of the Premier and has successfully maintained our Premiership status ever since. However, I think the time is right to make a change and, for this reason, I had talks with Jeff last week. We all wish him well for the future."

With no footballing reason given to me, I can only assume that my dismissal was down to a personality clash between myself and some members of the committee, especially knowing what I do about the earlier proposal that I should be sacked. This, of course, is just my opinion. But let's look at the facts. On the day I was dismissed, Barnstaple Town had won four of their first six league games, with one draw and just one defeat, and we were still in the FA Vase. We were sixth in the Premier Division table with a game in hand over the teams above us, and two games in hand over leaders Frome Town. If we had won those two games in hand, we'd have gone top of the league. Was my dismissal a footballing decision? I think not.

Doug Green was one of the committee members I had never really got on with. In my opinion, he had become too powerful for a committee member, and we never saw eye-to-eye. I didn't agree with him, and he didn't agree with me. I just felt that there were too many non-footballing people on that committee. At the same time, there were also some extremely dedicated and hard-working individuals. I've already spoken about Lee Barrow's fund-raising efforts out in the community, but I can't go without mentioning Jane 'Mrs Barnstaple' Huxtable. She worked herself into the ground for the club. You'd see her taking the money on the gate, then she'd be going around the ground selling raffle tickets. After the matches, she'd be in the clubhouse raising funds through ticket sales and other competitions. At the same time, she helped run the supporters' club. Every sports club has its unsung heroes and heroines, and Jane was certainly one of those at Mill Road.

My wife's cousin's husband Bob took the case on for me, and soon after I received a letter from the club with a settlement offer. I thought it was derisory, to say the least. With the money I had loaned the club for expenses included in my calculations, I felt that I was owed £5,800 to settle my contract. The figure I was offered was £580. There wasn't an issue about me not having paid tax, because my contract stated that the club would pay it first. I left it in Bob's hands, and it dragged on for quite a while as we waited for a reply. In the end, we sent our correspondence direct to Steve James and we soon got a letter back from the solicitors. Finally, the case was proceeding.

Bob and I had already discussed the possibility of taking the club to a tribunal if things didn't start moving, and it got very close to one. A tribunal hearing was only three or four days away when I got a letter from the solicitors apologising for the delay, and saying the club would honour the full amount owed, as long as I signed an agreement, witnessed by an independent solicitors, confirming it would be the end of the matter, with me making no further claims. I agreed, and went to a solicitor in Chipping Sodbury where I was asked if I understood the terms of the agreement. I said yes, the solicitor signed it and earned £150 for her efforts. I would have signed it myself for nothing ... more money wasted!

It's a shame it got so petty, but I heard from the solicitors that they had received the cheque and that I needed to go over and sign for it. When I looked at the cheque afterwards, I noticed that it was a personal cheque from Steve James. I wish Steve had seen me and spoken to me personally at the Barnstaple Hotel before all this started, because I'm sure there would have been a way to sort it out without going down this route. I liked Steve, he was a nice guy. Instead of the full amount of £5,800, I would more than likely have accepted a cheque for, say, £2,500 and just walked away from the club. But, knowing what I did about the earlier proposal to sack me, thanks to the copy of the minutes I have on my desk as I write, I wanted to fight it all the way. For me, the biggest disappointment was that the money had to come from Steve James, who I had a lot of time for.

I'll leave it up to you to form your own opinions about what happened. Obviously, I've got my own opinions and I've aired them in full here. But I must stress that's what they are... my opinions, and nobody else's. Some of the club's committee members clearly had their own opinions too, and one of those was that I wasn't the right man to manage Barnstaple Town. At the same time, they obviously thought Pete Buckingham was the right man to take the club forward, because they offered him the job after my dismissal, which he accepted.

Pete and I never really spoke again after this whole episode, because I was expecting him to step down in protest over my sacking. When I was assistant to Les Alderman and he left Trowbridge Town and Mangotsfield, I felt I had to go with him because we were a team. I believe the situation was different at Bath City, because Les left out of choice rather than a falling-out or disagreement, and also at Stroud when John Evans was sacked – after all, I barely knew John and had only gone up there to help out in the short-term. But again, whether Pete was right or wrong not to follow me out the door at Barnstaple, it is all down to opinions. I'll let you decide.

Although it was a very disappointing end to my time at Barnstaple Town, it wasn't all doom and gloom. I have some very good memories and we had some great laughs. Needless to say, the end-of-season tours were good fun. As is usual when a group of young lads go away for the weekend, lots of beer was necked and young ladies were spoken to! We also had our own little outings as a management team, namely Lee Barrow, Dave Cooke, Dave Griffiths and I. The first year we went down to Cornwall, and took in Plymouth Argyle's end-of-season do along the way. It was a little quieter than the end-of-season nights I'd been used to in the Western League, but it was still very enjoyable indeed.

We also had two end-of-season tours to Spain. Both were fantastic jolly-ups, and on one boat trip I've never seen any one man snore the way Cookey snored! He was sound asleep and the noise was unbelievable. He even tried to tell us he wasn't asleep when we woke him up. It was a very good holiday, though, made all the more memorable because we were staying in an all-inclusive hotel. Also enjoying the unlimited booze and food were Hibernian FC, a Scottish amateur rugby team and a ladies' hockey team from Crawley. The drinking games that took place took me all the way back to my Abbotonians days. In fact, the more I think about it, it's just as well the Abbots weren't there – it would have been total carnage!

Sadly, though, I never got the chance to finish the job at Barnstaple Town. I'll write a bit more in depth about this later, but it's one of my biggest disappointments in football that I wasn't able to fulfill my ambition of taking the club into the Southern League. I'm still confident that, if I had been allowed to manage the club the way I had wanted to do, and bring in the players I wanted to sign, Barnstaple Town would have been the first side to bring Southern League football back to North Devon, not Bideford.

Barnstaple Town at the start of the 2003/04 season. Pictured (back row from left) are me, physio Dave Griffiths, Steve Rowlands, Aaron Harper-Penman, Richard Bray, Jon Vaughan, Simon Ovey, Lee-Roy Cochrane, Russell Jee, secretary Dave Cooke and (front row from left) Tom Marsh, Lee Eate, Jake Barwick, Keith Shapland, Ross Middleton, Mark Thomas, Chris Webber, Ashley Cole and assistant manager Lee Barrow. PICTURE: NORTH DEVON JOURNAL

A work in progress. This is how Barnstaple Town lined up the following year. Pictured (back row from left) Jake Crush, Jake Barwick, Richard Hevingham, Dominic Rivans, Mike Symons, Jon Vaughan, Aaron Harper-Penman, Mike Hedden, Simon Ovey, Rob Guppy, Danny Robinson, Ross Middleton, physio Dave Griffiths and (front row from left) Darren Parish, Mark Thomas, secretary Dave Cooke, me, main sponsor John Brend, chairman Roy Lucas, assistant manager Lee Barrow, Alan Chapman and Ricky Marinaro. PICTURE: NORTH DEVON JOURNAL

Former Plymouth Argyle manager Paul Sturrock's visit to Barnstaple Town was a very memorable night. Pictured here are (from left) Kevin Summerfield, Dave Cooke, John James, me, Paul Sturrock, Lee Barrow and Geoff Crudgington.

Putting pen to paper... Lee Barrow and I sign contracts with Barnstaple Town, watched by Dave Cooke, Doug Green and Roy Lucas. This was the contract that cost the club so dear when they decided to sack me.

12... The county comes calling

THE fall-out from my dismissal at Barnstaple Town and parting of the ways with Pete Buckingham left me without any involvement in football for several months, because the previous season I had also decided to end my four-year spell as joint manager of the Devon FA's county side. It was back in the summer of 2001, when I was still at Torrington and Pete was in charge down at Elmore, that the pair of us went along to be interviewed for the joint position. The interview was a success and, a couple of years later with us at the helm, Devon were celebrating their first South West Counties Championship triumph in nearly 30 years. I haven't really had much chance to talk about this chapter of my footballing journey yet, but now is as good a time as any.

The South West Counties Championship was an annual competition that Devon's senior squad competed in, along with eight other county sides split into two leagues – one of four and one of five. Sides would play each other once in the league format, and the two sides topping Group A and B would meet in the final to decide the Championship winners. As well as Devon, there would be entries from Cornwall, Somerset, Gloucestershire, Hampshire and Sussex. Guernsey would enter a team, as would the Army and the Royal Navy. It was always an extremely competitive tournament.

After being offered the jobs, Pete and I sat down to try and work out which players we wanted to call up to play for Devon and make them a force in the South West Counties Championship. However I don't think either of us realised just how tough a task it was to get players to represent their county. I assumed that any player we got in touch with would jump at the chance to play representative football for Devon, but it wasn't like that at all. Pete and I had to sell the county to players, and we had to work very hard to persuade players to get involved. It was almost like being in charge of a club side!

By now I'd built up a good amount of contacts with Devon-based players from my time at Torrington, and likewise with Pete at Elmore and Bideford before that. So we set about naming a squad for our first game in charge of Devon, which was an away match in Group B against Guernsey in October 2001. I called up four of my Torrington lads – Karl Madge, Trevor Haslett, Karl Baggaley and Peter Trego –

and Pete brought in Elmore players Damon Palfrey, Nick Woon, Steve Rowlands, Mark Thomas and Andy Reader. We also had two quality Taunton Town players in goalkeeper Ryan Draper and centre-half Darren Hawkings, who were both Barnstaple lads and had become FA Vase winners with Russell Musker's Taunton side a few months earlier. Barnstaple Town duo Danny Harris and Kevin Squire, along with the Dawlish Town lads Jamie Day, Shaun Friend, Steve Blurton and Jason Heath, completed our first ever Devon squad.

Although most of these lads knew each other from when they played against one another, they had no experience of playing on the same side. So with the Devon FA's permission, we arranged a Friday night get-together for the squad at Clyst Rovers, which is a club based near Exeter Airport. Pete and I thought it would be a good idea to get the players together and hold a good training session before flying out to Guernsey the next morning for the game, so we booked everyone into a hotel nearby.

As the Friday evening approached we had about seven or eight players pull out of that squad, for one reason or another. Straight away we were up against it in terms of numbers but, after more than a few frantic phone calls, we were able to draft in some replacements and I think we eventually travelled to Guernsey with a squad of 18. The Friday night session actually went very well, and the training was done in a very professional manner. Everybody went to bed early so we'd be fresh for the flight and the game, and I felt the preparation had gone pretty well.

The weather, however, had other ideas. We were all up bright and early, and arrived at Exeter Airport only to find out that our plane was forced to land in Bristol due to fog. Devon's officials were starting to panic, because time was a luxury we didn't really have. The flight company arranged for a coach to pick us up and whisk us up the M5 so we could board the plane at Bristol. That was just great for me – I'd had to come down the M5 the previous evening! To be fair to the players, they stayed in good spirits throughout and were laughing and joking all the way up to Bristol. I think there were only two or three other people on the coach, and they were kept very entertained by all the singing and jokes.

At Bristol Airport, several of the players made the most of the duty-free shopping during the short wait before boarding the plane. I'd flown to Guernsey from Bristol before, so I knew where the aeroplanes would be on the runway. As we all got on this little bus to taxi us over to the plane, I was pointing out which one was probably ours. To my surprise, the bus then took a sharp turn to the right and started heading towards some sheds at the far end of the airport. I'd always just assumed that these sheds were where repairs were carried out. We then pulled up alongside what has to be the dirtiest and oldest aeroplane I'd ever seen! It was in a shocking state.

On taking my seat, I noticed that Kevin Squire was behind me, and he wasn't looking at all happy. "Don't worry Kevin," I said. "This plane did us proud in the war, so I'm sure it will get us to Guernsey no problem!" I didn't know it at the time, but Kevin had never flown before and he was absolutely bricking it! I now know exactly what they mean when they talk about a white-knuckle ride. I've never seen a person go the colour that Squiresy went, or a pair of knuckles that white as he gripped on to the arm rests! I think he stayed in that frozen position for the entire 35-minute flight, and didn't speak to anyone!

The same couldn't be said of Nick Howe. Nick was another Elmore lad who we'd drafted in, and he was thoroughly enjoying himself. As the stewardesses started wandering down the aisle asking the passengers if they needed anything, I heard a familiar-sounding voice over the in-flight speaker system. "Bing bong, this is your captain speaking, our flight attendants are coming around offering drinks, and please let them know how you'd like your T-bones cooked." Howey had only gone and commandeered the in-flight announcement service while nobody was looking! One of the stewardesses nipped along to the back of the plane where the microphone was, but she was too late. All the players were back in their seats, desperately trying to keep straight faces and look innocent.

A few minutes later, with the girls and their trolleys back in the aisles, we heard the 'bing bong' again. "Don't panic if you see fire engines on the runway at Guernsey," he told everyone. "One of our prop engines is on fire, but it shouldn't affect our landing at all." By this time, poor Kevin Squire was about ready to fill his pants! But it certainly kept the rest of us entertained – well, maybe not the stewardesses – and took our mind off the travel delays we had encountered.

It really was a race against time, and we only managed to arrive at Guernsey's ground about 45 minutes before kick-off. After the professionalism of the previous evening's preparation, it had all turned into a bit of a disaster. We couldn't even request a delayed kick-off, because a local Channel Islands television crew were there to cover the match and the TV time slot had already been agreed. They asked us to be as quick as we could, and we obliged and we somehow managed to get the game under way on time.

The first 40 minutes that followed served as a stark reminder of the importance of professional preparation. It doesn't matter what level of the game you are playing, be it in the Premier League or at the lowest rung of the local non-league ladder. You have to warm up properly and, thanks to our flight fiasco, we weren't able to. As a result, Pete and I were facing the prospect of having to give our first ever Devon half-time team talk to a side losing 4-1. As it happened, Steve Blurton pinched a goal just before the half-time whistle so that made it 4-2 at the break.

Walking off at half-time, I wasn't too downhearted. Obviously I didn't want us to be trailing 4-2 but, considering our preparation, it was clear that the lads were finding their feet in the last 10 or 15 minutes of the half and I felt confident we'd be the stronger of the two sides in the second half. Nick Woon, a striker who Pete had signed for Elmore from Taunton Town about ten days before this game, had scored our opener in the first half. He netted two more in the second half to complete his hat-trick and bring us back to 4-4. Then, with seven minutes to go, that man Squire – the one who had been so terrified on the flight over – curled a fantastic effort into the top corner to make it 5-4 and seal our first Devon win. It was a remarkable turnaround, and we were all whistling and singing the Great Escape tune when we made it back to our coach.

Back at our hotel in Guernsey, it was time to shower and smarten up for the evening do, jointly organised by the two FAs. A representative from each association gives a talk about what they are doing for football in their county, and then they talk about the game. I've been to more than a few of these evenings, and they're always okay as long as there's a few people there having a laugh. On this occasion, I remember that the food there was absolutely superb. When it was finished, all the players sorted out taxis to take them down to St Peter Port for a night on the town. Even Pete Buckingham, complete with his 1970s-style leather trouser suit, was off down town with the boys thinking he was a teeny-bopper again... fair play to him!

At breakfast the next morning one player, who shall remain nameless, was missing and I was getting a bit concerned. I shouldn't have worried, because I knew he was a level-headed lad and not a complete drunkard, but you can't help but worry when you've got a flight to catch that morning. Finally he appeared at the hotel and, as soon as I saw him, I asked where on earth he'd been. "On a boat," was the surprise answer! It turns out he'd met a young lady in one of the bars and she'd suggested they go back to her dad's boat in the marina. They had climbed down a ladder on to this boat, not aware that the tide was on its way out. When this lad had decided to get off the boat and come back to the hotel, the tide had gone out and the ladder was out of reach! He ended up having to stay on the boat until the tide came back in to let him get off! It was one of the more memorable excuses I've been given when collaring a player for being late back to the hotel!

Spirits were very high on the coach back to the airport at Guernsey. All the lads were talking about what a great game it was, and what a good night out they'd had, and there were a few more little stories coming out. But I'm a man's man ... I know that what happens on tour, stays on tour, so I'm not going to name and shame anyone in this book! But it really was a thoroughly enjoyable trip, and it wasn't over yet – we still had the return flight and another 35 minutes of sheer terror for our match-winner Kevin Squire! If any of you have flown from Guernsey, you'll know what a small airport it is and that there are a lot of places to hide ... as the mischievous Nick Howe soon discovered. There was a microphone by every desk and, as we were waiting to board, I heard another 'bing bong' from Howe. "The flight to Glasgow has now been delayed by 20 minutes." A couple of minutes later, there would be another 'bing bong' from the other side of the airport. "The flight from Gatwick is now landing on runway two." Howe had a field day, sending the people at the airport into a complete frenzy, and I still don't know how he didn't get caught!

When we landed at Exeter, we all shook hands and said we'd see each other again for the next game against The Navy at HMS Drake in Plymouth a month later. Once again we fought back from going behind to score five goals and win, this time 5-3. We had called up

Bideford's Robbie Gough for this game, and he struck an equaliser from 20 yards after we'd gone 1-0 down early in the first half. Steve Blurton added two more in the second half, both from the penalty spot, and we were looking good at 3-1 up, only for things to get a little tense when a speculative Navy shot took a big deflection off Danny Harris past our goalkeeper Peter Trego. However, 3-2 became 5-2 with two goals in four minutes from Kevin Squire and Steve Rowlands, who picked up his county cap that day after making his 15th Devon appearance. Although The Navy pulled back a consolation in stoppage time, we'd won two out of two and were top of our group.

Next up was a game against Hampshire at Cullompton Rangers in December 2001, and we ended up having to settle for a 2-2 draw after conceding a late equaliser with around 15 minutes to go. Hampshire had taken the lead, but Dawlish's Jason Heath had finished off Alan Chapman's cross to score our equaliser, before Squire put us 2-1 up. Despite being unable to hold on, we were still leading our group after three games because no other side had managed to win twice. We were top with seven points from three games, while Sussex had won once and drawn twice, so were second with five points. Sussex also happened to be our final group opponents, so it was effectively a winner-takes-all clash between the two counties at Dawlish Town's Sandy Lane ground on March 9, 2002.

Goalkeeper Ryan Draper, Sean Friend, Alan Chapman and Darren Hawkings were all suspended for the game, and Damon Palfrey was injured, so that hit us hard. On top of that, Sussex were a very professional outfit and they beat us 2-1 to leapfrog us at the top of Group B and go into the final against Group A winners The Army. It was very disappointing to get so close and then have nothing to show for it, but both Pete and I were confident that we had plenty to build on for the 2002/03 challenge.

By the time the first Devon game of the new season had come around – we were at home against Guernsey at Liverton United's ground – I had been installed as the manager of Barnstaple Town. Two of my players there, goalkeeper Jon Vaughan and defender Darren Edwards, were brought into the squad to join up with the regulars from the previous season. It was vital to make a winning start, and that's exactly what we did, beating Guernsey 4-2 with two

189

goals from then-Exmouth Town striker Jamie Densham and one apiece from Dawlish Town duo Heath and Blurton.

A lot of heavy rain during December and January left us facing our next two group games within a week of each other, starting with a narrow 1-0 win over The Navy at HMS Drake. The game had already been postponed once when our ground at Elmore was ruled unplayable again, so we were forced to concede our 'home' advantage and go down to Plymouth. Blurton got the game's only goal from the penalty spot. A week later, we went to Somerset and lost 2-1... and I still don't know how we didn't win it. We hit the crossbar three times in the opening half-hour before Densham finally put us 1-0 up just before half-time. Somerset nicked two goals in the second half and we just couldn't get back on level terms. I can remember Squire somehow having an effort cleared off the line near the end.

As it was, we knew we had to win our final group game at Gloucestershire at Almondsbury in February to be guaranteed a place in the final. We came so close to doing it – Squire had two great chances in the second half, but was denied by their goalkeeper – but ultimately had to settle for a 0-0 draw. Would seven points be good enough to top the group? As it turns out, it was ... on goal difference! The Navy also ended up with seven points, but had a goal difference of +1 compared to ours of +2. It meant Devon were through to the final of the South West Counties Championship, and had the chance to win the title for the first time since 1976. All that stood in our way was Group B winners Cornwall.

Any cup final is special but, for me, this one was even more so. Not only was it my first final as a county manager, but it was also being played at Mill Road – the home of my club side Barnstaple Town. It was a cold and drizzly day in North Devon, but we had a big support from all the Barnstaple fans, who were there to see six of the club's players involved – Jon Vaughan, Nick Bowrah, Lee-Roy Cochrane, Karl Curtis, Darren Edwards and Kevin Squire. Cornwall also brought a lot of fans up, and they were confident that they had enough quality to beat us. Their manager Ray Nicholls had some good players in his side. St Blazey striker Andy Watkins went on to play for Plymouth Argyle before spearheading Truro City's charge up the non-league ladder, and there were other very good players in there like Glynn Hooper and Jamie Morrison-Hill. Devon were the underdogs, but that suited us just fine.

Lee-Roy in particular was outstanding on the day for us in defence. He'd been top quality for Barnstaple in the few months since he'd joined from Ilfracombe, and he was just as impressive on the county final stage. Lee-Roy made an absolutely crucial goal-line clearance from Morrison-Hill in the first half, while Jon Vaughan pushed a Luke Hodge header on to his post – they were two important moments for us because they helped us get to the break at 0-0. Cornwall may have just shaded the first half, but we were holding our own. Pete and I encouraged the lads to keep working hard, and promised them their chances would come.

About 15 minutes into the second half, a chance did come, and it went our way. Steve Rowlands sent a free-kick into the Cornwall area, looking for a Devon head. Instead, the ball deflected off a Cornwall defender, Leigh Underhay, and nestled itself nicely in the back of the net. 1-0 to Devon! Cornwall upped the tempo in their search for an equaliser, but I was never overly worried. I had confidence in the players to see it out, and they were coping admirably with that task.

By now, with Cornwall pushing forward, Kevin Squire was seeing very little of the ball up front, so I decided to take him off and send Darren Edwards on. Darren gave us an extra defensive body on the pitch to soak up the late pressure, but he was also a big lad who we could send forward when the chance arose to get the ball back into the Cornwall penalty area. That opportunity soon arose when we won a corner, about two or three minutes after Edwards had come on. Up he went, and nodded the corner across the face of goal, where fellow Barnstaple defender Lee-Roy Cochrane was able to blast home from six yards and double our lead. The place erupted! It was the 87th minute and we were 2-0 up in the South West Counties Championship. Surely it was all over?

The answer was no. Andy Watkins was always a threat to us with his pace and, with stoppage-time looming, he was brought down in the box by Simon Hill as he attempted another raid into our area. Luke Hodge scored the penalty and suddenly it was 2-1, with a fired-up Cornwall hell-bent on getting an equaliser in the two or three minutes of injury time. But they couldn't do it. Why? Because we were better than them on the day. We were the more composed in defence, we took our chances at the other end, and we deservedly raised the trophy. In fact, we must have been out on that Mill Road pitch celebrating for a good 15 or 20 minutes after that final whistle went. They were great scenes. I firmly believe we were the better side. To this day, Cornwall feel they deserved to win that final, but I disagree totally.

Twelve months later, Cornwall were given their chance for revenge against our Devon side. Once again we topped the two groups in the South West Counties Championship, but this time Cornwall would have home advantage in the final, with the game being played at St Blazey. We had a fantastic group campaign, though, and won all four of our games to go down to Cornwall with a 100 per cent record for the 2003/04 final.

Carl Cliff-Brown, a talented but temperamental striker who at the time was playing for Clyst Rovers, came into the Devon set-up during this campaign and scored all four of our goals in our opening two group wins, against The Navy 2-0 and Gloucestershire 2-1. However, by the time of our third group game in early March against Wiltshire at Elmore's ground, Cliff-Brown had become unavailable. He had secured a Southern League switch to Tiverton Town, where he had been put on contract by their manager Martyn Rogers. We still managed to beat Wiltshire 2-1, with a 12th-minute opener from Kevin Squire and a penalty from Mike Booth. Actually, Mike had blasted his first attempt against the crossbar, but the referee ruled that he had to retake it because the goalkeeper, Bath City's Justin Shuttleworth, had moved too early. Mike made sure he didn't make the same mistake twice, and doubled our lead.

Another trip over to Guernsey completed our Group A campaign, and we signed off with a professional 3-0 win. Exmouth Town's Dougie Jane scored two, and set up Squire for the other. Meanwhile, across the water at Bodmin Town's Priory Park ground, Cornwall got the win they needed against Dorset to top Group B. So the two deadly rivals were set up for a rematch, and I'll be bluntly honest about it, Cornwall were the better side and deserved their 2-0 win over us. I've always prided myself on being an honest manager... if I knew we were outplayed, then I would say so. And on this occasion, I'll admit that we were second best. The St Blazey centre-half Chris Hudson headed Cornwall into a 1-0 lead early in the second half and, not long after that, Jason Heath was sent off for us. It was a double hammer blow for us, and when Ian Gosling tucked a second goal past Jon Vaughan, I knew it was over. It wasn't that we didn't have our chances – Jamie Densham and Jason Reeves both came close to snatching an equaliser before that all-important Gosling goal, while Torrington striker Lee Langmead and Bridport Town defender Tom Gardner had the best of our chances earlier in the game. It wasn't to be, though, and Cornwall deserved their day of celebration. Now I knew exactly how they had felt 12 months earlier.

To be honest, I had started to get the feeling that my Devon days may be numbered. I wasn't planning on resigning, and I didn't think I was going to be sacked. Instead, there were lots of whispers going around about the Devon FA's future in the South West Counties Championship. Money was tight, and county officials were seriously considering whether or not to withdraw from the competition. In the end, the FA searched hard for sponsorship to help fund Devon's 2004/05 campaign, but there were heavy cutbacks. The most notable one came in terms of travel. We were no longer able to travel to away games by coach, and it got to the point where we had to drive ourselves to the game at Sussex with groups of five lads per car.

The professionalism and preparation that had been so important during our first three seasons had now vanished, so it was no surprise that we were unable to reach a third final in succession. We still gave our opponents some good games, but we just fell that little bit short. Our away game against Gloucestershire at Almondsbury was a prime example. We were 2-0 up through Perry Carpenter and Tom Barwell, but conceded three to trail 3-2. Rob Guppy and Richard Blake both scored to put us ahead 4-3, yet still we threw it away in the latter stages and lost the match 5-4.

A disappointing season ended with a 2-2 draw against Cornwall at Exmouth Town, where Kevin Squire scored both goals for us. I had already decided that it would be my last game as Devon's joint manager but, despite the anti-climax of that final season, I must go on record to say what an honour it was to manage a county side for those four seasons with Pete Buckingham. Knowing my name will always be in the record books of South West Counties Championship-winning managers makes me very proud indeed. On a completely personal level, it also gives me the right to say that I've managed club sides in four different counties (Devon, Somerset, Wiltshire and Gloucestershire) as well as a county representative side. There can't be many, if any, other managers in the English game who have done this. I believe Frank Gregan has managed clubs in four counties, but has never taken charge of a representative team. If I'm wrong, no doubt someone will tell me!

It's a great shame that the South West Counties Championship no longer exists for senior sides. Other county FAs echoed Devon's sentiments about the costs involved in sending their senior squads around the country for these fixtures, and several withdrew. I think the last senior championship took place in 2007/08. Now it only exists for women's and youth teams. Given what all these local clubs and players are charged for suspensions and things like that, I cannot believe that there isn't enough money floating around to be able to keep senior representative football alive at some level. Look how popular the corresponding competition is in rugby. I would fully back any moves to bring the competition back, but I can't emphasise enough the importance of giving county managers more control in picking their sides. They must make sure that the FA side's senior managers have the authority to take players from clubs. In the end, Pete and I didn't have that luxury. We encountered a lot of opposition from certain club managers who were unwilling to let us select their players, and it made the job all the more difficult.

Devon celebrate winning the 2003 South West Counties Championship after beating Cornwall 2-1 in the final at Mill Road, Barnstaple.

Pete Buckingham and I with the South West Counties Championship Cup after Devon's triumph in 2003. It was a very proud moment.

13... Career over – by text!

THE biggest problem about being put on 'gardening leave', as they seem to call it in football management terms these days, is that you have to turn down all offers from other clubs. I soon discovered this in the weeks and months that followed that phone call from Barnstaple Town chairman Steve James, informing me that I'd been dismissed as the club's manager. While I had been sacked and would no longer be anywhere near Mill Road or Doug Green, my hands were tied with regard to finding a new job. I had to wait until my contract had been settled and, as I explained a couple of chapters ago, that turned out to be a long and drawn-out process.

While these legal negotiations were ongoing, I took the opportunity to get clued up on the Bristol football scene again. I'd just spent the best part of ten years managing in North Devon, so I was keen to take the chance to go and watch a few Southern and Western League games around the city. Welton Rovers were one of the clubs I made a point of visiting. My old pals Chris Mountford and Mike Ford were in charge there, so I knew I could go along, watch a decent game of football and have a chat and a pint in the clubhouse afterwards before going home.

I went to several Welton games while my contract settlement was being negotiated with Barnstaple Town and, although they didn't have the greatest of league seasons – I think they ended up in mid-table in the Western League's Premier Division – they did reach the final of the Les Phillips Cup. This final was the last game of the 2006/07 season, against Willand Rovers. Unfortunately for Chris, he was due to be away on holiday in Portugal at the time of the match, so Mike gave me a call and asked if I would be willing to join him in the dugout and help him out. As luck would have it, my financial dispute with Barnstaple Town had just been settled and I was free to take Mike up on his offer and help him out for the day. We didn't get the result we wanted, and lost 2-0 to Willand in the final.

That game marked the end of a very strange season for me, one that had started with such high hopes down in North Devon. I had a strong-looking Barnstaple Town side who were up among the top group in the Western League, and I felt more confident than ever of launching a Southern League promotion push. Within the space of a month, though, it had all gone sour and I was on 'gardening leave'. It left me in limbo for the best part of seven months. I wasn't able to get my teeth into anything else football-related, and I wasn't used to just watching the game as a spectator. Chris and Mike at Welton knew me well enough to understand that I hadn't enjoyed my time out of the game, and called me up for a meeting during the summer before the start of the 2007/08 season. They had an interesting proposition for me.

The three of us met in a pub for a pint, and Chris told me he wanted me to join them at Welton Rovers. I politely pointed out to Chris that he was already manager at Welton, and that I'd never wanted to do anything else other than manage. My brief spell at Calne Town, and the fact that I really struggled not being a manager, backed up that claim. "With all that in mind, what do you want me to do at Welton Rovers?" I asked him. Chris said he wanted me to come in and be director of football. It's a job title that has become quite popular among the top clubs over the past few years, but I didn't really know how such a job could be done at Welton Rovers. "Basically Jeff, you'll do anything you can to help me!" said Chris.

I thought a lot about it, and about my age. I was in my 60s now, and wasn't sure whether I wanted another challenge of starting at a club from scratch, so I agreed to give it a go. To be honest I quite enjoyed the role. I was responsible for making sure all the players were signed on, sorting their money out each week, arranging the pre-season friendlies and giving Chris as much help and support as I could. All the work involved building towards our first Western League Premier Division game of the season, which was at home against the division new boys Truro City.

This was easily going to be the toughest fixture for us, and every other Western League side, during the 2007/08 campaign. A couple of years earlier, Truro City had been taken over by Cornish-based property developer Kevin Heaney, who pumped a load of money into the club with the ambitious aim of making them the first ever Cornish club to play in the Football League. They were storming through the leagues at an astonishing rate, as Team Bath did a few years earlier.

I'd already had one pretty major run-in with Truro a couple of years earlier, when they were playing the Carlsberg South Western League. It was at the start of their revolution, and they were beginning to attract the type of players who were far too good for that standard.

197

The former Plymouth Argyle midfielder Joe Broad was a good example. He'd left a pro career at Walsall to sign for Truro, and there were plenty of others too. One of them turned out to be Shane Tolley, who was scoring a lot of goals in my Barnstaple Town side that season and was clearly on their radar. They announced through the press that they'd signed him, and Shane had informed me that he had accepted their offer. But there was one small thing that was missing ... I was adamant that Barnstaple Town, as a club, had received no official approach. I had certainly not waived the seven-day notice of approach, which sometimes managers do to help a player move on. Even though players could have a dual registration with a side in each league, I felt certain that we should have received seven days. After all, this was no dual registration. We were losing one of our best players.

I submitted an official complaint to the FA after Tolley had made his first appearance for Truro City, a brief introduction as a late substitute in their 4-0 win at Penryn, alleging that an illegal approach had been made. It seemed I had good cause to be annoyed. The case was heard and Truro City were later docked three points. Now, those three points had the potential to be the difference between getting promoted to the Western League – which they were banking so heavily on achieving – and staying in the South Western League for another season. When the points were taken off, it left them out of the top two promotions positions and eight points behind Liskeard Athletic with a handful of games to go. Somehow, they still managed to overturn that deficit and take the runners-up spot on goal difference from Falmouth Town, who had also been deducted a point during that season.

From then on, there was no stopping Truro and they won three successive titles, as well as an FA Vase at Wembley Stadium. The second of those three titles was the Western League Premier Division, a campaign which started with a narrow 2-1 win over our Welton Rovers side at West Clewes. Had it not been for a clanger from our centre-half Jason Hughes with about five minutes to go, we would have grabbed a point. With the talent that Truro had on show that day, it showed that this Welton side weren't far off being able to compete with the best sides.

Full-back Mark Thomas was one player who I helped to bring in at Welton Rovers. Tommo had ended up being my captain at Barnstaple

Town, and I had a lot of time for him. He was a good lad, and he obviously had a bit of time for me too because he walked out of Barnstaple Town in protest at my sacking. It was a good addition to get him on board at Welton and, other than that Truro blip, we made a pretty encouraging start to the league season. We won three and drew one in our next four games, including a 2-0 win at Barnstaple Town on a blazing hot Saturday in August. It was strange being back at Mill Road in the other dugout, and seeing Pete Buckingham a few yards down the touchline with the Barnstaple bench. It was also good to see some old faces in the clubhouse after, although certain committee members made sure they kept their distance!

As the games went on, though, I got more and more despondent with just standing in the changing room and saying nothing. Much like my time at Calne, I had lots of opinions on what was happening on the pitch, but didn't feel like I was entitled to share them with the players. At times when he was giving a pre-match or half-time team talk, Chris would ask me if I had anything to add, but he had his ideas on the game and I had mine. At the end of the day, he was the manager and I didn't want to interfere with that. I carried on helping out behind the scenes and went to meetings for him, but I wasn't entirely happy.

We had an away game at Corsham Town in the middle of October on a Tuesday night, and I thought the players were absolutely fantastic when they overcame a 2-0 deficit to fight back and claim a 2-2 draw there. Rob Dumphy and Jason Hughes got the goals that evening and, had I been in charge, I would have been congratulating them on their fighting spirit. Chris didn't share my optimism, and kept them in the changing room for a good half-hour after the game and tore strips out of them. He knew I didn't agree with how he'd approached it, and called me up the next day to discuss things. "This isn't really working out, is it?" he said. I totally agreed with him, and that phone call effectively ended my spell as director of football at Welton. I'd like to stress that it was nothing personal between Chris and I. We were very good friends, and we're still very good friends to this day, there's no doubt about that. We just didn't click as part of a management team.

Because we still got on well, I told him I was always available if he needed any advice or suggestions, or if he needed any help on a more informal basis. A couple of months later, he asked if I could go over to watch a player for him at Odd Down, who were bottom of the Premier Division table and struggling like hell. When I got there, I bumped into one of my old Bath City directors Mike Russell, who was now chairman there. I had a drink with Mike after the game, and he told me they were under pressure to sack the manager there due to their rock-bottom position in the table. I told him that, with the side they had, a bottom-place finish was almost inevitable. He then looked at me and said a very funny thing. "It's a shame you won't come, but then we couldn't afford you, could we?"

I laughed. "Put something in front of me and I'll see what it's all about." The money side of football had never mattered to me, not in my younger days and certainly not at my age now. All I ever wanted covered was my expenses, and a little bit of beer money. After a while, I was persuaded to take the job on and I've got to be totally honest, it was the worst decision I could possibly have made at that stage of my career. I've got to tell the truth here... I'd just spent ten years in North Devon, and the band of players who I knew in and around Bristol had all finished playing. Sure, I had watched a few Welton Rovers games and helped them out for a bit, but my contacts among Bristol footballers was nowhere near as strong as it had been ten or 15 years ago. All the players coming on the scene now were young lads who I'd never seen before, let alone spoken to.

I took the job on without really knowing any players who I could bring in to help the club. I wasn't able to just pick up the phone and speak to people, which I had always relied so heavily on when I'd taken on squad rebuilding tasks in the past. Odd Down were all but relegated anyway when I took over, and sure enough we finished bottom of the Premier Division table that season. In the longer term, it probably did the club good to go down and rebuild from scratch in Division One. One player I did know, of course, was Mark Thomas, so I took him there with me as coach to help with pre-season training ahead of the 2008/09 season.

I put a call in to the old Bristol Rovers goalkeeper Brian Parkin, who was coaching at Team Bath alongside the manager Ged Roddy and assistant Andy Tilson. By now, Team Bath were an established Southern League side pushing for promotion to the Conference South, so I was rather hoping they may have some players on the fringes of their first-team who may benefit from coming along to Odd Down for a loan spell. Brian said he had about two teams full of them! In the end, we took about six or seven young lads on board to give them some competitive experience in the Western League.

We started off okay. We were losing more games than we were winning but, even in defeat, we were scoring goals and showing glimmers of promise. We'd lost 3-2 at Cadbury Heath, 3-2 against Bradford Town and 4-2 at Keynsham Town. A point from our opening game against Roman Glass St George, 1-1, was later followed by our first win – a 4-2 success at Shepton Mallet – and we also had an excellent 4-3 win over Shrewton United at the end of September.

I had let the club know I was preparing to take a six-week holiday to New Zealand during the season. It was something my wife Jo and I had wanted to do for a while, so we could get the chance to meet up with friends we had made some 30 years ago when we were last over there. I was also able to meet up with a few of the blokes who I had played football with, so it was a very enjoyable trip. When I arrived back at Odd Down, I couldn't believe what I'd missed.

I was informed that there was a new chairman coming in to take over from Mike Russell, and there was also a new secretary because the former secretary had sadly died from cancer. The new secretary was really struggling with the demands of the job and didn't really know what she was supposed to be doing, and the whole scenario just didn't seem right to me.

Despite this, we actually put together our best form of the season in the final few months. From January 1, 2009, through to the end of the season, we only lost six of our last 18 games. At the end of March, we won three games on the trot – beating Portishead Town 2-0 and 3-1, and Hengrove Athletic 1-0 – and had lost just one in seven. That all came crashing to a halt when we went to Shrewton United and lost 3-0. After the game, the new chairman was having a chat with me and told me he thought the club needed to be taken 'in a new direction' next season. I asked him to tell me exactly what he meant by a new direction. "Getting these Team Bath lads in is all well and good," he said. "But they don't spend any money in the bar, and they don't come to any functions." Immediately I suggested that the best step forward for the club would be to appoint a local manager, and he agreed.

It was a perfectly amicable chat and, at the end of it, I said my goodbyes to the players and committee members. They were a little taken aback... I don't think they were expecting me to leave there and then! There were still three league games left to play, but that was my lot. I left the clubhouse at Shrewton and it proved to be my last involvement with Odd Down. It was short, not particularly sweet, and there are no real stories to tell or laughs to share. Like the new chairman had said, the majority of the lads were on loan from Team Bath and would disappear as soon as the game had finished. The only times you saw them were at training, on the pitch or in the changing room! It was a very hard season, and I was glad to get out of it.

The whole Odd Down experience did have one major effect on me, though, with regards to thinking about my future. Before taking the job on, I had been perfectly happy with the thought of retiring. To be honest, I had strongly considered retiring after leaving Barnstaple Town. I was now 64 years old and I felt I'd done more than enough within the game. When I got home that night, I told Jo that I'd done my lot and that I had retired. She looked at me in that disbelieving way, as she could tell there was something about the idea of retirement that didn't sit well with me. She was right too. There was something really eating away at me. I had done such a lot in football and I'd got so much enjoyment out of it, so I really didn't want to sign out on a bad note. I wanted to retire, leaving a good team that I had enjoyed working with for a full season. That hadn't happened at Odd Down, and I really felt that it was the wrong way to say goodbye to a game that had given me so much enjoyment over the best part of 50 years.

I was at home with Jo one evening in July when my phone went and, with football still in my mind, I was very happy to hear the voice on the other end of the line. It was Ian Hill, who was a quality centre-half in his time and had played a good standard of non-league football and had also managed. Ian had spent a lot of time at Dawlish Town, and he was ringing to ask me if I would consider taking on the job there. Dawlish had just finished fourth in the Western League's Premier Division, but the young player-manager in charge, Adam Shearer, had only taken the role on a temporary basis until the end of the season. He wanted to stay at the club as a player, but didn't really have the time needed for management due to work and youth coaching commitments. I was so taken aback by the offer, especially because Jo was sat next to me on the sofa and I knew I'd told her a month or so earlier that I had retired. "Thanks for the call Ian, but I've decided to retire so I'll have to say no," I said.

Jo asked me what the call was about, and I told her that Dawlish Town had just offered me the job. "See, I told you that you hadn't finished," she said. "What?" I said. "You just heard me speaking to them, I said no!" When I woke up the next morning, I was already having second thoughts about rejecting the Dawlish approach so quickly. I walked up into the village to pick up the morning papers and I couldn't stop thinking about whether I'd been a bit hasty, so I gave Hilly a call and asked him if it was too late for me to reconsider. Hilly said he'd get in touch with the committee members involved in searching for a new manager, and said he'd get back in touch with me. When he did call back, he told me that one of the club's directors would be getting in touch with me shortly to discuss it further.

After a couple of days, the phone went and we arranged a meeting. This meeting was later delayed, and then rearranged, due to one of the committee men working away and not being able to make it. Further delays followed, and I started to get a bit impatient. It had been dragging on for nearly three weeks and we were getting closer and closer to the start of the season, so I called back and said that the meeting needed to happen soon or I wouldn't be interested. "Don't worry about pre-season," said the voice on the other end of the phone. "We've already got the team here, we just need you to come and manage it."

I'd been around long enough to know it wasn't as easy as that. Pre-season isn't just about building the squad, it's about fitness and developing team understanding and awareness. Anyway, my call seemed to do the trick and a meeting was hastily arranged for the Thursday night with all the necessary committee men present. I laid out my terms and conditions very plainly at the meeting. I wanted everything to be right. They were asking the right questions, and I must have been giving the right answers, because the chairman Dave Fenner finished by asking me how much I was going to cost them.

I was completely honest with them, and told them straight that they couldn't afford me. I didn't mean it in an arrogant way in terms of my actions of managing the club, but rather the consideration that Dawlish's ground at Sandy Lane is about 110 miles from my front door! Basically, I was facing a 220-mile round trip in a BMW 7 Series every time I had to come down for a match or training. Considering the petrol costs at that time, it worked out to be at least £50 per trip. If I was running a little bit late and had to put my foot down, you'd be looking at £60! I spelt it out to them plain and simple. If I was needed two nights a week for training, and a home match on a Saturday, you'd be looking at £150 for fuel before considering any managerial expenses. They said it wasn't a problem, and told me that they wanted to gear Dawlish Town up for Southern League football so needed to be as professional as possible. With that, the deal was done and I told them I'd be down for training on the Tuesday night.

That evening, I was introduced to the two players who had been taking the training sessions since the players had reported back for pre-season training. Chris Porter and Dean Coppard were the two lads in question, and they told me that they'd had around 15 or 20 turning up to each session. What they didn't tell me was that, although there were 15 to 20 players at training, not one of them had signed on! The first day of the Western League season was only about two weeks away, and not one of them had been registered as a Dawlish Town player.

After meeting Chris and Dean, I then had to speak with every player individually and discuss the wage structure with them. I needed to find out as quickly as possible who was on board, and who wasn't. The harsh reality of those meetings was that there were about five or six lads there who felt they were worth far, far more money than I, Chris, Dean or Dawlish Town were prepared to pay them! Even at those meetings, I heard mutterings from players saying that they'd have to go and speak to one of the directors. I understood that one of the players had an expenses deal that was nothing to do with the football club, and instead was set up through one of the directors, so I needed to find out from the chairman exactly what the score was.

The chairman Dave Fenner told me that he sponsored his son Craig, who was a good centre-half for Dawlish, while other directors sponsored other players. I told him I felt that certain other players simply weren't worth the money they were being sponsored for. That was just my honest opinion, based on what I'd seen at training so far. I don't want to go into the specifics of exactly how much players were being paid, but I know for a fact that there was one player at Dawlish Town, at that time, who was getting more money than players I knew at Tiverton Town who were travelling all around the Southern League. This didn't go down well with me, especially as I didn't think the player in question was worth that much to the club.

I had to go back down for the next training session and hold more talks with Chris and Dean about the players that we had, and we finally came up with a squad that we were happy to go ahead with. Chris was to be my assistant manager, and Dean would continue as a player-coach. I felt a couple of the players played more for themselves than the club, so I knew that needed changing, but I also knew there was some real quality there. Craig Fenner was a very good centre-half, while Dean Coppard himself and young Dougie Ford were also good defenders. Gary Fisher was an absolute class act to have in central midfield, with several years of Southern League experience at Taunton Town under his belt, while Dean Stevens had a magnificent left foot on him. Up front, young Joe Bushin was as hard as nails and only knew one thing – how to score goals. Another striker was Jules Emati-Emati, a lad from Cameroon who had recently moved to South Devon, and he was absolutely superb too.

I knew the basics were there, but finding a goalkeeper was a top priority. I signed Steve Johns, who played for Pete Buckingham and I at Barnstaple Town. At the same time, I signed Steve's good mate Aaron Harper-Penman who I had also brought into the first team at Barnstaple. I knew Aaron could play at centre-half or in midfield for me, so straight away I had a couple of extra options. I then signed a striker who had moved down from up north, Ricky Lee, along with a couple of youngsters who had been in Chris Porter's Torquay Boys' Grammar School side that had won a national cup a couple of years earlier, Matt Micklewright and Freddie Smith. One other name I mustn't forget is Radley Veale. He was another outstanding talent who could play in midfield or up front, but the lad was a farmer and wasn't always available. Martyn Rogers had liked him enough to sign him for Tiverton Town a couple of years earlier, but Radley's work commitments just didn't mix well with the travelling schedule of Southern League football.

I was perfectly happy with the squad at the start of the season, although I was less pleased with the complete lack of pre-season preparation. I was worried it may take us a fair few games to find our feet, but the side seemed to find their rhythm almost instantly. We were top of the league after our first four games, with the fourth win an impressive 3-2 defeat of reigning Western League champions Bideford. Joe Bushin further underlined his goal-scoring potential with a hat-trick, scoring the winner in the last minute. He'd also scored a hat-trick in the previous game, a 5-2 midweek success against Wellington Town.

The first break from league action came with our first game in the FA Cup, an extra preliminary round tie against Division One side Elmore, which we won 3-0 thanks to two goals from Dean Stevens and one from Bushin. That set up an away tie in the preliminary round against another Division One side in Bridport, managed by the former Reading player Trevor Senior. I knew we were struggling for numbers for that trip to Bridport, and we travelled with just 11 players and one substitute thanks to a combination of injuries and suspensions.

We drew the game 3-3 and I was quite happy at that point to take them back to our place. Although they were in the division below and many people thought we should have won comfortably, Bridport were actually a decent footballing side. As good a quality as that is to have, it's also probably the reason they haven't returned to the Premier Division sooner. Division One can be a tough and hard league, and sometimes you need that little bit extra. Anyway, on that Saturday we had matched them and came away with a 3-3 draw thanks to goals from Bushin, Stevens and Gary Fisher. As I said, I was happy enough with the result considering the limitations I had in terms of selection, and I went into the bar at Bridport in high spirits.

I was just having a chat with a few people about the game, when one of the directors who had been at my initial interview started chirping on about the standard of the side I had put out, and also about their commitment. I asked what he was on about, and he told me that half the team had been out on the lash the previous night down at the Dartmouth Regatta. I asked him if he was sure about his allegation, which he said he was, so I said I'd look into it. When it comes to problems like this, I'm never one to beat around the bush so I walked up to the players and pulled them all over to the corner of the Bridport clubhouse. "Right, let's get this out in the open straight away," I said. "Who was out on the piss last night?" Nobody rushed to give an answer, although Bushin did say he'd had his usual couple of pints on a Friday night to help him sleep. I explained to them what I'd just been told, and the players blew their tops and immediately rubbished the accusations.

I went back to this director and demanded a chat outside, where I set the record straight in no uncertain terms. "Don't you ever come and have a go at me in our clubhouse or in anybody else's," I said. "If you want to give me a bollocking, if you want to ask me questions, then pull me aside into a private area. Just be professional about everything you do, because what you've done today is very unprofessional." For me, the matter had been dealt with but unfortunately we still had to play Bridport again in the replay. I was still short of a few players, and we lost the game at Sandy Lane 2-1.

It was one of the few blips we had during the early part of that season, but disaster struck when I learned we would be losing Joe Bushin. I don't think there could be any argument about it, Bushin was the best striker in the Western League that season, so it was inevitable that he was going to attract attention from other clubs. Martyn Rogers was having a difficult start to the Southern League season with Tiverton Town, and I know he'd been tracking Bushin for a fair while. I finally received the notice of approach from Tivvy, and it was hardly surprising. Joe had just scored his third hat-trick of the season in a 3-3 draw with Ilfracombe Town, and in total he'd scored 14 goals for us. Given that we were only in early October, it was stunning form.

I would never dream of standing in the way of a player who wants to challenge himself at a higher level of football, and gave Joe my blessing to join Tiverton Town. He said he would always be available to play for us if his Tiverton commitments allowed it. In return, Martyn let us have a midfielder called Glenn Gould. While he was a talented young player, he wasn't a top goal-scorer and our squad just wasn't the same without Joe Bushin up front. After he left, our next six games included two wins, two draws and two defeats.

By this time, having seen the players in about 10 or 15 games, I'd also made my mind up about picking a new captain for Dawlish Town. I'd chosen Gary Fisher, and it was an easy choice to make. Gary's attitude was spot on, both on the pitch and in the changing room... he wanted to be a winner at all times. I'd also signed a strong centre-half in Paul Kendall to give us some extra strength at the back but, just when we had a couple of positives, we were dealt another massive blow. Joe Bushin's strike partner Jules Emati-Emati had also got himself among the goals in the early part of the season, and he was playing an even more crucial role for us after Joe signed for Tiverton. Sadly, he too attracted interest from a bigger club.

Conference South side Dorchester Town came in for him and, once again, I couldn't stand in his way.

Within the space of about three or four weeks, I had lost the Western League's two top goal-scorers. Bushin had scored 14 for us, and Emati-Emati wasn't far behind. No matter what team you are, if you lose your two strikers who are the league's leading scorers, then it's going to hit you hard and knock you back. We were no different and, no matter how many years of managerial experience you have stored up, you're never going to simply pluck another top centre-forward out of thin air. I had no choice but to go with what I had, and that involved sending Dean Stevens up front to play alongside the big man Ricky Lee. Ricky hadn't featured that much due to work commitments and was lacking match fitness, but we had to just ride it out the best we could.

To make things even harder, I had to urgently find a new goalkeeper. Steve Johns had injured his ankle, so I managed to sign Luke Purnell who had played for me briefly at Odd Down. Luke had been a young starlet with Weston-super-Mare, but was now at college down in Plymouth and I knew he would be a safe pair of hands to bring in while Johns was recuperating. All this upheaval was clearly having a real effect on our league form and, during December and January, we lost six games in a row.

Of course, losing our two top strikers was one of the key reasons for this, but I also put part of it down to the very good FA Vase run we found ourselves on. As a manager, you want to win every game, of course you do. But at the same time, you know you're not going to win every game, especially with a thin squad like we had at Dawlish Town. I made the decision to pick players to play in the league who maybe weren't quite good enough, just so that I could make sure key players would be available to give the FA Vase a real go. We ended up taking Dawlish to the last 32 of the competition, the furthest they had been in 20 years.

Our Vase campaign had started back in October, before we lost Joe Bushin and Jules Emati-Emati. We beat Liskeard Athletic 3-0 at Sandy Lane, with Bushin scoring twice and Dean Stevens also finding the net, and that booked us up with another home tie against Wimborne Town in the second round proper. Wimborne were a very strong side, and it was probably one of the toughest draws we could have had. They went on to win promotion from the Wessex League at the end of that season but, on that Saturday in November at our place, they were thoroughly outplayed. We put in a great all-round performance to win 3-1. Radley Veale's deflected effort put us one up at the break, and two goals from Jules put us 3-0 up. Wimborne threw everything at us in the final stages, and their player-manager Alex Browne snatched a late consolation. After a performance like that, I told the press that I didn't care who we got in the third round. I felt we could beat anybody, and I meant it.

As it happened, we were handed another home fixture in the third round, which was the last 64 of the competition. Another Wessex League side were heading to Sandy Lane, this time Brockenhurst Town. I didn't think they were as good a side as Wimborne, but we knew they would be up for a Vase game and they certainly gave us everything they had. It was the first Saturday in December, and the conditions were appalling. It was chucking it down with rain, the pitch had been cut up pretty badly and, to make it even tougher, Brockenhurst forced extra time when they cancelled out Dean Stevens' long-range effort with about ten minutes of normal time to go.

Luckily this game came just before Dorchester Town got in contact with us, so I still had Jules Emati-Emati and he played on his own up front. Quite what Jules made of the conditions, I don't know. Having come over to Devon from Cameroon, via Spain, I think there was probably quite a lot about the English weather that shocked him. At one of our midweek games, we had headed up to Ilfracombe Town in the middle of a storm one Tuesday winter night. Anyone who has been to Combe's ground will know it's on the top of a hill, right on the North Devon coastline. There's very little to protect you from the elements! Chris Porter was on the pitch leading the pre-match warm-up in driving rain and with rumbles of thunder. Suddenly, a bolt of lightning lit up the sky and struck the roof of a small building right behind one of the stands. What a noise it made. The crack was deafening. Poor Jules was bricking it! A few minutes later, another bolt of lightning shot down from the sky and wiped out all the power in the area. That meant no floodlights, and I think Jules was the most relieved of all that the game was abandoned!

It may have been a culture shock to him, but he adapted to the conditions well against Brockenhurst and did a fantastic job of leading the attack on his own. By extra time it was hard to even stand up in the mud, let alone hold the ball up and move with it. But Jules did everything we could ask of him, and finally got the goal his tireless performance deserved when he finished off a cross from our young full-back Luke Martin in the second half of extra time. We wanted to try and avoid the replay in Hampshire if possible, and tensions were eased a few minutes later when Radley Veale pounced on a goalkeeper slip-up to tap home a third. We won 3-1, and all eyes were on Monday lunchtime's draw.

All I wanted, again, was a home tie, and I got my wish. The next name out of the hat was a Derbyshire side called Gresley, who were one of the lowest-ranked sides left in the FA Vase. I knew not to get too excited by that, though. This side was basically the same side that had always been known as Gresley Rovers in the old Unibond Northern League, until going into liquidation. As a result, they had reformed several divisions down the non-league ladder as Gresley in the East Midlands Counties League, but their pedigree was plain to see by the fact that they had knocked out one of the Vase favourites, Spennymoor Town, in the previous round.

Gresley came down to Dawlish on Saturday, January 16. And if you thought the weather was bad for the previous round against Brockenhurst, you hadn't seen anything yet! It chucked it down, non-stop, all Friday night and all the next morning. There must have been real concerns about the match not going ahead, especially after the pounding our pitch took just a couple of weeks earlier. Obviously we had to do everything within our power to get the game on, because Gresley had already travelled down the night before. Fortunately, the pitch passed the morning inspection by a local referee, and the match referee also said he was happy for it to go ahead when he arrived at Sandy Lane in the early afternoon.

What a game it turned out to be. I can't think of many games throughout my 50 years in football that could surpass it in terms of drama and tension. It had it all. Well, everything except a Dawlish Town win. The score was locked at 4-4 when the referee finally decided he had no other choice but to abandon the game during the second half of extra time. The conditions really were horrendous. The torrential rain was driving down vertically, and it was coming down so hard that I couldn't see the opposite end of the pitch from my dugout. In the middle of the pitch, the players were almost ankle-deep in mud.

Every one of our players gave his all, which was even more amazing given that we played the best part of 90 minutes with ten men. Our centre-half Paul Kendall had been sent off midway through the first half after pulling down one of their strikers. It was Kendall who had put us 1-0 up just a few minutes earlier when he'd got on the end of a Dean Stevens free-kick, helped on by Craig Fenner. The sending-off hit us hard though and, within the space of a few minutes, Gresley had scored twice before we were able to reorganise and they led 2-1 at half-time.

Things looked like they were only going to get worse in the second half, as again we were under the cosh and Gresley scored a third on the hour. With 30 minutes to go, we were 3-1 down with ten men on a deteriorating pitch. It didn't look good at all, but we weren't finished and scored three goals in 11 unbelievable minutes to come back from the dead.

The horrendous weather had benefited us in certain ways, namely the postponement of Tiverton Town's game. It meant we were able to call upon Joe Bushin and another striker, Adam Mortimer, who was registered for both clubs and turned out for us when Martyn Rogers didn't need him. It was Bushin who started our fightback in the 68th minute when he got on the end of a Dean Stevens cross. Three minutes later, Mortimer let rip from distance and got us the equaliser via a fairly hefty deflection. The lads were buzzing, and I really believed we could go on and win it. So did Mortimer and Bushin, with the former charging down an attempted goalkeeper clearance and the latter slotting home a fourth Dawlish goal.

We only had 11 minutes left to hold on, but how we didn't get a fifth to kill the game off in the final minute, I'll never know. If there's one player you would never bet against scoring with an open goal, it was Joe Bushin. Gresley had committed everybody forward, even their goalkeeper, in a last-ditch attempt to find an equaliser when they won a corner. We were able to break quickly and, from my position in the dugout, I watched Bushin charge down the wing with the ball. Out of the corner of my eye, I could see that the keeper was struggling to get back. Gresley's defenders were frantically trying to get back too, with a couple chasing Bushin and another couple heading towards the empty goalmouth. Bushin cut inside and, spotting his chance, drilled the ball. Chris Porter and I held our breath, and I think everybody in the crowd did too. Everything seemed to happen in slow motion… even the driving rain seemed to stop for a brief second or two! Unbelievably, the net shook but the ball wasn't in it. Joe had hit the side netting. Due to the state of the pitch and the fact that it was almost impossible to stand up straight on it, he just hadn't been able to get the connection he was hoping for.

It was a blow, but all was not lost. We were 4-3 up going into stoppage-time and, seconds before that break, Luke Purnell had made an absolutely fantastic save with his fingertips to deny Gresley scoring from their best chance of the half. I kept waiting for the final whistle. Waiting and waiting. But it never came. We got to the sixth minute of time added on, and there was still no sign of it. Then, as we approached the seventh minute of injury time, it had to happen. They went and scored their equaliser following a desperate goalmouth scramble. What a sickening blow. Their players were going absolutely crazy with their celebrations, and all we could do was stand in stunned silence, with the pouring rain rolling down our faces. We knew we'd have no chance to try and snatch it 5-4. The referee blew for full-time just one second after we kicked off. It meant Chris and myself had the task of trying to pick the players up for another 30 minutes of battle.

They were out on their feet. The conditions had sapped every bit of energy out of them, not to mention the numerical disadvantage that we had. I've never known so many players to go down with cramp after that final whistle. Craig Fenner is a strong and fit lad so, for him to go down in agony, it shows how hard they had worked. It was no surprise that the action slowed down in extra time, and I think it was the 111th minute when the referee finally decided enough was enough and abandoned the game. However I still can't work out where he found seven minutes of injury time from. There hadn't been any injury stoppages of note, and I think there had been five substitutions made. If you give each of those 30 seconds, that's still only two-and-a-half minutes. There was no point grumbling about it, though, we just had to get ourselves regrouped for a replay in Derbyshire. At least we thought we did. Several of Gresley's committee members were going spare in the main stand because they feared the game would have to be replayed, given that it had been abandoned and not reached its natural conclusion. A quick call to the FA soon calmed them down though… because 90 minutes had been played, we were all going back to Derbyshire in a week's time.

It was a quite stunning match, and one that I will never forget. It's just a shame that there were only about 300 or so people who saw it. Now that was an extremely good gate for Dawlish Town, who usually averaged around 60 to 80 fans while I was in charge. But it was such a good game, it deserved to be seen by so many more. We got to see a copy of the report in the local Derby newspaper, and Gresley's manager Gary Norton had said exactly the same thing. "It was an unbelievable match," he said. "I've been involved in a lot of games, but I can't remember a time when I have gone through such a range of emotions." I know how he felt!

The game was there for us to win, not just at Dawlish but also at Gresley in the replay. But on both occasions we let ourselves down. At Sandy Lane, that open goal would have put us 5-3 up, instead of drawing 4-4. And in the 120 minutes at Gresley, where we drew 1-1, we missed a penalty in the 88th minute that would have earned us a 2-1 win.

Their top scorer Brian Woodall opened the scoring in the replay after just seven minutes, and we found ourselves 1-0 down. We also had to do without the suspended Dean Stevens, which was a major blow. Stevens usually took most of our free-kicks and set-pieces so, in his absence, I gave Radley Veale those duties. Midway through the first half, he smashed the crossbar with a free-kick as we started to get back into the game. We were more than a match for Gresley, and in the 68th minute we were awarded a penalty that Veale drove home – but only after it had hit both the post and the goalkeeper! It was 1-1 and anybody's game, but it should have been ours with two minutes to go when the referee pointed to the spot again. He'd seen a handball after Fred Smith had whipped a cross in, and we had a golden chance to book our place in the last 16 of the FA Vase. Radley was suffering badly from cramp, so we thought it was safest that he didn't take this penalty. Instead, Adam Mortimer stepped forward but unfortunately the keeper saved it.

After that, it started to feel like maybe it wasn't to be for us. In extra time, we battled hard but just couldn't carve another chance like the one we had wasted in the 88th minute. In fact, Luke Purnell was excellent in goal as Gresley threw everything at him in the extra 30 minutes. Ultimately, though, the two sides could not be separated after nearly 240 minutes of intense football, so it all came down to a penalty shootout. The way the two games had gone, I just knew that this shootout wasn't going to be simple, and how right I was. After 14 penalties, we were still no closer to deciding a winner! Both sides had missed one each, and it was locked in sudden death at 6-6. A minute later, our FA Vase dream was over. We'd missed, they'd scored. That was it.

The worst moment for me was walking back into the changing room and seeing the two young lads who had missed their penalties, Dougie Ford and Fred Smith, sat in the corner in tears. I headed straight over to them and assured them that they should hold their heads up high. "You two should stand up and be proud of yourselves," I told them, in front of everybody. "At least you walked forward to take a penalty. There are far more experienced players than you in this room who still haven't taken one today, so be fair to yourselves and get your heads up... you've done nothing wrong." Even with those words, I knew the pair of them were going to be feeling terrible on the long coach journey back to South Devon. We decided to take a few quid out of the players' kitty and stock up on a load of bottles of beer from the Gresley bar. It helped them deal with the heartbreak of that defeat, because they were able to have a drink and a laugh on the way home. I meant every word of what I'd said. I was proud of them.

That defeat knocked us out of our stride completely and, as we started playing catch-up on all the league games we'd missed out on during this run, we started losing a few. After one defeat, I said to Chris Porter that we needed to draw a line under what had happened this season, and start planning a rebuild early. We decided to start looking for some good young players, bringing in full-back Kris Davis and midfielder Sean Adderley. Jules also came back to us after it didn't work out for him at Dorchester, and we staged a mini-revival. A 1-0 win at Corsham Town was followed by a 0-0 draw at Ilfracombe and two wins against Longwell Green Sports and Radstock Town.

Any momentum we had started to build, though, came grinding to a halt after that Radstock game. It took the best part of three hours for us to get there on a cold Tuesday night from Dawlish, and we'd won 1-0 when Davis scored his second goal in two games since joining us. However the chairman Dave Fenner called all the players together after the game and told them that times were tight and the club would not be able to give them their midweek travelling expenses for the rest of the season. When you've just battled hard to earn three points for the club, and you're facing a three-hour trip home and the prospect of not getting back until 1am, that's the last thing that any of the players wanted to hear. I wasn't happy with the way the players were told, and I told Dave so. I felt it would have been better to break it to them after a home game. I think Dave just wanted to get it off his chest as quickly as possible though.

With hindsight, that impromptu meeting was probably the beginning of the end of my time with Dawlish Town. I'd said at the first meeting we held back in pre-season that I didn't think the club could afford my travelling expenses, and it looked like I was going to be proved right. In truth, I don't think the club could even afford the expenses for Chris Porter as my assistant, even though he lived fairly locally. Strangely, though, at a committee meeting held in Torquay a short while later, there was even a suggestion that Chris and I may get offered three-year contracts. The pair of us talked it over and, although the idea sounded great in principle, we were both more than a little sceptical about whether the club could really afford to do that.

As the 2009/10 season came to a close, there were no signs that things were going to get any better. Things were breaking down, the changing room got flooded, and there were times when we were going to games with 11 players plus Chris Porter as substitute. Chris could certainly play a bit, but we were keeping things as tight as possible just to keep the wage bill down. Again, I don't want to start quoting exact figures, but I will say that during some games towards the end of the campaign, it was about 40 per cent of what I'd started with back in August. I was saving as much money as I could for the club by taking the smallest squads possible, and I'd also earned them a few quid in prize-money from that FA Vase run. But it still wasn't enough. Crowds and gate receipts were going down, officials expenses were going up, and times were tight.

After a summer off, I made my first pre-season visit back to Dawlish on a Monday night in June. I met with Dave Fenner, and he introduced me to the new youth team manager, so we sat down and discussed how we wanted the youth team to benefit the senior squad in the longer-term. All the right things were said, but I just had a hunch that something wasn't right. I don't know what it was, just a gut feeling I guess. I've always been the type of person who sometimes reads too much into these things, so I put it to the back of my mind, said goodnight to everyone and jumped in the car ready for my 90-minute drive back to Bristol.

Tuesday was a normal day of work, and I sat down on the sofa in the evening to watch one of the World Cup games on the television. We'd moved training forward to the Monday night so the Tuesday evening was free for the game, and I happily watched it at home before going to bed. As I climbed into bed, my mobile phone went and it was a text message from Dave Fenner. I started reading it. I can't remember exactly how it went, but it was along the lines of 'Jeff, Dave here, I'm feeling shit about this but I need you and Chris to resign with immediate effect'. It then said he'd call me at a later date. I just sat there and looked at it, stunned. Jo was lying in bed, and asked what it was. "Oh it's just the chairman at Dawlish," I said. "He wants me to resign with immediate effect, and Chris Porter too."

Jo knew I had told him that I didn't think the club could afford me a year or so earlier, and so it proved. I totally understand that the club shouldn't try and live beyond its means, and have no problem with that whatsoever. However I couldn't believe I was getting this information via a text message and not through a face-to-face chat. I'd certainly never been sacked via a text message before! I also couldn't understand why Dave hadn't just spoken about it to me in person. After all, I was sat at a table with him just 24 hours earlier. Mobile phones will be the curse of society. They allow people to hide behind their phone, rather than talking to other people in person. To this day I've had no thanks for what I'd done for Dawlish over the previous season, and no explanation why I was being sacked.

My son Paul and his family live in Dawlish, and Paul did ring me up the following week to tell me that Dave Fenner had admitted in the *Dawlish Gazette* that he was wrong to sack me by text message. In the story, Dave said that he hadn't discovered that the club budget needed slashing until the Tuesday morning and, because he was away in Scotland for work, he wasn't available to tell Chris and I in person.

In the report, Dave was quoted as saying: "I will put my hand up and say I didn't deal with it the way I should have done. I'd love to have looked him in the eye like I normally do and say 'we've got a problem'. The same goes with Chris. But I was under immense pressure from outside the box in terms of the finances. When I saw Jeff on the Monday evening, everything was fine, but on the Tuesday I had a meeting with a third party and the rug was pulled from under us. I had to make a decision. Being the chairman, decisions are based on what we know at the time. I dealt with it the way I did because I was away from home. But in this situation there is still light at the end of the tunnel as I'm hoping Jeff will still work with us. I feel that he's got a lot more to give to football, outside of being a team manager."

Of course, I know it came down to reducing the budget and cutting out my travel expenses from Bristol, and I understand why they needed to do that. But it would have been nice to have discussed it in person. As a bloke, I had always got on well with Dave. He was a nice enough chap, and fair play to him for holding his hands up to his mistake in the newspaper. But I still would have appreciated it more if he'd have said it to me, face-to-face, before one of the local reporters.

Needless to say, I didn't take him up on the offer of staying involved with the football club. As I said earlier, it was costing me at least £150 per week in petrol, so there was no way I was going to take any sort of voluntary position. When Dave spoke to the *Dawlish Gazette*, he also explained that my replacement, Adam Kerswell, was willing to do the job for nothing. Credit to Kerswell for that, but he lived locally and didn't need to fork out hundreds of pounds a month on fuel. Having said that, though, I do know he only lasted a few months before walking away from the club in October.

I felt especially sorry for Chris Porter. Chris is a cracking lad, and I enjoyed every minute working with him during that one season at Dawlish. It was a privilege to have him as my assistant, and I'm sure he'll go on to better things as a coach or manager. Although a text message dismissal was a disappointing way to finish my time at Dawlish, I'm not bitter about it and it was a fantastic and much-needed experience for me. I desperately needed that extra year to forget about the frustration of the job at Odd Down, and I really, really enjoyed my time with the players at Sandy Lane. It was an absolute pleasure to manage some extremely talented lads like Joe Bushin, Jules Emati-Emati, Gary Fisher, Dean Stevens and Craig Fenner. As a centre-half, I'm convinced Craig could play Southern League football with no trouble at all. I'd also equalled my best ever display in the FA Vase, and experienced two of the most amazing cup-ties I'd ever been involved in.

When I put my mobile phone down on my bedside table after reading that text message from Dave Fenner, I knew that it was my time to go. It was 55 years since I'd won my first medal in football with Whitehall School. I thought back on some of the memories and experiences that I'd built up over the half-a-century since then, but I kept telling myself as I laid down in bed: "Be grateful for everything, and retire gracefully." There and then, as I said goodnight to my wife, I knew the time was right to end my football journey.

My first visit back to Mill Road after being sacked as manager of Barnstaple Town. That's me in the away dugout as director of football with Welton Rovers. Pete Buckingham is in the background. PICTURE: NORTH DEVON JOURNAL

My last job was a season-long stint as manager of Dawlish Town. It was a great way to sign out, and I thoroughly enjoyed working with my assistant Chris Porter (right).

14... A long managerial journey

DURING my time in football, both in the dugout and with my boots on, I've run into some great managers who have done fantastic jobs in non-league football. Some I've got on with, others I haven't. Some, I'd even like to think I've helped to get them where they are today. Now I've finished taking you through my football journey, I thought it would be a good time to highlight a few of those managers who have played an important part in my life, either through playing for them, leading sides out against them, or just watching them develop their own managerial career. If you don't know them already, you'll recognise the majority of the names I'm going to mention from chapters earlier in the book.

I can't start anywhere else other than with my first manager Jackie Pitt, during my three seasons at Bristol Rovers. He only stood about 5ft 6in tall, but he was a hard man and very disciplined. You always listened to what he had to say, and you certainly wouldn't dream of ever daring to argue with him! At that age the players needed a certain level of discipline. Jackie was dealing with a bunch of 16, 17 or 18-year-olds who were within touching distance of being professional footballers. Players needed to know that they had to work hard for that honour, and to be respectful too.

When the chips were down, though, Jackie would always be in the front line with you. As disciplined as he was, there was a friendly side to him too and he was forever taking us out for coffees. Part of our trainee duties would be to carry out work at the ground at Eastville on a regular basis, and Jackie would always be there with us, telling us some fascinating stories from his professional playing career. You don't play more than 500 games for Bristol Rovers across a period of 14 years unless you're a seriously good player. As a manager, though, you respected him and you listened to him. He was a professional footballer for most of his life, and he knew what he was talking about. At our age, it was vital to have that sort of person guiding us, trying to keep our feet on the ground while also trying to educate and develop us.

After leaving Rovers and entering the local semi-pro playing scene, the next big character I came across was Ralph Miller. He was a totally different character to Jackie Pitt, and I learned more swear words in my brief time playing for Ralph than I had during about 20 years of living in Bristol! He was also a disciplinarian, but didn't have the professional background that Jackie had. As a result of not really having played at any top level of football, Ralph's type of discipline usually involved him storming about the place and bossing people around. That's not a criticism, because it didn't worry me in the slightest as a player. I was always prepared to take it and do what was asked of me on the pitch. At that time, I had no idea that I was going to go on and become a manager but, looking back, I was able to take parts of his approach to non-league management and use them myself.

Brian Birchall needs no introduction in this book. Not only was he one of my best mates and 1974 FIFA World Cup travel partner, but he was also one of my long-standing colleagues during my playing career. We started playing together in that Iron Acton side that won the 1969 Berkeley Hospital Cup and, when he started his own managerial career, I followed him to several clubs. As a non-league manager, Brian was the complete opposite of Ralph Miller. He was a tactician, he never shouted or raised his voice in the changing room, and I hardly ever heard him swear. Before a game he would read the side out, and then give us a team talk based on how the other side played – and how we should be playing against them. If it didn't go to plan, he would be there to put his arm around you afterwards. Brian always found that the softer touch got results. In the four years that I played for him at Hanham, we finished higher up the league than the club had done in quite a while, so he clearly had a point. While Ralph Miller had taught me when the right and wrong times were to read the riot act, Brian taught me a lot about trying to be calm with players. I saw how he used this style of man-management effectively, knowing the right occasion to put your arm around a player rather than give him a bollocking.

I finished off my Saturday playing career with Mick Millard, who was and always will be Mr Abbotonians. There's not a lot more I can say about Mick that hasn't already been said in my chapter on Abbotonians. Mick ruled the roost and oversaw everything from top to bottom at the club. You would do as he said, or you'd be out… there was no arguing, no ifs and buts, it was as simple as that! When it came to arguing with the opposition, Mick would always be right there alongside you. He earned the right to hold such an esteemed and respected position though, given the years and years of tireless work and dedication he put into building Abbotonians and taking them forward. Mick also gave me my first chance as a manager and, in my first couple of years as I was learning the ropes, he was always there for me to offer advice and assistance.

I must also mention little Les Britton, who was manager of our Clifton Wednesday side. Even though he was in his mid-50s, he played in a lot of the games too, so it was a different experience for me to be alongside a player-manager, rather than a dugout manager. Wednesday football for me was more about a laugh and a joke than serious football, but I still learned bits and pieces from Les. He was another tactician who would try to weigh the opposition up.

There were plenty of other managers who I played for, but it was characteristics from the above five that I took with me when I had to start shaping my own managerial style at Abbotonians. I tried to take aspects of all their styles – what I thought had worked for them – into the Abbotonians changing room with me. It must have worked because, little did I know it at the time, but it was the start of 31 years in football management!

Along the way I've run into a lot of top footballers who you can learn from – either by speaking to them, or just watching and observing them. One of those was the former Scottish international Joe Jordan. I'd seen Joe play for Scotland in the 1974 FIFA World Cup, and about 13 years later I was stood in the opposite dugout to him during a county cup competition at Ashton Gate. Joe was taking Bristol City's reserve team that night, while Les Alderman and I were at Mangotsfield United.

Funnily enough, I was watching Tottenham Hotspur's away game at AC Milan in the Champions League on the television the other night, and it reminded me of this particular encounter with Joe Jordan. The next morning, this Champions League game was plastered all over the newspapers. Not because Spurs had won 1-0, but because Milan midfielder Gennaro Gattuso had got involved in a right old scuffle with Joe on the touchline and had attempted to headbutt him. The image of an incensed Joe, mouth wide open and screaming with rage, going head-to-head with Gattuso – a man half his age – was all over the tabloids and on the news bulletins.

Joe may be well into his 60s now, but he's a hard man and Gattuso is either very brave or very stupid. I will say this to the Italian, though... I know how it feels! During our game between Mangotsfield and Bristol City's reserves, there was a point during the game when I too found myself going face-to-face with Joe. I can't even remember what sparked it off, but I can remember seeing the fire in his eyes and the veins in his neck bulging as we yelled at each other. It wasn't a pleasant experience, and I can verify that Joe Jordan does indeed get very upset on the touchline! However, I couldn't help but like and respect Joe. Yes, he gets upset, but he faces you straight on and says what he's got to say. Once it's said, that's it, forgotten. When the match was over that night, Joe was a perfect gentleman. He talked to us, advised us, and it was a great honour to be able to pick his brains after the game.

There were other managers who I'd regularly speak to for advice, even ones who I'd never worked with directly. One of those was Bobby Hope at Bromsgrove Rovers. We'd got to know each other well during my time at Trowbridge Town, when we met in the final of the Bill Dellow Cup. During the two legs of that final, I found Bobby to be an absolute gentleman, and we always stayed in touch. He was always on the end of the phone if I ever needed any help, and he was another one to have a wealth of professional experience and knowledge to delve into. He made the best part of 500 professional appearances for West Bromwich Albion, Birmingham City and Sheffield Wednesday in midfield, and even won two international caps for Scotland. Sadly we haven't been in touch for a long time and I've lost his number, but he was a person for whom I had a great amount of respect – both as a football manager, and a man.

My short spell as manager of the ill-fated Stroud side wasn't one of the most memorable jobs during my managerial career, but it did give me the opportunity to lock horns with another great character during the two games against Grantham Town. The man in the dugout next to mine was none other John Robertson, the Nottingham Forest legend who starred at the height of Brian Clough's success and had scored the only goal in Forest's 1-0 victory over Hamburg in the final of the 1980 European Cup. Robertson was hilarious, a real character. For 90 minutes I just kept hearing these little comments coming over from the neighbouring dugout, and all I could do was laugh at them. As soon as the final whistle was blown in our away game at Grantham, he came straight over to shake my hand. "I'll see you in my office straight away," he said. When I got there, he offered me the drink of my choice and was happy to talk about anything. I asked him some questions about his time in the pro game, and we chatted for ages. It was a real education, listening to some of his experiences and tales.

One of the stalwarts of the local Bristol scene I would regularly come up against was John Southern at Backwell United. Our paths first crossed when I was at Abbotonians, and we had both taken a similar path in management. Like me, he had started off in the Somerset County League and had built a fantastic side at Backwell that won the league four years on the trot. I've lost count of the number of barnies the two of us must have had during our time in opposing dugouts. He was a fiery bloke and we had some spectacular touchline disagreements over the years! But much like with Joe Jordan earlier, the respect between us off the pitch was always there. Even if we'd spent the previous 90 minutes tearing strips out of each other, it was all forgotten in the clubhouse. We would always enjoy a drink and a chat together, and I'm still in touch with John to this day. The two of us had a fierce rivalry, but a healthy one based on mutual respect and John was a very well-known character around West Country footballing circles.

When I moved down to Devon to take charge of Torrington in the 1997/98 season, I knew how tough it was going to be when I realised how few players were there. I knew the start of the season was going to be a backs-against-the-wall effort if we had any chance of surviving in the Western League's Premier Division. Ultimately, we didn't survive and went down. Things weren't any easier in the FA Cup either, because we were drawn away in the preliminary round to Bashley, who were flying high in the Southern League at the time. My wife Jo came from the New Forest originally, so I knew Bashley fairly well. I also knew it was a fairly small place, and that you'd miss it if you blinked while driving through it. With that in mind, I was more than a little surprised to find myself heading there for an FA Cup tie to take on a Bashley side managed by... Jimmy Case!

Jimmy Case was a top player in his day with Liverpool, and I couldn't for the life of me understand why he was manager of little Bashley. After all, he was a three-time European Cup winner and a four-time Division One winner with Liverpool, and had also gone on to play for, among others, Brighton & Hove Albion and

Southampton. As our coach arrived at the ground, we clambered out to see three of the nicest Mercedes cars you could possibly imagine parked outside of the club office. In front of each car, there were signs reserving the space for manager, chairman and president. It was clear there was some money floating about at Bashley!

I met Jimmy briefly before the game, and he said we'd have a longer chat and a drink together after the game, no matter what the result. That was fine by me, although they played us off the park. Little Torrington were in nowhere near the same league as Bashley, and we got hammered 9-0. We tried and tried, but even on our best day and their worst, we wouldn't have stood a chance. As we were walking off the pitch at the end of the game, Jimmy was very sympathetic and said he'd see me in his office shortly. When I got there, I've never ever seen so much drink in all my life... and as a former Abbotonians manager, that's saying something! We talked a lot about Liverpool, and the drink was flying down. By the time I got back to the Torrington team bus, it took all my concentration and effort get up the step. I could hardly stand up straight! But it was a very enjoyable hour or so I spent with Jimmy Case, that's for sure.

On the subject of my time at Torrington, that brings me nicely to a couple of managers I'd like to mention in Devon. These two blokes are complete opposites. I'll start with Bideford's Sean Joyce, who took over as manager at Bideford after a good career as a professional with Torquay United. I think Sean joined Bideford as a player initially after leaving Taunton Town in the late 1990s, soon becoming player-manager and, later, manager. He's been there for more than ten years, and he must have won more Western League titles than any other manager.

When I first met Sean, I must admit I found it quite difficult to get on with him. Whether it was his northern accent and mannerisms, I don't know. But over the years that I've been in the opposing dugout to him, he's always been a character that wants to win... but not at all costs. He wants to win the proper way, by playing the game of football, and I have a huge amount of respect for him for that. I've won a few against him over the years, and I've lost a few, but those games between Bideford and Barnstaple Town were always big occasions for everyone. Unless the weather decided otherwise, they would always be played on Boxing Day and Good Friday, and they were guaranteed to attract crowds approaching 1,000.

I'm very pleased to see that, after all those years of hard work in the Western League, he's now plying his managerial trade at a higher level in the Southern League with the Robins. I really do believe that, in the future, no manager will ever last longer at Bideford than Sean Joyce. It will also take a pretty magnificent effort for any other manager to win more Western League titles than Sean too.

Another Devon-based manager I'd like to mention is Clive Jones at Willand Rovers. I knew him as a player to begin with, at Bideford. He was a happy-go-lucky lad and went on to take over this club in the middle of nowhere called Willand. I'd never heard of them before, but we all have now… and a lot of that is down to the hard work and dedication of Clive Jones. Over the years he's worked and worked to take Willand up through the divisions, and at the end of the 2009/10 season they were runners-up in the Western League. The one team above them was Sean Joyce's Bideford, who finally opted for promotion to the Southern League. Willand is now a place where Western League sides do not like going to, because they know they're in for a very hard game. Years ago, they were just a village side playing county football, but Clive has turned them into a very strong, feared and respected outfit.

Finally, I can't talk about Devon-based managers without a mention for Martyn Rogers, who will go down as an absolute legend at Tiverton Town. I've known Martyn as an opposition manager and a friend for 20 of my 31 years in football management. What he's done for Tiverton Town is nothing short of phenomenal. After taking over in the early 1990s, initially as player-manager, Martyn took Tivvy to four Western League titles in five seasons. At the end of the decade, he achieved the even more incredible feat of winning back-to-back FA Vase finals at Wembley Stadium. Since then, he took Tiverton to the first round proper of the FA Cup twice, and along the way clinched two promotions to reach the Southern League's Premier Division.

Martyn stood down as manager of Tiverton Town after a difficult season in 2009/10, that saw them only just avoid relegation. As I write, he's now manager at Weymouth and I wish him all the very best there. But what an achievement, doing what he did for Tiverton. Just look at how many clubs I've been through during my 31 years of management. For the best part of 20 years, Martyn remained at one club and celebrated unparalleled success there.

We first locked horns on the touchline in the 1990s when he was at Tiverton and I was in charge of Chippenham Town. He was a strong and fiercely competitive manager, and always wanted to win. After Tiverton gained promotion to the Southern League, Martyn became a good friend and a very helpful contact for me. In my last year at Dawlish Town, Martyn's help was invaluable. Of course, he signed my top scorer Joe Bushin, but the advice and suggestions with regards to players was second to none. Of course, his main priority was to look after Tiverton Town, and that's why he wanted Bushin. But at the same time, Martyn was aware that Bushin was going to be a massive loss for us, and he went out of his way to help us. He loaned us another striker, Adam Mortimer, who went on to play an important part in our FA Vase run. He also recommended the centre-half Paul Kendall and midfielder Glenn Gould to me, and they too starred in our Vase games.

The last time I went head to head with Martyn in a game was the Devon St Luke's Bowl final in 2006, when his Tiverton side beat my Barnstaple Town side 2-1 after extra time at Mill Road. When the final whistle went after 120 minutes of back-and-forth action, Martyn was the first person to come over and shake my hand. He apologised for the cruel way in which we'd been beaten. Gestures like that show what an absolute gentleman Martyn Rogers is. I'll always class him as a good friend, and I wish him the very best of luck for wherever his career takes him next.

Over the years, I've seen a lot of my former players take their first steps into football management, which always makes me proud. Jamie Patch was one of the first to do so. Jamie played for me at Abbotonians, and went on to manage at Backwell United before taking Brislington from county football right through to the Premier Division of the Western League. He was a very technical player, and he's just as technical as a manager, and another lad who I have a great amount of respect for.

My old Abbotonians goalkeeper Dave Mogg, who joined us after being released from Bristol Rovers, has had a bit of a rough time as a manager, in my opinion. He went to Hallen, where he had no money at all and worked himself into the ground. He then went to Taunton Town as an assistant before ending up at Yate Town, where he was recently sacked. There's usually a fair amount of turmoil behind the scenes when a manager gets the bullet, and I believe this was the case with Dave leaving Yate.

Tony Ricketts played for me at Bath City, and he never dropped below the top level of non-league football as a player. He continued that trend as a manager. He played more than 700 games at Conference level in his career, and went on to manage Bath City before earning himself a job in charge of Bristol Rovers Ladies. This side at the time were playing in the FA Women's Premier League Southern Division, and Tony took them to the runners-up spot behind the division's only professional side, Fulham LFC, in his first season. A year later, they won the league at a canter. I believe they were crowned champions with a quarter of the season still to play. I only ever knew Tony as a player, and I've never been in an opposing dugout to him. But given the quality of players he's consistently worked with, both male and female, he's clearly earned a huge amount of respect from them to get the results that he did.

Another of my former goalkeepers, Steve Fey, has had a long managerial career too, spending 10 years at Clevedon Town. Before that, he had spells at Almondsbury and Old Georgians, where he cut his teeth as a manager. Steve was my first goalkeeper at Abbotonians before shooting off to play a higher level of football, and he did an equally good job as a manager. I know he recently tried to get back into the game but, for whatever reason, he couldn't get a club. I have no idea why, as he did very well in management for the best part of 16 years. However, like me, he's now permanently retired from management.

Those players just mentioned all played for me during the earlier chapters of my managerial career, however there are several younger lads who moved from the pitch to the dugout in more recent times... and they're still there now. They are the second phase of managers, who I've managed, including Andy Black, Jeff Meacham, Barry Yeo and Richard Fey.

After reading the chapter on Trowbridge Town, you'll be fully aware what sort of antics Andy Black got up to as a player for me. But I have to say he's a totally different character now he's taken on managerial responsibilities. He's strict, no laughing or joking, but he's won the Western League and has managed at Southern League level. He's now back at his original club, Cadbury Heath, and he's determined to take them into the Premier Division of the Western

League. I went to watch one of their games recently, and I got the impression that a little bit of the 'old' Andy Black character may be coming back.

Jeff Meacham started off his managerial career as Steve Fey's assistant at Clevedon Town, and did a lot of work behind the scenes there. He's now gone his own way and is manager of Brislington in the Western League. Like a lot of clubs at that level, money is hard to come by these days and Jeff is finding it very hard work. But whenever you see him, he's still the same Jeff Meacham that I knew 20 years ago when he played for me. He's always up for a laugh and always cracking a joke, and he's always at the bar! It's no surprise that we still enjoy a regular pint and a chat together.

The two youngsters that I'm going to mention now are the very last of my players to become managers, and both were with me during the Torrington years. Barry Yeo is still in North Devon as manager of Ilfracombe Town, while Richard Fey is also a Western League Premier Division manager with Bristol side Bitton. I got a chance to stand in the opposite dugout to Barry Yeo during my season with Dawlish Town. I can assure you that, for 90 minutes, Barry is an extremely strict manager. He's a big lad, 6ft 2in tall, and always commanded respect as a centre-half in his playing days. He commands just as much respect as a manager, and fair play to him for that.

Richard Fey is now learning that you need that little bit of a serious side to your personality when you become a manager. As you'll know from the Torrington chapter, Richard was always the heart and soul of the party and team spirit at Vicarage Field. He took his first steps as a manager at Cadbury Heath, but now he's at Bitton and he's doing a very good job, so much so that he's been given a three-year contract there. Although I've officially retired from management, I have said that I'm always available to help Richard if he needs me. I've scouted FA Vase opponents for him this season, and I'm always on the end of a phone if he ever needs to bounce an idea off me or ask my thoughts on something. I know Richard will do a great job for Bitton in the longer-term too, because he's a workaholic. He puts everything into it, and deserves every success that I'm sure he will get in the future.

There are two other managers I'd like to mention, who I have shared a dugout with. The first, of course, is Les Alderman. I started as his assistant at Trowbridge Town before going joint-manager with him, and we went on to Mangotsfield United and Bath City together. For those five or six years that we were together, I could not have worked with a greater gentleman than Les. He was always trying to help people out, and I do believe that this was his downfall at the end of the day. In the end, there were people out there who were trying to take advantage of his kind nature.

I've never known the reason why he walked away from Bath City, and I wouldn't dream of putting him in an awkward position where he feels he's got to tell me his reasoning. However, I have a feeling that certain players and committee men had upset him there, and he felt that he was being taken for a ride. Wherever Les went, he was always able to get a very good sponsorship backing, and I have a feeling that he feared he was only there for that reason. Again, Les has never told me this... it's just the feeling I got. If that was the case, then it was completely untrue, because Paul Richards wasn't that sort of chairman and Les had a great deal to offer as a football manager. I still keep in touch with Les to this day, and I always will do.

The final honourable mention must go to my old buddy Mike Ford, who I first came across when he was assistant manager at Welton Rovers. We struck up an immediate friendship and, over the past two decades, he's been my assistant, my coach, my youth coach and the eyes in the back of my head at a number of clubs. If there's one thing I regret, it's having that beer-fuelled argument with him down at Torrington and losing his friendship for 18 months. Thankfully, we've been able to get past that and we're now back being the great friends that we always used to be.

At the age of 72, as I write, Mike is still very much involved with the game and is currently the assistant manager at Shepton Mallet. He's still got the same passion and enthusiasm for football that he had when I first met him. His coaching manual is unbelievable, and I mean that literally. I saw him recently and he produced this book while we were recalling our time at Chippenham Town. Despite it being about 15 years ago, Mike pulled out this book where he'd written details of all the players who played for us. He'd analysed the positions they played in, how they performed, and everything was there... years and years of knowledge and experience, in the pages of this book. It was fascinating. I'm sure that, if his legs allowed him to do it, he'd still be out in the middle of the pitch coaching the Shepton Mallet lads now. Obviously, at the age of 72, he tends to use his mouth more than his legs these days! But through this book, I'd like to thank him for his friendship over the years.

15... Secretaries and chairmen

I T'S the managers or the players who are the usual headline-grabbers for any football club, however there's a lot of work behind the scenes that often goes unrecognised. There are no harder-working committee men and women than those who become club secretaries for non-league sides. They don't get paid, yet they are always on the phone, they are always sorting out all the necessary club administration and paperwork, and they always still find time to help players and management. Some are better than others, and I've worked with several of these unsung heroes over the years. Having just written a little bit about some of the managers I've worked for and against, I thought it would be a nice idea to do the same for the secretaries. After all, without their hard work and dedication, there probably wouldn't be a club left for me to manage!

Also, for every secretary you work with, there's a chairman you have to answer to. As we all know from watching the professional game, a club chairman can either be an absolute hero or a villain of the worst kind imaginable. On many occasions, he can go from one to the other in a very short space of time! As well as mentioning my secretaries over the years, I'll also take a quick look at the many chairmen who have been brave enough to take me on. I'll tell you what I think they did right, and what I think they did wrong!

As we know, my managerial career started at Abbotonians, and there was a bloke there called Roger Tarrant who was a complete workaholic when it came to the club. His main role was that of secretary, but there wasn't a job he wouldn't turn his hand to if required. You would see him marking the lines out on the pitch or sorting the kit out as regularly as you would see him carrying out his secretarial duties. To this day, he's still very highly regarded at Longwell Green for his dedication and effort. My chairman was Mick Millard and, once again, there's nothing more I can say about the great man that hasn't already been said in earlier chapters. Mick was a man mountain, what he said went, and he truly was Mr Abbotonians.

After Mick sadly passed away, and Abbotonians had merged with Longwell Green, George Threader took over as secretary. George had been the secretary at Longwell Green and, ultimately, it was our big pre-season falling-out that led to my resignation as manager. It's a shame it all blew up with George, because I have to admit that his actual secretarial work was very, very good. But as I explained earlier in the Abbots chapter, I believed that George thought he was more important than he actually was, and that's ultimately what sparked the row we had that summer evening that resulted in me walking away.

The chairman who took over after the merger was Bill Holloway, who had been chairman at Longwell Green. Bill was the complete opposite to Mick Millard. But he was also a very quiet man, a gentleman, and he understood football. I played with him a couple of .times when he was at the very end of his playing career, but I know for a fact he was a very capable player in his day. He played for Welton Rovers when they were in their heyday, and a lot of the other top Western League sides. Bill had a tremendous understanding of the local semi-pro game, and it really was a terrible shame that he died so early.

Moving on to Trowbridge Town, and I can only remember the first name of the secretary, which was Pam. I can't for the life of me remember what her surname was. Anyway, Pam would never go to away games so, whenever Trowbridge were away, I used to pick up the secretarial duties. To return the favour, I always used to get her to do some of my paperwork when we had home games, so it all balanced itself out in the end! The chairman Les Doel was an honest, straight-forward gentleman. I still don't know to this day what he and Les Alderman had argued about, but my principles at that time told me to back Les Alderman by resigning with him.

When Les and I went to Mangotsfield, there was a lad there called Paul Britton who was an absolutely top-class secretary. He was fantastic at his job, so good that we made sure he came with us to Bath City when we took over. Paul went on to become secretary of the Gloucestershire FA, and later took a position with the English FA at their Lancaster Gate headquarters. He went right up the ladder, and I can't say I'm surprised after seeing how efficiently he did the job for me at Mangotsfield and Bath. Paul enjoyed a good laugh and, even though he sadly passed away fairly early in life, he had more than a little bit of good luck in his time. He won about £180,000 on the Littlewoods Pools. I can still remember Paul hosting a very enjoyable party, free of all charge, at Mangotsfield when he found out that news. Now that was a lively party! It was a long time ago that he died, and I think he was only in his 40s. It was a terrible shock for everybody who knew him.

The chairman at Mangotsfield was Ralph Miller. In my chapter on my time there, it probably seems like I've run Ralph down a fair bit with my criticisms. But I played for Ralph when he was a manager, as well as managing for him when he was a chairman, and I'll say this for him... he was an absolute fanatic about football. He loved it. He worked hard every day of his life for Mangotsfield. I wrote earlier in the book how impressed I was with the summer work that had been done at Cossham Street when I was there. Well, that was all down to Ralph's dedication. It was Ralph's breeze blocks that were put up around the ground.

It sounds such a harsh thing to say, but Ralph's main failing as a chairman was the fact that he was such a good manager! When he finally 'went upstairs' and took over as chairman, he just couldn't let it go. That managerial instinct was still inside him, and it was constantly forcing its way out... much to the frustration of Les Alderman and I, who were desperately trying to manage the club in the way we wanted to. Even though he was chairman, Ralph was still itching to run the side. Behind the scenes, his work rate as a chairman was superb. Come 3pm on a Saturday, it wasn't so good!

When we went on to Bath, Paul Britton came with us as secretary and he was basically doing the job professionally. He was able to do that thanks to the huge sum of money he won. After that, Paul was able to pack in his job with Rolls Royce and concentrate on doing what he loved... working in football. Although the role of secretary at Twerton Park was only a part-time one, you were guaranteed to see Paul there every day of the week. That commitment, coupled with the time he gave up to do the job, is what helped him do it so successfully. It's also why he ended up with a desk at Lancaster Gate and fair play to him, he thoroughly deserved it.

During his time with us at Bath City, I know for a fact that Paul also helped out the chairman Paul Richards a lot, and did some work for his business too. Paul Richards was a lovely bloke as well, and a great chairman to work for. He was also a top-class businessman, and that rubbed off in every aspect of the way he conducted himself around the club. Whether he was in the boardroom, the president's lounge or sat in the stand, he was a complete professional. After all the club's guests and visiting officials had left Twerton Park on a matchday, Paul Richards would then join us in the players' bar and you'd see a completely different side to him. He was a man's man, and he'd have a laugh and a joke with everybody. On numerous journeys home from away games, he would instruct the coach driver to pull over if he saw a country pub that he liked the look of. The next thing you knew, chairman Paul would be taking a group of 20 footballers and officials into the pub and treating them to steak and chips.

My brief spell at Stapleton was far from memorable and not much more enjoyable, but I couldn't write this chapter without giving a mention to Trevor Lewis. Trevor was a very hard-working bloke, and it was him who was pumping the money in to keep the club going while I was there. From what I saw, I always felt he was being taken for a bit of a ride by some of the other people at the club.

I'm starting to sound like a bit of a broken record when I use the phrase 'hard-working' to describe all these secretaries, but that's what they were. I'm going to have to use the term again, I'm afraid, this time to describe Arthur Wimble, who was the secretary for me at Chippenham Town. Arthur was a single man, and he was also at retirement age so had a lot more time to give to the club. Every day, you could find him cleaning the changing rooms, the committee rooms or the bar. The place was always spotless. On the other hand, I haven't got many good words to say about the chairman Doug Webb. He was fairly good to me for three years, but when the chips were down, I didn't like the way he behaved towards me when I was asked to reapply for my job.

By now, I was managing back in the Western League and I'd have a lot of dealings with the league secretary Ken Clarke. I've been critical of the Western League's committee in the past, and I believe there should be more 'football' people on the board, but any criticism I've made certainly doesn't apply to Ken. He's always been fantastic at his job, and he is as helpful a league secretary as any manager could wish for. He knows the game, he knows the league and I was always happy to help him out if ever I could. Although I've not worked with him in a manager-club secretary role, Ken definitely deserves a mention.

Graham Avery was yet another hard-working secretary who I met when I ventured down to North Devon to take over at Torrington. But now we've come to talk about Torrie, I must say a few words about the best chairman I have ever worked for. Winston Martin once told me during one of our end-of-season tours in Dublin that he would never ever sack me. I believed him, and I still believe what he said to this day. Winston was a man who had complete trust in me, and backed me in every decision I made. As a football manager, you couldn't have wished for a better chairman than Winston. If Torrington had been a club in a big town, then I think it's a safe bet to say that I would have never left. The committee, led by Winston, were impeccable, but the only thing stopping it being a perfect job was the location. Year in, year out, it was such a struggle to find the money for expenses. It was always Winston's hard graft that would somehow help to raise the money, but I just couldn't see Torrington ever going any higher. I was getting older, and I just felt I had to take the chance to go to a club where I saw Southern League potential.

That's why I accepted the offer from Barnstaple Town in 2002, which is when I became very good friends with Dave Cooke. I knew Cookey before taking the job at Mill Road, as our paths had crossed at plenty of games during my time in Western League management. But our friendship really took off when we worked together at Barnstaple, and I've since been to Spain and Dublin with him on jolly-ups. At this point I'd like to add that other people came too… it wasn't just Cookey and I! On a match-day at Mill Road, you'll always find Cookey in his little secretary's hut by the main entrance to the ground. He'll no doubt be in there, chomping on his cigar and dealing with some sort of club business. Before and after the game, he'll be in the clubhouse sorting out everything that needs to be sorted.

The chairmanship at Barnstaple Town was a bit more complex, and I went through four different acting chairmen during my five years there. The last of those four was Steve James, but sadly I never got the chance to work for a full season with him. He took over midway through the 2005/06 season, which was my last full campaign in charge. It was Steve who then had to call me up while I was in Guernsey, about a month into the following season, and inform me that I'd been sacked. It was a shame I didn't get the opportunity to work with Steve for a longer period of time. I felt he had the potential to be a top-class chairman for me, and he still can be for Barnstaple Town. If anything, I'd say that perhaps he needs to work on his own and trust his own football instinct, and not listen to what people around him are saying.

After my brief spell as director of football at Welton Rovers, the main factor in my decision to return to management with Odd Down was their chairman Mike Russell. I didn't particularly warm to the club on the times that I visited there, but I liked Mike and he was really up against it there. I considered myself retired when I finally decided to take the job there and help Mike out. When I joined, I soon found out that he was another one of these unsung heroes who was doing it all. He cleaned out the changing room, he made sure the money was always in the wage packets, he poured the beers behind the bar, and he was a very nice man. Away from the club, his wife was very poorly and, on top of everything he was doing at Odd Down, he then had to go home and care for her. I have nothing but admiration for people like Mike. It is hard work being a manager, but nothing like the responsibilities these chairmen have got, trying to keep their club afloat in such testing times.

We now move on to my last club, Dawlish Town. I haven't got a bad word to say about the secretary Sandra Walmsley. She was as straight as a die, and very sharp at her job. I had no chance of fiddling any crooked team sheets with Sandra on the case! I covered my sacking at Dawlish quite extensively a couple of chapters ago, so there's not too much more I can say about my chairman Dave Fenner. It was the one and only time in my career that I've been sacked by a text message! I've already criticised Dave for the way he handled that whole situation, but I would say that, chairmanship aside, he's actually a decent enough bloke who I got on quite well with. I wish both Dave and Sandra the best in the future, and that wish is extended to all the people I've mentioned here who are still with us. I hope they enjoy the rest of their years as much as I'm planning to enjoy mine!

16... Let them have their say!

YOU will have noticed by now that are three names that keep cropping up in this book whenever there is a good tale to be told. These are the three characters who account for some of my favourite memories within the game, and that's largely down to their drinking prowess and ability to have a great time wherever they go. Throughout my career, I've had more laughs with Derek Jones, Jeff Meacham and Richard Fey than I could possibly remember. Between the three of them, they have been ever-present in the best part of three decades of my life, and we're all still great friends to this day.

I've been speaking to Derek, Jeff and Richard an awful lot since deciding to write this book, because I knew they could help me recall some of our finest moments from years gone by. I can't tell you how many laughs we've had remembering some of our experiences. Some have made this book, but many are quite frankly unprintable! On one occasion I met up with Richard at a pub in Bristol to chat about our time at Torrington together over a few pints … all in the name of research, of course! At one point we had a visit from a very disgruntled businessman, who informed us that he had to call a halt to his meeting because they couldn't hear each other speak over our fits of laughter. I politely told the gentleman in question that we were in a public bar and, if he wanted to hold such an important meeting, then he'd be better off booking a conference room. He stomped away, and the laughter quickly resumed.

With the book nearing its conclusion, I thought it would be a good idea to get the three of them together so we could all have a good laugh together. We're all in contact regularly, but it's always good to get the four of us sat around a table of beer – and writing this book gave us all the perfect excuse! Richard's the youngest of the four by quite a distance. In his early 30s, he's only half my age, but it doesn't matter a bit. We are all united by our experiences together, and our love of the game that we put so much of our lives into.

Anyway, the main outcome of this beer-fuelled evening in the Premier Inn bar at Emersons Green – other than a few sore heads the next morning – was an invitation from me to the three of them to contribute towards this book. After all, I've told a lot of stories about them over the previous chapters, so it's only fair that I give them the opportunity to write a little bit about me. I told them they could write anything they wanted, good and bad, and assured them that the first time I'd see it was when the book was put together. If any of them decide to discuss my weaknesses, then I reckon cider might get a mention or two. But now I'm just waiting to see which one of them has stitched me up good and proper! So without further ado, I'll hand over to my long-time friends Derek Jones, Jeff Meacham and Richard Fey.

DEREK JONES

I was 16 years old when I first met Jeff, and I'd just been released by Bristol City. I started playing for Hanham Athletic and Jeff was there as a player. He was playing at right-back, which was where I thought my best position was, but Jeff kept me out of the side. The manager at the time was Brian Burchill, God rest his soul, and when it became clear I wasn't going to get a place in the first-team, he released me. I then went on to play for Brislington and Clevedon Town, which is where I met Steve Millard. Steve and his dad Mick were well associated with Abbotonians by that time, and he asked me to join them up there. I've pretty much been there ever since!

I had one season away at Cadbury Heath, but came back to Abbotonians when Jeff took over from Steve Millard as manager. Knowing what Jeff was like from his days with Hanham, I knew we were going to have a bit of fun when he took over. That's what my Saturday afternoons were all about… having fun. Sometimes we had too much fun, like the trip down to Holsworthy for the second leg of the Sutton Transformer Cup Final. What a craic we had down there, but it was a nightmare the next day!

I think, of all the cup exploits we had, the Somerset Cup down at Backwell was the most memorable. What a piss-up we had that night. We'd beaten Bishop Sutton 3-2 and we used to have quite a big following back then. Everyone was just rolling around, drinking whisky out of the cup, and we ended up at the local nightclub, Chasers. I knew the owner Fred Britton fairly well, and managed to persuade him to let us all in for free. In we all went with the cup, and what a night it was. We had some great times. We took things seriously when it came to kick-off time, but we knew how to enjoy ourselves too.

The team spirit at Abbotonians was fantastic, and it carried us through. We weren't exactly the best team with the best players, but all the lads at the club would have died for each other. If any of the players had a problem, all the others would be there to back them up, and that was the type of attitude that Jeff was looking for. He was a fairly young manager in those days, and he was one of the boys really. He always talked a lot of sense, and he always got the best out of the players. He is definitely one of life's characters, and the whole team was full of people like that. The banter and the piss-taking used to reach unbelievable levels. We were all so scared to say or do anything out of line, because we knew we'd be in for it from all the other lads! It all made for a great atmosphere.

On the way to that cup final, I always like to remind Jeff that I was the penalty shootout hero when we knocked out Wells City. We didn't have floodlights back then, and it was getting really dark by the time we got to penalties. I remember all the people with cars next to the pitch switched their headlights on, to try and stop the referee from calling it off! They were taking the nets down at the other end, and I was the last one to take a penalty. I put the ball down on the spot, started my run-up and just shut my eyes and hit it. The goalkeeper dived to his right, and the ball went to his left, bounced three times and bobbled over the line. I stood there with my hands in the air as all the lads ran over and jumped on top of me. It was a great moment, and definitely the most pressure I've felt in football just before taking that kick.

I said earlier that Jeff was like one of the boys, but he could hand out a bollocking too if someone deserved it. You just had to take it if you wanted to stay in the side. You had to play how he wanted you to, or not at all. Whenever Jeff did dish out a bollocking, it was always forgotten straight after… that was the type of team we were. What gets said in the changing room stays there, and in the bar he'll buy you a pint. That's the way it should be.

The best thing that we did under Jeff was to start training with Forest Green Rovers. It got us more football-orientated on training nights because they were a good side, but the Forest Green lads all liked a drink afterwards too. The two clubs were very close together, and the fact that we beat them 1-0 in the match to help them prepare for their FA Vase semi-final shows what a good side Jeff had put together at Abbotonians. We all went up to Wembley Stadium to watch Forest Green play in the final, and that was one hell of a night out in London. A lot of us had a Sunday League cup final on the Sunday with Embletonians, so we all had to motor back down the motorway with raging hangovers. We lost it too, but I reckon we would have won it had we not had the hangovers.

We were in the hotel bar that night after the Wembley game, and I can remember being at the bar with Jeff and a few others. There was this display cabinet stacked full of bottles, wine and spirits, and when none of the staff were looking we slid the doors open and nicked as much booze as we could! Jeff and the rest of us pegged it back to the rooms, where we thought we'd neck all this free booze we'd just pinched. But only when we opened the bottles, did we realise they were all full of cold tea and water! We were fairly well gone by then anyway, and we were just rolling about with laughter. What a craic it was. The next morning driving down the motorway, we were feeling rough but there was all the usual banter and several of the lads were hanging their arses out the windows. They were good times.

I'm still with Abbotonians now, or Oldland Abbotonians as we're called these days. The most important thing that I've taken from Jeff is the importance of a team spirit. I saw what wonders it worked for us back in the early 1980s, and it's something I still believe is vital for any club today. Oldland have got that team spirit today and that's why they've been successful lately. You can't have prima donnas in the side. There are players out there who just wind other players up... they shout and ball at the younger lads when, in actual fact, they're no better themselves. There would always be the odd player who thought he was better than what he was, and Jeff soon brought them back down to earth. He was a great leveller, and still is a great friend. It was non-stop laughter back in those days, and it still is whenever we meet up. They were very good times.

JEFF MEACHAM

I didn't even drink before I met Jeff Evans! I was a young lad, 17 or 18 years old, and I just didn't like the taste of the stuff, but that soon changed when I got involved with Abbotonians. I was first introduced to Jeff at a game I was watching. I assumed he was just part and parcel of the committee at Abbotonians, but I noticed how close the team were, and how they'd all be having such a good laugh together. Whenever they were sat down around a table having a good time, Jeff always seemed to be the focal point of it. You could tell that everyone respected him and enjoyed his company, and I soon realised that he was an important part of Abbotonians.

As time went on, Jeff took over from Steve Millard when he moved on. I moved on as well, to Glastonbury, but always stayed in close touch with Jeff and I didn't have to think twice when he asked me to come back and play in a Gloucester Amateur Senior Cup semi-final for Abbots. I decided to tell Glastonbury that I'd hurt my foot at work, so I explained to the manager that I'd dropped a brick on it and there was no way I'd be able to play for them on Saturday. Instead, I was shot off to meet up with Jeff and Abbotonians! I scored in the semi-final, and ended up staying with them for the rest of the season. We went on to the final at Bristol Rovers' old Eastville ground, and Jeff left me out of the side! It was one of those things, and Jeff was doing what he thought was right for his club, which was fair enough.

When Jeff was at Trowbridge Town with Les Alderman, Les had asked him to try and sign me. As soon as the phone went and I knew it was Jeff, I didn't have to think twice about going to play there. I knew what Jeff was all about… I knew we'd be having a great laugh there, but also taking the football seriously and playing at a good standard. Jeff told me that Les would sort out my money, but I told him straight away that I wasn't worried about the money. I was there because I knew what the team spirit would be like, and I wanted to be part of it. Obviously we all wanted to win, but the fun that went with it was fantastic. Jeff was always very big on the social aspect after the games, which was good.

I had a great time at Trowbridge, both on and off the pitch, and it helped me get a move to Bristol Rovers, and Weymouth after that. By the time I got to Weymouth, Jeff had taken over at Bath City and it wasn't long before he was on the phone again. I was under contract at the time, but the two clubs set up a deal and I joined up with Jeff for a third time. When I first joined Bath, I was in the middle of serving a suspension for something I'd done in a Sunday League game. We only had a brief time together at Bath, and that was the last time we were ever in the same team together, but we've stayed good friends ever since. I was a teenager when I first met him, and I'm nearly 50 now. It's a long, long time. Jeff was always keen on the social scene, and he still is. When I told my wife I was going to meet Jeff to chat about his book, she told me to book a taxi. I said I'd drive and wouldn't have a drink. "Yes you will," she said. "You're going out with Jeff Evans!" Even she knows what he's like, and appreciates what he's about.

When I finished playing, I went to be assistant manager to Steve Fey at Clevedon Town for a number of years, and then joined up with Jamie Patch at Backwell United. I was also Jamie's assistant at Brislington, but now I've taken the main job there. I would always run into Jeff in opposing dugouts when he was managing teams like Torrington, Barnstaple Town and Dawlish Town. In a weird way it was good that Jeff went down to Devon to manage, because it meant there was always a familiar and friendly face for us when we travelled down there for games. All the Bristol players liked Jeff too, and they always used to enjoy seeing him down there. They always used to laugh at this little thing he did with his glasses, when he'd push them up his nose with his finger. They'd all be watching out for it in the clubhouse, and would be in hysterics every time he did it!

The three times I played under Jeff were all at very different standards of football. Firstly it was county football with Abbots, then it was Southern League stuff with Trowbridge, and then it was for a Bath City side trying to get into the Conference. No matter what the standard, Jeff was still very keen on the social side of building a team spirit, but he also got the right people in around him and took the football as seriously as possible. Jeff was involved in a lot of football over the years, and knows a lot about the game. He also knows a lot of players, both in Bristol and in Devon. Bath City was a big jump up in standard, but he stuck to his guns and still put the emphasis on the social side, and that's what I respected him for. When he was managing with Les, Jeff did a lot of the running around and was always on the phone to this player and that player, persuading them to sign for him. That's what he was good at.

In our teams, we had good players, but more importantly we had the right players. That's what I'm trying to do now at Brislington, it's what Jeff has passed on to me. Jeff always wanted players who were desperate to win, but who were also willing to have a laugh together afterwards. You've got to have the fun in football. You've got to enjoy it, and appreciate it, and Jeff taught me that. He soon got me off the milk too! That's all I used to drink when I was young, until I met those lot. Jeff told me to drink cider, but I soon knew I didn't like that, so I've stuck to lager since!

I've got plenty of drinking stories that stick in my mind from cup finals or weekends away with the team, but I think I'll keep them in my mind for now... they're probably not safe for publication! The double-header weekends away with Trowbridge Town were absolutely superb. We'd all want to go out and have a few beers after the first game on the Saturday night. With Jeff, we didn't usually ask whether we could go out or not. It was always 'how long can we stay out for?' There was one occasion when we all got back to the hotel after a few beers and Andy Black had lost his room key. We couldn't get him into his room, and Jeff had the room opposite, so he said he'd climb out his window and climb in through Andy's window to let him in from the inside! "No, no, no Jeff, you'll kill yourself," we were all saying. In the end, someone had to leg it down to reception and get the master key to stop Jeff climbing out of this hotel window!

The Wembley trips with Jeff and the guys were brilliant. I was the youngest one of the group, so it was definitely an experience for me. They always used to take turns in driving, but I was only a young lad at the time and didn't have a car. Steve Fey always prided himself on having an immaculate car. It was absolutely spotless. Jeff always used to like winding him up about it. "You wait until we're all pissed up in here on the way back home, Feyer," he'd say. "This car's going to get in a right old state!" Jeff used to smoke the odd cigarette back in those days, and I can remember one time he was having a bit of a joke at Steve's expense by waving this cigarette about. He kept pretending to push it into the roof of the car. The trouble was, Feyer drove over a bump as Jeff was doing this and the cigarette end went right into the roof, burning a hole right through the material! Feyer went spare, but it was brilliant, we were just in hysterics in the back seat.

After watching the England games up there, Jeff would use his contacts to get us into these VIP bars where the players would go for their post-match drink. Being a young lad, I was a little bit 'raw', shall we say. We were all sat down having a few beers after one game, and Phil Neal was stood nearby. Jeff and the guys were having a good laugh and swearing away, when I thought it would be a good idea to have a bit of a dig at Neal. "Don't swear in front of stars," I said, making sure he could hear it. He came right over to me, and said: "What did you say, punk?" We managed to calm the situation down, and I always wonder why I said that. I guess it's because I was young! We had great times in those bars after the England games, though. I don't know how Jeff managed to get us in each time. It was a real eye-opener for me at that age, and it was just an education to be going out with them.

Nothing will ever change when we all get together. When I knew Derek Jones was coming as well, I thought we'd need to end up writing another book with the amount of stories he's got! There are stories upon stories, and it's been a brilliant laugh knowing Jeff all these years.

RICHARD FEY

I've known Jeff Evans all my life. Even though I was only two or three years old, I can always remember Jeff coming round to our house. He was good mates with my dad Steve, who played in goal for him at Abbotonians. I'm 33 now, so you're going back 30 years. When Jeff used to visit, usually on a Friday, I'd be in the kitchen and my mum or dad would always ask me: "Who's the big fat man?" "It's Jeff," I would answer as a little lad. Then one time, they asked me that question and, as I answered, Jeff jumped out from the corner to surprise me. It terrified me! I ran off to my bedroom crying, and locked myself in my room! I'll never forget it. Little did I know at the time, but 20-odd years later he'd be shouting at me every Saturday afternoon!

Fast forward to when I was about 17 years old and, as a young goalkeeper, I'd just been released by Bristol Rovers. I packed in football for a year after getting that news, and of course Jeff could sympathise with exactly what I was going through because the same thing had happened to him. I started playing again as a goalkeeper, but I got messed around by Bristol Manor Farm and was told I wasn't good enough. After that, I just wanted to have a laugh with my mates and ended up playing as a midfielder for Hanham Athletic's third team.

After a while at Hanham, I heard from Jeff, who was trying to persuade me to go down and play for him at Torrington. He told me he didn't have a goalkeeper and that he needed me to sign immediately. Eventually he turned up at my house and kept on at me, telling me that he'd pick me up the next morning and take me down for the game at Torrington. I don't think Jeff was going to leave the house until he got the answer he was looking for! In the end I said I would and signed on for him, and the next day we went down to

North Devon and I played in goal for him. We lost 4-1, but it could easily have been double that and I had a blinder. After the game, Jeff told me he needed me to play for Torrington for the rest of the season, which I did.

Although we got relegated at the end of that first season, it really took off from there and those years I had playing for Jeff at Torrington were fantastic. To be honest he's like a father to me, having known him for as long as I can remember and having played under him too. I've been away with him, I've shared rooms on tour with him, and he made me his captain at Torrington. After being released from Rovers and then my time at Manor Farm, I went off the rails a bit and just wanted to have a laugh and enjoy life. But Jeff took me under his wing. He'd talk to me on the phone and offer advice, long before I finally signed for him at Torrington.

The first time I ever went to Torrington, I couldn't believe what the place was like. It was in the middle of nowhere and, when I walked into the changing room, it was so quiet. Slowly but surely, the atmosphere started to pick up. I started really looking forward to Saturday mornings again, even the two-hour trip from Bristol down to Devon. We used to have a right laugh in the car on the way down, and after a while we started winning a lot of games, so the spirit was good and we'd end up staying over at the hotel and having a good night out with a few beers.

After that, Jeff kept signing great characters. One by one, they'd join us and the atmosphere in the changing room was unbelievable. In all my time playing, and now as a manager, I've never known a team spirit like it. That's what Jeff did so well at Torrington. Although we had fun, Jeff was also strict when he needed to be. In all the games I played for Torrington, I had one or two nightmares and Jeff would always let me know about it. But if you'd done well, he'd also be the first to tell you.

A lot of my mates in Bristol couldn't believe it when I first signed for Torrington. They'd never even heard of the place! Every pre-season, I'd get calls from Bristol clubs asking me to come along to training, and they couldn't understand why I was going down there every week. But the travelling became as much a part of it. Every Saturday was the same. Jeff would pick me up in the morning at Bristol, we'd stop for a coffee in South Molton, and get to the ground for 1.30pm. We'd play the game, stay in the clubhouse until around

6pm, over to the Barnstaple Hotel for a few beers, and then get changed to go out on the town. We used to have some cracking laughs, and stagger back to the hotel at around 3am or 4am in the morning!

The journeys down the M5 were a good laugh. We used to pick up a lad called Geraint Bater, who I knew in Bristol and had persuaded to sign for Torrington too. His dad Phil is the manager of Mangotsfield United in the Southern League. Ger and I used to get a copy of the *Western Daily Press* while we were waiting for Jeff, and it became a standing joke in the car to go over the classifieds and ring up for some random item. One time, I called up a woman who was selling a bird cage and, after finding out a bit about it, I asked her if I could fit my baby in it! She started having a right go at me, she was going ballistic, and Jeff had to pull over because the tears were rolling down his face. He couldn't see through his glasses! I think we ended up beating Hallen 5-0 that day.

On the way home, the fish and chip shops gave me just as much entertainment. I always used to make sure I was the first one in there and, without fail, I'd unscrew all the lids to the salt and vinegar. The next person to come along, which was usually Karl Madge, Karl Baggaley or Lee Gitson, would end up getting a pot of salt on their food. It took them about 14 weeks to work out it was me, and I ended up getting banned from the chippy!

Those lads were just a few of the characters that Jeff brought in. Barry Yeo was another great lad in the Torrington changing room, and I still keep in touch with him to this day. We see each at least twice a year on the touchline, as he's the manager at Ilfracombe Town now. There were two local North Devon lads who came in, Darren Polhill and Gary Bedler, who settled in with us straight away and were a brilliant laugh. Out of all of them, though, I think the funniest lad in the team had to be Danny Robinson. Barry and I were the clowns of the dressing room, but I took to Danny straight away because he'd always be up for a laugh and never took himself too seriously. I remember one game, he turned up wearing women's underwear for a laugh! All the boys were in absolute stitches, but that was just the type of atmosphere we had down there.

Wherever we went on our end-of-season tours, be it Jersey or Dublin, I would always end up sharing a room with Jeff, including the tour when he had a set-to with a bouncer on the door of one of the bars. It was probably my fault, because Barry and I had just chucked Dave Newsome into a bin for a laugh, and the bouncer had seen us doing it. When we got to the door, this bouncer said he wouldn't let Dave in because he stunk! Jeff immediately stuck up for Dave – he will always back his players – and it ended up all kicking off. I jumped in to help, and we were all told to leave. I ended up going for a stroll and a kebab with Jeff that night, and it must have been well past 2am by this time. That Ireland trip where we missed the flight home was unbelievable too. I don't know what the bus driver was playing at. Jeff's wife Jo has been brilliant over the years, though. We all had to ring home to say we wouldn't get back on time, and in the end we were almost two days late home after that trip. Jo has always been as good as gold about stuff like that.

Becoming a manager has all happened quite quickly for me. I'm still only 33, but I'd hurt my knee and, although I could have carried on playing, the doctors warned I may struggle with it later in life, so I decided against it. I got the opportunity to take over at Cadbury Heath, which I took, and Jeff was the first person I called. I actually asked him to come along and be my assistant manager, but he was at Dawlish Town at the time and said he wasn't interested. I then took over at Bitton, and asked him again to come along with me. He was still at Dawlish, and gave the same answer.

Funnily enough, my first game as manager of Bitton was against Dawlish Town. I hated it. We won 4-0, but I hated every minute of it! The excitement and adrenalin in the build-up to the game was second to none, but when it came to the game, it was really difficult seeing Jeff in an opposing dugout. Ideally I wanted it to be a draw! We were going nowhere in the league, and nor were they. We won 4-0, but the two of us had a good few pints together after the game!

I only had about seven games at Bitton at the end of that season, and the final match was the return encounter down at Dawlish. We won 3-0 then too, and I hated every minute of that game too because Jeff's chairman was over by the dugout and I felt bad for him. After everything he'd done for me, and all the advice he'd given me over the years, I felt terrible for putting him under any extra pressure with his chairman. I didn't want to be the one to take six points off him. But he told me after the game that the experience was a learning curve for me. I don't think Jeff would have felt the same me towards me, bearing in mind he's got 50 years of experience behind him!

When he finished at Dawlish over the summer, I asked Jeff again if he'd come along and assist me. He told me he'd drawn a line under his football management career, and that he'd done his shift, and fair play to him. I still make sure I speak to him every day for advice. He helps me with ideas and opinions on players, on formations, on teams we're going to be playing. We played a game at Bitton the other week and drew 1-1. After it, Jeff phoned me up and gave me a bollocking for making a wrong substitution! That's just Jeff. He wants me to do well, I know he does, and that's why he helps me.

He went and scouted a few of our opponents in the FA Vase this season and the information from both him and his son Clive, who's also a great bloke, has been second to none. He went to watch Downton play in the Wessex League, and they were a side who hadn't lost in 25 or 30 games. Jeff came back to me with a report on their formation, the way they played, their set-pieces, everything. It worked. We went down there and beat them 2-0. Jeff comes to watch at Bitton quite a few times now. I'd much rather have him in the changing room with me than sat in the stand, but he's made his decision to retire and I respect that. It's a great privilege for me to have Jeff available for advice any time I need it, and that's why I speak to him every day. Not many people have done what he's done in the game, for as long as he has, and I'll always value everything he says to me.

We're still enjoying a few beers together after all these years! That's me with Richard Fey, Jeff Meacham and Derek Jones during one of our 'meetings' to research this book!

17... See you in the clubhouse!

MUCH like any career in this unbelievable game of football, I've experienced a truckload of highs and lows throughout my 50 years. It's been such a huge part of my life for half a century, I really did wonder how I was going to cope when I decided to retire after my time with Dawlish Town. I didn't have a clue how I was going to react. Sure, I'd had spells out of the game before, so the first few weeks weren't going to be a problem. But how would I feel, say, three months down the road? What would I be thinking come December and January, with all the festive derbies, the big crowds and the exciting FA Vase runs beginning to take shape?

As it happens, the best thing I ever could have decided to do was write this book. It's really helped to ease me out of the game, and not sever all ties immediately. I think I first discussed the possibility of a book about five years ago with Chris Rogers, who was the sports editor with the *North Devon Journal* while I was manager of Barnstaple Town. At that time the game was keeping me busy enough, but we brought it up again a few weeks after I left Dawlish. By then, Chris was working for the *Torquay Herald Express* and he convinced me that a book would be worth doing. We met up to discuss it over a few pints when I'd returned from my holiday to Italy in September, and here we are nearly a year later with a book on my 50 years in football.

It really has been a fantastic project and, as I just said, it's been the perfect way for me to leave the game. Instead of constantly going over in my mind what I'm missing, being away from the game, I've been able to put my mind to this book. We divided my life and career up into a series of chapters during that first meeting and, since then, I've been hard at work going over old newspaper cuttings and match programmes, looking at results and league tables, and recalling all the wonderful times I've had. The best bit, though, has been the meetings I've had. It's given me the perfect excuse to catch up with my closest friends in football and just talk about our experiences in the game – with a fair few beers thrown in for good measure! It's been an unbelievably good laugh going over old times with them, and I've thoroughly enjoyed every minute of it.

As for ultimate highlights, I'd have to start with my first ever winners' medal when I was eleven years old and my Whitehall School side won the Coronation Cup. It was a first taste of success, and the pursuit of that very feeling is what has kept me hooked for so long since then. Representing Bristol Boys in national competitions was a real honour, as was signing for my boyhood club Bristol Rovers. A lot of promotions and cup wins followed in various guises during my playing career but, looking back, I've got to be honest and say that the real highlight for me was simply pulling on a football shirt. There was nothing quite like that feeling before a match. At 6pm after a game, all I could think about was getting back out there for the next one.

Winning all the medals I did with Clifton Wednesday, and with other senior sides, was fantastic, but the main thing I always remember about those days was how good the standard of football was. When Hanham Athletic played Bristol St George in the Bristol Premier Combination, you could guarantee that there would be 400 or 500 people watching. You wouldn't get those sorts of crowds in the Western League these days, let alone in the Bristol Prem. Of course, you were only a few steps away from the Football League in those days. It's no surprise to me that so many of the sides that I played against have since gone on to play at a very good semi-pro level at either Conference South or Southern League.

In my managerial career, the highlight has to be my year at Bath City. It was like going into the professional game. In the opposite dugout every Saturday, you could guarantee that there was a top-class manager and it was an opportunity for me to pit my wits against them. When I think back, it was absolutely fascinating.

Getting to manage clubs in four different counties – Devon, Somerset, Wiltshire and Gloucestershire – as well as a county side alongside Peter Buckingham is an achievement I'm also very proud of. I'd love to know if there's another manager in the English game who has ever done that. In all that time, it would be hard to single out any highlights. For me it was all about the thrill of being involved in football as a manager, being in charge of a team, pitting my wits against other managers, and coming out on top! I don't care if it sounds like I'm blowing my own trumpet, but you don't manage for 31 years unless you know what you're doing. I've even been offered a couple of jobs since I announced my retirement, which I politely declined. I can assure you all that I have definitely retired this time!

As far as disappointments go, the biggest of the lot had to be the day I opened that letter that told me I wasn't going to be offered a professional contract with Bristol Rovers. At the time it was the biggest disappointment in my life but, if I look back at it now, would I have been in management for so long had I made it as a pro player? I'm not so sure I would have been involved in the game for as long as I have, had I had a professional playing career. There aren't many ex-pros who come down and manage at the non-league level, and stick at it for any real length of time. Sure, there are a few exceptions, but quite often ex-pro players would manage a local side for a year or two, and then they'd be gone. So although my Rovers release was a major disappointment at the time, I can look at it now and see that out of something bad, comes something good. I may have missed out on a professional playing career, but I feel I've had the best of it too in terms of management.

In my managerial career, having to tell chairman Paul Richards that I was packing in as manager of Bath City has to go down as one of my lowest moments. It was such a hard decision to make, but it had to be done. Due to my work commitments, I just couldn't give the Bath City job the time it needed. Sometimes life has a horrible habit of kicking you up the arse, and this was one of those times – especially because, at the time, I had no idea that I would be leaving that company anyway within the next 12 months. I know you can't change things now but, had I known I would be leaving that job soon anyway, would I have thought twice about leaving Bath City? Absolutely! I ended up working on my own, and could have quite easily carried on at Twerton Park.

For me, the other major disappointment was how things ended at Barnstaple Town. I absolutely loved it there. I feel that if the chairman had only listened to the players and the manager, and not to other people, then Barnstaple Town would have been the first side to bring Southern League football back to North Devon, not Bideford. I still feel sure that Barnstaple Town could attract gates of 500 or 600 if things went well in the Southern League. But there we go, it's all in the past now. Although having to leave both Barnstaple and Bath were disappointments, let's keep it in context. They weren't massively devastating because I soon found other jobs and was able to stay involved in the game of football for 50 years.

One of the biggest, but best, decisions I made was to take the job at Torrington. Being based in Bristol and knowing the non-league scene there like the back of my hand, I think a lot of people in and around the city raised an eyebrow when I took over a club that was a two-hour drive away, and effectively in the middle of nowhere. I went to watch a game at Longwell Green a few weeks ago, and I bumped into Martyn Grimshaw there, among others, and we all had a good chat. They kept asking if I had definitely packed it in, and I told them I had. "Jeff, have you ever actually managed in Bristol?" one bloke then asked me. I had to really think about that one! Of course, I had, firstly with Abbotonians and later on during my brief spell with Les Alderman at Mangotsfield United. But take those six years away from my 31 years of management, and you're left with 25 years of managing away from Bristol. In that time, I'd been to Wiltshire with Trowbridge Town and Chippenham Town, Gloucester with Stroud, Devon with Torrington, Barnstaple Town and Dawlish Town, and Somerset with Bath City, Welton Rovers and Odd Down.

Of course, although I spent a lot of time outside of the city, a lot of those clubs are still in Bristol's fringe areas. Knowing the Bristol football scene wasn't a problem. The biggest difference between managing up there and managing down in Devon was the ratio of clubs – and therefore competition – within a small area. By competition, I don't just mean local derbies on the pitch. I'm talking about rivals in terms of trying to sign players, attract sponsorship and supporters, all things like that. In the Bristol area, if you were trying your hardest to sign a player, you could be sure there were 15 other clubs working just as hard.

It was totally different when I moved down to Torrington, it was like a breath of fresh air. The biggest thing that struck me was the difference in attitude towards the clubs. Players got really excited about playing for the town, and it took me a while to get my head around that. I couldn't understand why they didn't want to play for Exeter City or Plymouth Argyle. After all, in my day every young footballer in Bristol grew up wanting to play for either Rovers or City. Instead, the local lads were really proud to play for their town. Don't get me wrong, it was great to have that sort of attitude from the players. I just found it strange.

One of those players was Barry Yeo, and he actually explained it to me. It was basically because of North Devon's location. It's tucked away up there and, although it doesn't look very far away from Exeter or Plymouth on a map, it's still an hour or a two-hour drive respectively. Barry told me that, when they were growing up and going through junior and senior school, the lads were never able to get involved with the pro circuit. All they wanted to do was play for Barnstaple Town, because that was their top club going through school. Barnstaple, Dawlish and to a lesser extent, Torrington, were town clubs. Chippenham and Trowbridge too… they were all town clubs. The players wanted to play for their town, and the town was proud of the home-grown players.

I've helped out Richard Fey a little bit behind the scenes at Bitton this season when he's asked me to, and seeing the pressures he has to work under makes me feel so very lucky for being able to manage so many town clubs. It is so cut-throat for Richard at Bitton. Within a square mile, you've got four Western League clubs. If you open it out another mile or two, you've got eight Western League clubs. There are only so many chimney pots all around the place… there are only a certain amount of players to go round. It's such a hard job to find players.

Look at Barnstaple Town though… they should be in a world of their own. Look at the number of people who live there, and the size of the town. There's only one club in the town, and they should be the top dogs. Barry Yeo has managed to do it with Ilfracombe Town. He's used local players, who all want to play for the town, and he's built a top Western League side on the back of that attitude. In terms of playing resources, there should be a world of difference between Barnstaple Town and Ilfracombe Town, and the likes of Bitton, Longwell Green, Cadbury Heath and Oldland Abbotonians – four Western League sides all within a mile of each other.

Of course, Torrington proved to be a different matter altogether. Okay, so they were a town club, but they just didn't have the size or support of nearby clubs like Bideford, Barnstaple or Ilfracombe and sadly were forced to withdraw from the Western League a few years ago. Their reserve team, who played local football in the North Devon League, then became the club's first team. I felt so terribly sorry for the club and everyone there when I heard of their situation. But knowing how the club was run, I do have to say pulling out of the Western League was the best thing that could have happened to them.

When I was managing Torrington in the Western League, if we got crowds of 50 or 60 for a home game, we were delighted. That was the maximum we could realistically hope to get, unless it was a derby game against Ilfracombe Town. We'd maybe get 200 or 300 for that fixture but, as a one-off each season, it wasn't enough. We just weren't getting enough money in through the turnstiles, so that meant all the money had to come from behind the bar or from sponsorship. Nowadays, playing in the amateur North Devon League, Torrington are still getting their 40 or 50 people through the gate, but there's no pressure on my old chairman Winston Martin to find a wad of extra money each week to pay the wage bill. It must be a huge relief for Winston, because I know just how hard he worked for the club in all the years I was there as manager.

As I was getting ready to send this book off to the press, I also learned that Dawlish Town had folded on the eve of the 2011/2012 Western League season. Reports in the newspapers said the club were issued with a winding-up order due to debts of around £60,000. They owed money to brewers Carlsberg Tetley concerning the clubhouse, and were also in debt to landlords Teignbridge District Council. I have already written about my serious concerns regarding Dawlish Town's financial situation during my brief spell there, so news of the club's demise didn't come as any great surprise. It's another sad story, though, and once again we have a town that has lost its football club.

In the end, with clubs like Torrington and Dawlish who are struggling financially, common sense has to prevail. I would also argue that something needs to be done with regards to the non-league structure of football in the South West to help these clubs out. It's okay for all the Bristol-based clubs playing in the Western League... they only have to make the long trips down to Devon two or three times a season. But the Devon clubs have to do it every other week, and it's a huge drain on expenses.

I would suggest that the time is right for the remaining Devon clubs like Willand Rovers, Elmore, Barnstaple Town and Ilfracombe Town to consider a move to the South West Peninsula League. But for clubs like those to consider making such a switch, it's imperative that the Premier Division of the Peninsula League is placed evenly with the Premier Division of the Western League, in terms of where they are in the non-league pyramid. Currently, the Western League's top division sits on step five, while the Peninsula League's Premier is step six – the equivalent of Division One in the Western League.

In my opinion, the South West pyramid should be restructured so that the Premier Division of the South West Peninsula League is pushed up to step five. That way, any team finishing in the top two can apply for promotion to the Southern League, should they have the facilities and the finances in place. At the moment, Peninsula League winners can only apply for promotion into the Western League's top flight.

If only a group of people within the FA could lock themselves in a room, sit down and map out a fairer and more regional non-league structure, I'm sure we would see huge benefits in South West football. Promoting the Peninsula League Premier Division to step five would breathe new life into the Devon clubs I mentioned earlier. They could switch to the Peninsula League without fear of dropping down a level, and I'm sure they would be better off financially. You'd get bigger crowds, because there would be more local games, and you'd make a huge saving on travelling costs because the miles would reduce dramatically.

When I first played Western League football all those years ago, it was for Bristol Rovers Colts, and clubs in the division then were effectively only a couple of promotions away from the Football League. Nowadays, a club like Barnstaple Town would not only have to win the Western League, they'd also need to go through two Southern League divisions and two Conference divisions to get there. Why, with all these extra leagues, are clubs in Devon still expected to travel to Bristol or Wiltshire all the time? The only solution, as far as I'm concerned, is to bring the Peninsula League up to step five and watch the clubs reap the benefits.

I often get asked if, with the benefit of hindsight, I would do anything differently over the course of my career. The topic that is usually the first to be mentioned is my time at Bristol Rovers. During the last three months of my stint at Eastville, I ended up playing as a goalkeeper rather than at right-back, where I'd played for the previous two-and-a-half years. I was a competent goalkeeper, able to do a job as an emergency, but there was no way I was up to professional standard with the gloves on. Those three months should have been when I was working my socks off as a full-back to show the Rovers just what I could do. Instead, I spent it between the sticks and I never got my chance. I do put that down as part of why I didn't get a professional contract. Why did I have to play in goal? And why, of all times, did it have to be in the most crucial three months of my possible career with Rovers? Perhaps I should have been more disciplined, and maybe not so helpful and accommodating. I was a right-back, therefore I should have played at right-back... maybe I should have told them that.

On the other hand, how many professional football managers would like getting ultimatums from a 17 or 18-year-old lad? It was a difficult situation and, for whatever reason, it never quite happened for me. At the time, you feel you're doing the right thing, or else you wouldn't have done it. As the years go on, it's human nature to look back on things and wonder if you should have done it differently. I've lost count of the times I've thought 'if only I'd pulled that chairman to one side' or 'if only I told him not to listen to such-and-such a person' over the years!

At the end of the day, though, I've had a wonderful 50 years in football. It's been absolutely superb, and I've loved it. So with that in mind, would I do anything differently? Probably not, if I'm being honest. In answer to this book's title, I don't think I'd have had more fun as a professional either.

Don't get me wrong, I would have loved to have been a pro footballer. But I just don't think I would have stayed involved in the game for so long, had I gone down the professional route as an 18-year-old. I knew professionals who had their playing career but, unless they were able to stay on in the professional game as a manager, they didn't stay involved past their mid-30s. Some came back down to manage at a non-league level, but very few stayed there for long. One thing's for sure, none of them have come back to the non-league game and stayed involved for 31 years like I have done. So even though I was absolutely gutted when I didn't gain a professional contract, and the experiences that come with it, I feel I've gained a lot more in the longer term. All the friends I've made, the laughs I've had and the memories I've got are irreplaceable.

As I said earlier, writing this book has been the best way possible to help me retire. In the past eight or nine months, I've had one hell of a laugh, remembering what I've got up to. It's helped me truly appreciate what I've experienced over the last 50 years, and for that I'll always be immensely grateful. When it is my time to finally head upstairs, I just hope there's a football pitch up there! Of course, during the research for the book, there have been a lot of stories told that couldn't possibly be reprinted without my lawyers being put on red alert! Who knows, maybe next year I'll release the uncut version... now that would be an entertaining read! Until then, if you see me at a game, buy me a pint and, if you're lucky, I may tell you one or two!